Telling the Truth as It Comes Up

Selected Talks & Essays 1991–2018

Alice Notley

The Song Cave

The Song Cave
www.the-song-cave.com

Cover photo by Kirby

Design and layout by Janet Evans-Scanlon

ISBN: 979-8-9878288-1-6
Library of Congress Control Number: 2023945422

FIRST PRINTING

Contents

What Can Be Learned from Dreams?

Is Dream something godlike inside you? One splits so easily into dialogue with it.

One would like to dream what one fancies one needs, for example. You have learned that you can suggest topics to Dream to be dreamed about. Dream will sometimes let you dream about those topics—but not in any way you have imagined, you suddenly have information you are not sure you know the use of, though it's unforgettable. When I was writing an essay about the soul last week, I suggested to myself before falling asleep that I would like to dream about "the soul"—which I was imaging as armless legless, a baby bundle, or luminously amoeboid, a lit cylinder shape, etc. Instead I dreamed of two "souls" that were very tiny people, perhaps less than a foot high, one was my dead brother, one an unidentified woman with long blonde hair who was somehow thrown dangerously into a small bush which my brother then leaped into too in order to rescue her. That was all. What might I do with this information? In dreams everything is made personal, you are constantly reminded that you are not pure and lofty, though your concerns may be; the real dead and living are present there, always to remind you that you miss them, or that you hurt, that you're anxious, that you feel inadequate. And that some other part of you is always thinking about everything. But what do I do with this depiction of the soul, so contrary to my images, and actually now, so unforgettable? They were doll-like slips of beings long-legged like Barbies, but graceful and agile. Have I made the soul, in my thinking and in my essay, seem like a small human—or do I secretly feel that, really, the soul is diminished, a diminished thing, in contrast to the "total being" with body and personality? Or does the dream suggest that perfection is small rather than large; has a personal aspect rather than not? Etc. I don't know what the dream means. Does Dream know what it means? The image of the tiny figures entering the bush one after another has haunted me all week.

People often give over their problems to Dream, without knowing it, without remembering dreams, without knowing that there is a problem, or that an old problem is being dwelled on. I have become aware, during bereavements, that I repeatedly dream about high places like mountains or tall buildings, being high up on or in them, and then coming down. The summit is some sense of psychic danger, the descent is relaxation from threat. Over and over I have dreamed of snowy Alps (always snow), tall castles, high apartment buildings, airplanes—and then a few days later dreamed of a fall, a sliding down, a flying descent in air, and so on. This past week I awoke and realized I had had one of the descent dreams, in a mountain town, a sliding down past people at cafe tables—I slid on smooth metal I think; a curving literal slide. Had I been secretly upset or worried? Perhaps it was my brother, that I was thinking again of him—but my feelings awake had not been extreme, I had just been thinking. But asleep I was deeply bothered? Everyone has experiences like these. There is so much that it is handling for you, Dream, or the Unconscious—one can only be grateful and awed.

Dream is you, and Dream is not you. It does so much that you can't do. How dare you claim the making of your dreams? 'I dreamed that tiny people were souls.' Oh did you? You did that? Hah! Actually, you only witnessed it, or took part in the action. Well as a matter of fact, you were exactly in the dream, weren't you? How could you be in such an invisible-to-others reality, really there? You were really there. Your presence in a dream, while it is happening, is not nebulous—it never occurs to you, dreaming, to question that you are there—it rarely occurs to you that you are dreaming at all. Why don't you ask how you got to be in this room with wooden benches and tables, this pub you've never seen in waking life? Why don't you ask yourself why you're sliding on a metal slide past a cafe with outdoor tables? A dream is a vivid present without a recent past—how can that be? And the reality of a dream is a remembered one: you remember what it was like to be in it. You draw it out of a void. It "comes back to you." The quality of memory here is not the same as when remembering something from waking life; your memory fills a strange dark hole in time. Yet a dream feels real while it's happening, everyone knows this, everyone knows exactly what the present of dreaming is like.

Everyone also knows that dreams make their own time. In the morning you might awaken five times in an hour, each time having dreamed something epic as if hours had gone past. In five minutes, in two minutes, you might dream a very long and detailed dream as if a whole night had been wedged between two or three dots on a clock face. How can this be? Why does no one discuss it ever? Where do dreams come from? What in you makes dreams? And has an inventive story-telling ability that you don't have? Why are many dreams not connected to the daily life, to events and information scattered through the day (as scientists often insist they are)? How can I dream repeatedly of the same two friends together—Philip and Shelley—over the years, without knowing precisely why except that vaguely it might have to do with the idea of a shell and its filling? Why don't I know why that's important to me? But only Dream knows. Dream knows many things about me, about life even, that I don't. And things about language, and about artistic form, that I don't. Dream obviously knows a much more subtle form of allegory than the poets know—Dream is freer with transitions than a film-maker, being not bound at all by time and space—Dream can be better at character and relationship than a novelist, knowing hard secret feelings that are best left out of daily life.

I usually relate to Dream on a basis of asking it something, or asking what it means. But other people I have known have considered Dream to be a great personal entertainer, precisely because of Dream's "artistic qualifications." Dreams are their own form—like any other form, they don't translate well. When they are written down the language falls dead. As far as simulations go, dream sequences in films invariably seem hokey. In a play of Shakespeare's a dream is obviously "made up": Clarence's dream isn't a real dream, though it's beautiful, and "works." But it's a "play" dream in both senses of the word. Invented dreams are never as bizarre, spontaneous, unexpected, loose, as real ones, though they may be more "beautiful." Beauty seems a quality connected to the conscious mind; a dream setting may be very beautiful—or a dream detail—but the events of a dream will rarely be symmetrical, and a dream will not often have closure.

A dream is not well-proportioned, perhaps partly because it isn't governed by rules of time and space, but especially rules of time: when you make a poem, I think, you are always concerned with how much time for each word, each detail, each explanation, or run of words—in relation to all the others. A dream is a jumble of places and times: the stresses don't fall into place. Or a very long and sagging expanse of small detail—you were in it much longer than the telling might suggest. In fact, you meandered all night hopelessly. It was not well paced. Another characteristic of art that dreams do not share is a sense of emotional appropriateness. You may feel nothing when someone dies in a dream, or when a murderer chases you. You may feel a great deal though, without preface, in a bleakly aspected house; or when flying, you may feel calmly happy—but why not surprised? But emotions tend to be kept separate from their real situations—as if the situations were better scrutinized that way, not necessarily as if they were less painful that way. Dream is as much a thinker as anything else.

The form of art that is most dream-like is myth, which explains origin in terms of rather "automatic" sequences of images. A woman falls from the sky, loons hold her up awhile, until a turtle is found to support her upon the great water which lies below the heavens. Then various animals dive to obtain mud from beneath the water, one succeeds in bringing up a small mouthful, which is molded to the shell and then spreads until earth is formed. Later when the woman dies, pregnant with twins (good and evil), plants sprout from her bearing the vegetables people will eat. In other words, something falls, something must catch it, something must be found to support it. That something isn't earth yet, where is earth? Dive down further to get some. It is a small amount, but it grows bigger. She lies down on it to give birth, and dies of the impatience of the evil twin to be born (he pushes through her abdomen.) Then plants sprout from her. Each picture or action suggests the next, without bothering about realities of space and time: a chain of "childish" imaging. Compare a split-second dream I had recently: I first (before I dreamed) lay awake trying to relax muscle by muscle. As I slid into sleep (suddenly, instantaneously) my muscles became the muscles of two giant naked women I could see wrestling across the room from me, a dark ancient chamber lit by a torch on the wall. Then I heard three words spoken, "Rahab Rachel Remodel" and awoke. That dream too is a consecutive train of pictures and sounds, a chain. Or take the sliding dream I have mentioned. The logic of it could seem to go: "I must descend again. From what? A mountain? Do I see snow? Yes, at night. Why here's a slide to descend on! It curves and twists going down though. Oh here's a cafe. With outdoor tables. Oh look, a woman is naked at a table. Can that be all right? . . . "

In both myth and dream, anything might happen. In a myth Coyote plays a game with some birds in which his eyes are plucked out of their sockets and then dropped back into them. Is it so different for me to dream that I feel a fluttering down the back of my shirt and then a succession of bats fly out? Or that I pull a long purple string out of my ear? In myth, too, there may be little suggestion of emotion: it is a rational thing actually, a form of logic. One suspects that dream told the ancients, the "primitives," the answers to their questions about origin. We don't have such a satisfying relation to Dream. Dream seems to give us answers all of the time without our ever knowing what the questions are. We don't seem to think we should ask it anything—we think we should ask science and philosophy about origin. And we think we should ask psychology about dreams. We rarely ask ourselves anything.

But that myth about the falling woman isn't true, someone says. Oh it isn't? What does it say again? Something came from heaven towards earth, but earth actually was yet to be formed. Various beings wanted it to be formed for this one being who came from heaven, and when it had been formed, and she became fertile with both good and evil, she died and became food for human beings. I.e., something interesting and desirable came out of the divine void and initiated a chain of events which resulted in a world in which food must be cultivated and eaten, in which there is both good and evil. That isn't true? Is it true that there was a Big Bang? Maybe. But what does that fact mean to my life? Absolutely nothing. It has no resonance, it's sterile, basically because it refuses to say the words "good and evil," especially "evil." Our human imperfection does not necessarily follow from the establishment of dimensions, of space and time. One is not ethically imperfect simply from bodily being. How can anyone be interested in a theory of origin which does not contain a seed of an explanation of the millenia-long subjugation of women and men, a hint of what has lead to the grotesqueness of war and the cruelty of slavery? It would have been just as easy to be good; it still is. Anyone knows she can be reasonably good—so why won't everyone be good together? Why are many animals polygamous? Is evil just another evolutionary accident? Then why won't it accidentally go away since it's "evil"? Is territoriality in animals, is animal combat, an example of a "good thing"? Are animals necessarily "good"? Is nature necessarily "good" or even "neutral"? Is there evil in nature from the beginning? If there is evil from the beginning, why not at the Big Bang? What is the principle of evil? Why is there no new explanation of origin which includes Mind, and which explains Dream—which seems to become more and more mysterious as one talks about it?

What again is Dream for? Is this tentative or casual relation one has with it the only one one might have with it? What if you wanted to find out what Dream knows? If you repeatedly asked Dream a question like 'What is the best way to live?' what would it say? Something complicated, ambiguous, tied to the pain of your own life—It would never say, Make money, Become successful. Rather it would tell you a strange story which you would refine somewhat as you tried to interpret it according to conscious wishes which would never really mesh with it. You would be constantly saying to it, 'Aren't you saying I should become great? greater?' and it would be answering, 'The pain of this house makes these artichokes slice your hands . . . ' If you see what I mean. I don't know very much about the dreams of the outright wicked—nightmares? Or nil. But my point again is that dream does not tell you what you want to hear, or what you expect to hear. It makes you think, it divests you of righteousness, it casts a shade of hidden motivation, or hidden concern, on your waking life. Its stories and sayings are never "clean," do not contain "classic outlines," because you do not. I dreamed "about" my brother last night, but he wasn't in the dream, I unfortunately couldn't see him (why not? why never?) There was a grave in a cemetery with a rosebush of blue and red (I think) roses growing on it, that was, in some respect, his, or our, place. A young couple came to look at it—it was suddenly after the Iraqi War*—and instead of a rosebush there was a heavy plaster face. I indignantly asked the couple if they had a friend buried there—No—Then I said, "It is the place where my brother . . . " Then the dream becomes awkward, something like " . . . where we spoke together about his part in the Vietnam War." I flashed more anger at them. End of dream. But you see, it can't be his grave—that would be a lie—or artistically a grander, simpler conception: the new war has crushed and obscured his grave. No, this is the grave of my conversation with my brother about what happened to him in the Vietnam War, his telling me that he understood his guilt, that he knew he had been used by the government, the military, etc., and our feeling, finally, close, in our thinking about these matters. For all this has been superceded by the Iraqi War and the shallow rhetoric surrounding it in regard to it and the Vietnam War—"we've put all that behind us, by winning this one, we've buried Vietnam." In the symbolism of the dream the Iraqi War is a slab of plaster laid down in place of a natural thing, a rosebush, which we had made grow over time. Suppose a world leader were in touch with his dreams? Would he finally have the delicacy of understanding necessary to conduct a conversation, a real conversation, with foreigners, with others? without leaping to Action? The classic outlines of action, of war, always arise out of a simplification, which is a falsification, of reality. Dream is not noble, or courageous, or heroic—Dream is messy, embarrassing, truthful, sometimes clairvoyant (if you've suffered enough), sometimes full of exquisite release (if you've suffered enough). But Dream will tell you what you really know, if you're humble enough to ask. Be-

* First Gulf War, 1990-1991.

cause what you think you know, is a source of danger to others.

Is there shame in this society, is it a present possible feeling? Is there some way to pull a psychic plug so that shame leaks out from whatever void it's been relegated to and into everyone's dreams? Could we have a national dream of nakedness and guilt? . . . Actually only one by one, individual psyche by individual psyche, could such an event take place. And one by one is the only desirable change there can be—each in her own privacy of Dream facing Infinity, knowing she is whatever she is (including whatever nationally she is part of).

One and one we fall asleep and dream clumsy wondrous things. Can't we attend to them better? Can't we look inside ourselves for answers to our ultimate questions? For it is each of us who dies singly—and what good is an answer from an outsider as to what a right life is up to that point? Don't you know something too? What is it? Is it a dream? "I dreamed that the tears of General X, after the Battle of Y, had turned to jade, to small pieces of red and white jade . . . " That is knowledge, moral knowledge.

First published in *SCARLET,* No. 5, Sept. 1991.

The Poetics of Disobedience

For a long time I've seen my job as bound up with the necessity of noncompliance with pressures, dictates, atmospheres of, variously, poetic factions, society at large, my own past practices as well. For a long time—well in fact since the beginning, since I learned how to be a poet inside the more rebellious more outlawish wing of poetry; though learning itself meant a kind of obedience, so like most words the Dis word, the Dis form, cannot be worshipped either—and that would be an obedience anyway. I've spoken in other places of the problems, too, of subjects that hadn't been broached much in poetry and of how it seemed one had to disobey the past and the practices of literary males in order to talk about what was going on most literarily around one, the pregnant body, and babies for example. There were no babies in poetry then. How could that have been? What are we leaving out now? Usually what's exactly in front of the eyes ears nose and mouth, in front of the mind, but it seems as if one must disobey everyone else in order to see at all. This is a persistent feeling in a poet but staying alert to all the ways one is coerced into denying experience, sense and reason is a huge task. I recently completed a very long poem called *Disobedience* but I didn't realize that disobeying was what I was doing, what perhaps I'd always been doing until the beginning of the end of it, though the tone throughout was one of rejection of everything I was supposed to be or to affirm, all the poetries all the groups the clothes the gangs the governments the feelings and reasons.

I seem to start with my poem *The Descent of Alette* these days, whatever it is that I am now seems to start there. It was for me an immense act of rebellion against dominant social forces, against the fragmented forms of modern poetry, against the way a poem was supposed to look according to both past and contemporary practice. It begins in pieces and ends whole, narrated by an I who doesn't know her name and whose name when she finds it means appendage of a male name; her important name is I. I stand with this, and with the urgency that saying I creates, a facing up to sheer presence, death and responsibility, the potential for blowing away all the gauze. In two subsequent narrative poem/proses, *Close to me . . . & Closer (The Language of Heaven)* and *Désamère* I felt myself pushing against ideas of reality as solely what's visible and in what shapes and colors it's said to be visible, against the idea that religion is solely an organized affair, against the pervasive idea that one must not protest what everyone else has named the Actual—how can you fight Reality?—against the psychology of belonging, of aiding and abetting. *Désamère* especially is about not wanting to belong and the process of ceasing to belong to the extent that's possible. All three of those works are characterized by emphatic though variable metrical patterns, in the prose as well as the poetry parts; two are very quirky as to physical presentation; all three have narratives that tend to the fabular.

In a book that will soon be published, *Mysteries of Small Houses*, I was firstly trying to realize the first person singular as fully and nakedly as possible, saying "I" in such a way as to make myself really nervous, really blowing away the gauze and making myself too scared of life and death to care what anyone thought of me or what I was going to say. Saying I in that way I tried to trace that I's path through my past. In a more subsidiary way I decided to go against my own sense that certain styles and forms I'd participated in formerly might be used up, that autobiography was, that the personal-sounding I (as opposed to the fictional I) might be, against the rumor that there's no self, though I've never understood that word very well and how people use it now in any of the camps that use it pro or con—I guess I partly wrote *Mysteries* in order to understand it better. I came to the conclusion, in the final poem of the book, that self means 'I' and also means 'poverty,' it's what one strips down to, who you are when you've stripped down.

It's possible that my biggest act of disobedience has consistently, since I was an adolescent, been against the idea that all truth comes from books, really other people's books. I hate the fact that whatever I say or write, someone reading or listening will try to find something out of their reading I "sound like." 'You sound just like . . . ,' 'you remind me of . . . ,' 'have you read . . . ?' I read all the time and I often believe what I read while I'm reading it, especially if it's some trashy story; intense involvement in theories as well as stories seems difficult without temporary belief, but then it burns out. I've been trying to train myself for thirty or forty years not to believe anything anyone tells me. Not believing, then, became the crux of *Disobedience*, which is my most recent completed book. Not believing and telling the truth as it comes up. One of the main elements in the poem is an ongoing fantasy in which the I, who is pretty much I, keeps company and converses with a man very much like the actor Robert Mitchum and that of course is not strictly believable. On the other hand it's fun, and it stands for something a sort of truth, about how we do have stories going on in our consciousness and unconsciousness all the time and about how we're always talking to some "you" mentally. I wouldn't expect you to take this book as the truth, I would expect you to go with it, given that you like to read. I find the act of reading puzzling at the moment, since in a book I've been working on since *Disobedience* I ask the reader to read despite the fact that I'm not really entertaining the reader or being clear in any of the traditional ways I can think of. I think books may imply a readership that simply likes to read, which may sound obvious but it's something I myself have only just thought of. But back to *Disobedience*. It asks the reader to read a lot of pages, about 230 A4 pages in verse, but it's fairly easy to read and it makes a lot of jokes. It's very feminist but men seem to enjoy it a lot, it possibly contains a rather virile approach to things riding roughshod and shooting at every little tin duck that seems to pop up. As I implied earlier, *Disobedience* didn't exactly set out to be disobedient; it set out actually to try to do the kinds of things I'd previously done in different poems all in the same poem, that is tell a story, interact with the so-called visible or phenomenal the despised daily, and explore the unconscious. But it got more and more pissed off as it confronted the political from an international vantage, dealt with being a woman in France, with turning fifty and being a poet and thus seemingly despised or at least ignored. The title popped up in a dream, a real dream I had towards the end of writing the work, in connection with a comic poet I know: it was the title of his book in the dream and I realized later that there was probably nothing more disobedient than being a comic poet, since no one's ever sure if that's good enough, particularly the academy unless you've been dead since the 14th century or unless you've also written a lot of tragedies. I myself wouldn't want the limitation of being only one kind of poet, but I realize this comic business is something to think about. But more and more as I wrote *Disobedience* I discovered I couldn't go along, with the government or governments, with radicals and certainly not conservatives or centrists, with radical poetics and certainly not with other poetics, with other women's feminisms, with any fucking thing at all; belonging to any of it was not only an infringement on my liberty but a veil over clear thinking.

It's necessary to maintain a state of disobedience against . . . everything. One must remain somehow, though how, open to any subject or form in principle, open to the possibility of liking, open to the possibility of using. I try to maintain no continuous restrictions in my poetics except with regard to particular works, since writing at all means making some sort of choices. But NO DOCTRINES. Rather I tend to maintain a sense that a particular form or set of rules at a certain point might serve me for a while. Like many writers I feel ambivalent about words, I know they don't work, I know they aren't it. I don't in the least feel that everything is language. I have a sense that there has been language from the beginning, that it isn't fundamentally an invention. These are contradictory positions but positions are just words. I don't believe that the best poems are just words, I think they're the same as reality; I tend to think reality is poetry, and that that isn't words. But words are one way to get at reality/poetry, what we're in all the time. I think words are among us and everything else, mingling, fusing with, backing off from us and everything else.

Since *Disobedience*, I've been working on this other thing, called *Reason and Other Women*, which isn't as friendly as *Dis* is, though it isn't meant to be unfriendly. It's just hard to read, in that you have to decide to sit down and read it word by word giving each word the rhythm and weight it requires. That sounds like poetry but this one tends to be in long blowy sentences all down the page. I am going at several ideas at once: one is that the world is intensely telepathic, infused with the past and continual thought of all the living and all the dead. I started out with that idea and with the idea of a Byzantine church as a sort of head, mine, full of icons and mosaics on ever expanding and shifting walls. But the church or head got bigger and bigger and more and more full of images and words until it expanded into a city. So at the moment, on page one hundred and something, I'm dealing with the idea that there are two cities or worlds at the same time, an ideal crystalline one and the supposedly real one. Generally I'm neither all the way in one nor the other, though sometimes it seems as if I'm nowhere near the crystal one and its reasonable opulence so I start beating hard at all the doors I can find in my mind. Then sometimes it seems as if the supposedly real world just isn't there or here at all though I know if I stop typing and go outside it will get me. This work is also very disobedient, in a way it picks up where *Disobedience* left off; but it doesn't lecture as much or shake its fist so, is less interested in the so-called real than in denying its existence in favor of the real real. You can't fly unless you're not on the ground and this one really flies sometimes.

I think I conceive of myself as disobeying my readership a lot. I began the new work in fact denying their existence; it seemed to me I needed most at this point to work on my own existence, so I couldn't afford to cater to them if they got in the way of my finding out things. But this is a work of mine, it should be published sometime. I'm now in a predicament I can't get out of, a form I can't manage for the reader, which just keeps leading me on and leading me on. It's predicated on leaving in as much mind fuzz as possible, that is being open to all that is out there in all telepathy—not a very organizable entity, the entity. Too wordy too long; and I've allowed in a lot of notions from my dreams again, have allowed odd images to take on the weight of truth; and I'm stubbornly involved again in what you might call mystical conceptions, but aren't those a no-no? except in icky New Age territory, yuck. The reader likes you to tell her/him what she/he already knows in a familiar form whether in mainstreamese or avant-gardese, but then there is the individual reader who is often not like that at all, who prefers poems to talking about them and has strange individual experiences with them. That's a very scary idea. It's possible that the reader, or maybe the ideal reader, is a very disobedient person a head/church/city entity her/himself full of soaring icons and the words of all the living and all the dead, who sees and listens to it all and never lets on that there's all this beautiful almost undifferentiation inside, everything equal and almost undemarcated in the light of fundamental justice. And poker-faced puts up with the outer forms. As I do a lot of the time but not so much when I'm writing.

Written for a conference on Contemporary American and English Poetics, held at King's College London, Centre for American Studies, on February 28, 1998. First published in *Civil Disobediences*, ed. Waldman and Berman, Coffee House Press, 2004.

Williams And

I'm resisting writing this talk because I want what I've learned from Williams to stay put, flat down underneath: I am after all myself. But I still have that funny feeling, thinking about Williams, that no one ever gets it, they're still not getting it. Anthologies continue to make antiseptic selections from Williams' tidier-looking rectangles; books by non-academic poets tend to make the same selection, on the grounds perhaps that these books are for teachers, or poetry lovers, who must be amateurs who can only love what they've already been told to love. Or a bit from *Paterson*, yeah, as Big Poem. ("But is it Great?") Meanwhile poets who have been influenced by him, either directly or indirectly (and oh they never seem to acknowledge how much of what they do has come from that indirect influence) prefer to argue Pound or Stein or Pound versus Stein, because it's more fun to argue. To anguish and rage over Pound's flaws, and to defend Stein against the ever obvious Philistines who have no idea that we women sound like her because she sounded like us (not because we're imitating her). But it's from Williams that we—I'm not including academic poets, who seem to have gotten more of the call to tidiness from him—have gotten all our permissions to mix prose and verse (Stein was certainly no verse writer), balancing the two and tilting the balance this way or that way, how far? to make things more dangerous. How prose-y can you get? How piercingly poetic can you get? on the same page? How broken can the text be and still be unified, in how many ways can it be broken, within the poetry part, within the prose part, as well as between the poetry and prose parts? That comes from Williams. But he still does it better than most of us, because of his obsession with measure: we are obsessed with the subject, or philosophy and theory, or ourselves, when we use those broken forms; many of us are shitty musicians.

What else comes from Williams? The large un-self-centered voice, rigorous and energetic—never poeticizing itself as in Whitman, and in many of us —including everyone and everything therefore in a truly democratic way: how we all broke into poetry finally. His voice let us in. But those of us who also choose to be "un-self-centered" are usually not so truly democratic—because to be democratic right now seems to mean only something about words, being inclusive as to words (Williams is the origin of the emphasis on words as well, but by words he didn't mean abstractions and dull phrases, he meant those edged things that draw blood.) Williams made room for us, Williams and no one else, in terms of our having the guts to speak despite being who we were, which was not the right ones. Not the kind of people who become po-ets. It doesn't matter how some one poem offends someone now—oh he's just so . . . —it's just so . . .—When in the introduction to *Selected Essays*, you see a man who naturally admits women as equals in poetry, more naturally than many do now—because now it's always about making a point, not about poetry, and the inclusive men make the point because they must, or in order to get a little more power over other men. Not simply because Marianne Moore's poetry has always been part of them. (But isn't she out of fashion? She has five pages in the Norton, two of which are the introduction.) Williams had minimal power, a fact which killed him so slowly that its maiming made his poetry better, much better than anyone else's poetry of old age.

So as you see I can still get up a polemic. I would like to add that I find the introduction to Williams poetry in the *Norton Anthology of Amer-*

ican Literature (1995 edition) offensive—earth mothers? simple verse forms?; that I'm pretty sick of red wheelbarrow, Queen Anne's lace, Breughel's Kermess, all the poems anyone can talk about. Those sleek short works that enable the teacher to say That Thing. So, what this comes down to—mess and measure in O'Hara's words, who owed so much to Williams, and through whom we owe Williams (as through Schuyler, Olson, Creeley, Baraka, Oppen, Zukovsky, Ginsberg, Levertov) immeasurably. And through me, younger etc. Okay I will, that is acknowledge it again. Though as I began by saying I too hate this. But this is mess and measure, not tiny rectangles—the fact that Williams measured his messes, always had, and then upon seeing the Real mess others were making, tried to organize measure a little. No one took the point . . . Or has taken it; let's talk about that. Let's talk about his sound a little.

From *A Folded Skyscraper* (1927)

3

The Winds

flowing edge to edge
their clear edges meeting—
the winds of this northern March—
blow the bark from the trees
the soil from the field
the hair from the heads of
girls, the shirts from the backs
of the men, roofs from the
houses, the cross from the

church, clouds from the sky
the fur from the faces of wild animals, crusts
from scabby eyes, scales from
the mind and husbands from wives

4

In my uncivilized, amputated country thinking (I exist in a matrix of confusion) tobacco fed, looking for the number on a house down by Guinea Hill, thinking of Horace's (Quintus Horatius Flaccus) dictum: No wine, no poetry; undrunk no poetry—drunk in the caboose of my coupe, looking out dizzy from the smoke—thinking of poetry—just before the lights came out on the wires and pulleys and the poles, like cactus flowers (in a desert) as I often have the habit of thinking—thinking of Ezra Pound, our greatest and rightest poet, how excellent he is in his self-deception—opposed with a laugh to my fervent, my fierce, anger to have a country—speaking of his work, deriding me, saying that in the end his artificial pearl will be longer to last than anything I have made with all my striving—writing the greatest American poems today, his pearl-like cantos, so purely American—his self-deception that he had found poetry in the quattro cento in Dante, in them all of those old countries—when as a fact he had found poetry—how right he is a United States poet—when he thinks he has found poetry in the Renaissance, in his self-deception—for he HAS found poetry, an artificial pearly Pound, exile,—he has welded his material, he has what he has discovered, he has taken what there at least is—driven from my country that I strive so wildly to possess, he has taken the false, the make shift—the thing that they here—made him take—not the thing I want, but the thing I want.

That's only the first sentence of part 4. That of course is not typical Williams—as if You knew what it were, Queen Anne's Lace, red wheelbarrow? 'She's chosen something She sounds like'—why not? The prose, which obviously takes its sound cue from the poetry, suggests the drunken mind, and is about thinking, as well as about himself and Pound, organized into clauses separated by dashes, clauses expertly manipulated to contradict each other, or mean two things at once, because that's what's true here, both sides of the argument. But this prose isn't poetry though it very nearly is, it's coming close to that edge that the wordier feet of the variable-foot poems will walk, that fantastic border across which poetry and prose touch fingertips. Each clause, though, is prose. One thing I like about this is that you would never find it in an anthology (not even *Poems for the Millennium)*, it's an awkward bastard thing—and it bitches another poet by name—not nice, not pure (Everyone's a purist finally.) Does it sound like a poem? Very much so. It's a fugue, anthologists prefer canons ("The Kermess")—or pure litany (the "So be it" section from *Paterson*)—certainly anything where you can tell the prose from the poetry (*Paterson*). Aside: There isn't a single variable foot poem in the Norton, not even a section of "Asphodel." Williams somewhere defines music, 20th century poetic music, as structural, and he is a master of complicated structures (not just *Paterson*, but "The Desert Music," and all these shorter heterogeneous works); elsewhere he writes that he comes nowhere near Pound's fine ear. They could both follow their minds, their flow of thought, to the end the form made as it itself was being made up. Pound's purity of ear, refined by his immersion in other languages, is unsurpassed. Williams is consonantal, strict, particular; all that detail but within the larger newly invented shape; he is much more structurally inventive than Pound. Large play of music across different structures—what was that lit crit word of our youth? Juxtaposition—but this is a juxtaposition of musics rather than images or simple vocabularies. This was the sound of our century. The different ways we all spoke trying to force those voices into the same poem, the same project of this "uncivilized, amputated country": the measure must be one for amputations, and for a prose-like sound, the sound of our speaking, because we can't have single simple measures as in older cultures.

Williams' structures are the true precursors of "our" structures: sequential or series works with explanations (did I say Spicer, back there?); clotted-looking things which involve the inclusion of other people's words at great length (oh yes we're supposed to call it intertextuality and act as if the theorists invented it), the use of disjunction (naturalized), out-of-sequence syntax, and cut up and interspliced previously written texts; the poetry and prose form together, but very differently from Dante in that the prose doesn't explain the poetry but continues the work enabling a various trajectory; also the why-are-these-two-items-next-to-each-other kind of work. Have you read "Two Pendants For the Ears" recently? "Two Pendants For the Ears"—which again would never make an anthology, too long, without being weighty, as in proper usage of grand topic—and where does its unity come from (did the Norton really say simple verse forms?) "Two Pendants" is all in verse but is too, just too prose-like—because its structure is airy, diffuse; it's also diary-like, like much of William's most experimental work (Hello everybody again.) The first "Pendant" (because this work is for the ear? not the familiar puristic reasoning process) begins with a dream of a wounded tiger, upon a parapet, after a violent struggle with its trainer:

> at least they said
> it was a tiger though I never
> saw it—more than a shadow—
> for the night . . .

When I arrived
the people were underground
huddled into a group and terrified
from the recent happenings:
a terrific fight, apparently—
between the beast and
a man, its trainer, lying
he also, out there now
horribly wounded—perhaps dead . . .

Somewhat to the right
apparently unable to lift itself
and hanging upon
the stone wall, I seemed
to make out the beast and could
hear it panting, heavily . . .

How is it every line's beginning (not ending) is a surprise to the ear? Williams hears the man too, probably "mewing"—matter of factly stated, as is that the people are "underground," and says to the crowd, finally, "Has no one notified the police?" So Williams awakens and records the morning, the yard, details of household, a passage about women, girls and women—is it sexist?: girls whose "smiles vanish / at the age of four. Later they / sob and throw their arms about my / waist, babies I have myself delivered / from their agonized mothers. They / sob and cling to me, their breasts heavy / with milk, pressing my coat and refuse/to let go until their / sobs quiet . . . " —And next he's excoriating his "countrymen": "how can you permit yourselves / to be so cheated—your incomes / taken away and you, chromium / in your guts (rat poison) / until you are swollen / beyond all recognition . . . " Isn't that still true? So many of us are cheated of our incomes, these economics have never changed, this is a dis-unified country of amputations and so the poem must go anywhere that it wills in order to find its object. There is a feeling driving "Two Pendants For the Ear" which one finds out in the second "Pendant," called "Elena." Elena, Williams's beloved long-lived crackpot (psychic) mother from Puerto Rico is now dying, the refrain of the pendant is "Elena is dying"; but Williams can only proceed through the day-by-day, as if everything else is happening too. The story partly told through the voices of others, as they are surely always there, Williams's I is always in relation to others:

> Why just an hour ago
> she sat up straight on that bed, as
> straight as ever I saw her
> in the last ten years, straight
> as a ram-rod. You wouldn't believe
> that would you? She's not
> going to die . she'll be
> raising Cain, looking for her grub
> as per usual in the next two
> or three days, you wait and see

This pendant contains separate kinds of diction for all the voices outside, and all the voices inside Williams's head—he is after all in a "state," each voice its own music but gently similarly measured in such a way that that is the constant surprise of it, without interfering:

> a guerdon
> (a garden)
> and cries of children

indeterminate
Holy, holy, holy ...

A page later:

And Magazine # 1 sues Magazine
#2, no less guilty—for libel
or infringement or dereliction
or confinement

Elena is dying (but perhaps
not yet) . . .

A half-page later:

The river, throwing off sparks
in a cold world

Is this a private foight
or kin' I get into it?

This is a private fight.

Elena is dying.

In her delirium she said
a terrible thing:

Who are you? NOW!
I, I, I stammered. I
am your son . . . .

With the reference to the "private fight" we get the quasi-academic tie-in, the Point, of the tiger dream—but it doesn't come with an academic summary, you can imagine what that might be like: "I dreamt I fought a tiger / as my mother lay dying / Later she didn't recognize me. / I served her wine, where she was lying, / from her birthland, Puerto Rico . . . " Here, we get the real conversation, which seems spookily close to today's headlines not those of 1949:

>   Can't you give me
> something to make me disappear
> completely, said she sobbing—but
> completely!
>
>   No I can't do that
> Sweetheart (You God damned belittling
> fool, said I to myself)
>
> There's a little Spanish wine,
> pajarete
>   p-a-j-a-r-e-t-e
> But pure Spanish! I don't suppose
> they have it any more.

It is important that all of this, this process or experience, not be reduced to Poetry, but that it be a poem; Williams says, oh somewhere, that the "subject" (of or in a poem, that which he sometimes also calls the "object") is always fantasy and only the words count—you always make the poem up, but the right words won't come if you aren't where they are. They aren't in explanation, whether it's a bad summary-type-poem, or some pretentious-sounding opaque thing that backs up a theory—they're where they can kill. That isn't melodrama, and dying isn't melodramatic either, it's a form of living; that's what this poem's about. Imposing your will on another's death—twisting it to suit your poetic purposes—would be just that, an imposition, but this isn't—and not least because that exacting ear is involved, which measures experience by its own time. And Elena's dying makes its own time—she doesn't die in this poem, she has had a remission, but "Elena is dying." Dying is a time which will culminate in death, yet it floats and lasts, and can be divided down to the last or least incident within it if the poet, or patient wishes. Not a statement, or philosophy, it's living. Williams seems to detest philosophers as having become empty poachers on poetry, and I follow him there down to the smallest particulate of experience they can't pin.

Poetry has its own philosophy of time, bound up with stress as both a familiar musical beat and as a small pool of emphasis. That thought takes me to the variable foot, as that, finally, is what the variable foot is about:

> Relativity gives us the cue. . . .
>
> ("On Measure—Statement for Cid Corman")

And from "Letter to Richard Eberhart," 5/23/54:

> (approximate example)
>
> (1) The smell of the heat is boxwood
> (2) when rousing us
> (3) a movement of the air
> (4) stirs our thoughts
> (5) that had no life in them
> (6) to a life, a life in which
>
> (or)

(1) Mother of God! Our Lady!
(2) the heart
(3) is an unruly master:
(4) Forgive us our sins
(5) as we
(6) forgive
(7) those who have sinned against

Count a single beat to each numeral. You may not agree with my ear, but that is the way I count the line. Over the whole poem it gives a pattern to the meter that can be felt as a new measure. It gives resources to the ear which result in a language which we hear spoken about us every day.

Obviously a beat isn't a beat as we're used to thinking of it—a clock, or metronome, or heart, or something connected with the formerly fashionable breath; it's a mental stress or time, relative. (Though there's also a pulse-beat in those lines, a familiar sub-beat.) But Williams' beat is conceived of as being relative to the poet, the poem, the situation. To give "forgive" and "those who have sinned against" the same stress is exactly psychologically right: not all words are equal. They don't have neat borders. "Those who have sinned against" is a gluey unit, a puddle of stress. Equality is never about individual words, which is enslavement to the proliferative clock world (word word word word word: you now have a product!)—it's about how individual things are inside their own times. Time. Sexist example ("A Classic Picture"):

Therefore
she fusses with her hair

for
a woman does not want to seem repulsive,
unless
to gain for herself
she be hungry,
hungry!
as would be a man
and all hunger is repulsive
and puts on
an ugly face.

Equal weight to "for" and "a woman does not want to seem repulsive": "for" sets up the longer line, and the longer line gains by not being broken, by being one "beat." One doesn't think about that but about whether or not "all hunger is repulsive"— which could have been broken "all hunger is/ repulsive"— somewhat in the manner of the "Mother of God" lines, but to do that here would be pompous, rather than reflective (though both poems are reflective.) The poem is also annoying, and slight, but it's interesting that he throws into question the traditional "subject" reason for grouping words into lines, that is, that at least one thing, possibly more should happen in the line. "For"? Something does happen there, a logical thing, and the full line is as much the three feet together as the word "for," "Therefore she fusses with her hair for"— therefore she fusses with her hair for. That isn't the line though. The line is the three units floating together, but each foot is also a line. "Therefore/ she fusses with her hair/ for . . . " The stretching out process makes these ordinary phrases mysterious, as phrases. One thinks, 'Then they should be,' then the mysterious fibrous connection between matter and event and thought, our perception of which language tends to destroy, is restored. The variable foot looks like, somehow, particle waves, it looks like matter must, if we could only not see it according to our systematic noun-making eyes; the variable foot destroys the discreteness of previous poetry, the way previous poetry has made discrete word- and phrase- and line- shapes on the page and in the ear. But it looks so systematic! But it's less systematic than his messier looking poems, his Patersons and mini-patersons, really.

I have seen it
and so have you
when it puts all flowers
to shame.
Too, there are the starfish
stiffened by the sun
and other sea wrack
and weeds. We knew that
along with the rest of it
for we were born by the sea,
knew its rose hedges
to the very water's brink.
There the pink mallow grows
and in their season
strawberries
and there, later,
we went to gather
the wild plum.
I cannot say
that I have gone to hell
for your love
but often
found myself there

in your pursuit.
I do not like it
and wanted to be
in heaven. Hear me out.

("Asphodel, That Greeny Flower")

Why isn't this prose? Always the question with him—this especially this, and is that why these poems are still somewhat ignored? Too idiosyncratic these three's, and it's like prose the razor-edge of the words of the earlier poems has dissolved into these light waves, and into something really dangerously close to ordinary speech. But it's poetry because it sounds like poetry, the variable foot makes it poetry. Williams made his poetry easier and harder at the same time: the two together are always a great difficulty for people. Williams had worried here and there about works like the sagas and Homeric poems, how different they are from what he and his contemporaries were doing in that poetic music and action were fused into something so directly perceived that sophisticated readers now aren't sure they're having a proper poetry experience with them—where are the words? Where is ambiguity? Where is manifold meaning? Instead you have story, and sound, which creates depths that don't necessarily have to do with meaning, as living doesn't and flesh doesn't and ears and eyes don't. In the variable foot poems Williams robs the poem of the specialness of words and instead shapes matter, very ordinary matter, into an "object" which can be easily perceived. Via the ear, with no special skills, because syntax and punctuation are left whole and individual words are not squeezed and strained. It's a contemplative and discursive poetry, but it's something more because the experience of it is odd—I suppose one is "in" the experience in a way that's both physical and mental—which is what "direct" means.

Which leaves, to account for,
the tortured bodies
of
the slaves themselves
and
the tortured body of my flower
which is not a mustard flower at all
but some unrecognized
and unearthly flower
for me to naturalize
and acclimate
and choose it for my own.

("The Yellow Flower")

That's a nice description of poetic form, which is roughly the same as poetic music. My own feeling is that we aren't listening very hard right now to the sound of it—there's a lot of performance poetry but it tends to imitate music itself—as if that were a superior art because it has money behind it, not this other thing something like speaking, something like thinking, and something purely made up. A distortion into a new shape. The poem that's different every time (*Paterson*, "The Desert Music," etc.) is itself a form; this is a form too but it isn't structural, except in the three's—but would you always have to do that? How does one move on from the variable foot? Because if you imitate it you're marked as an imitator, whereas if you imitate *Paterson* mysteriously you're not. I'm not sure, I've done something myself, in *The Descent of Alette*, but unconsciously—the only way to go. I don't know, be mindful of it and of the fact, most of all, that it's meant to correspond to a change in your perception of reality, not just of poetry, or of the material (man-made) surfaces we're surrounded by. It's about the way we organize life into shapes and patterns and time, it's really about that—and what's beyond that. I think Williams's broken forms were about how modern life looked and felt in the United States; but the variable foot is more about what reality is despite what we try do to it.

First presented as a talk at Teachers & Writers, in New York, March, 1999.

All passages from poems are from *William Carlos Williams: Collected Poems*, edited by A. Walton Litz & Christopher MacGowan, Paladin Grafton Books, Glasgow, 1991.

Instability in Poetry

Truthfully, I informed Temple last summer that I would call this talk "Instability in Poetry" because I had discovered that my son, the poet Anselm Berrigan, in his handout for a summer course he'd taught at Naropa, had used a portion of a poem by me, and had, on the copy of the handout he'd given me, his own, drawn lines around the following lines:

> Come with me amid this instability
> permit me not to know what things mean yet.

The lines, I knew, were relevant to his esthetic and so his own generation, and I wanted that relevance somehow in this talk about my poetics. I decided to proceed with the word "instability" though I wasn't sure if it were applicable beyond the poem I was using it in, to which it is absolutely essential, and two other poems with which that poem makes up a trilogy. Not being sure if the word would work has itself created a certain instability or at least shakiness. But back to those two lines. They are from the long work *Benediction*, specifically from the first "poem" in *Benediction*, "City of Tingling"; *Benediction* is preceded by *Disobedience*, the first member of the trilogy, and *Reason and Other Women*, the second. The three poems are each between two and three hundred pages long.

Instability, in these poems, does not refer to instability of surface form. The poems which compose each long work are in a form invented for each, replicated throughout in a general way, both stable and loose-jointed. The basic forms are quite different from long work to long work. What is really unstable about the poems, and especially *Benediction*, is the world being created in them. *Benediction* posits a city, an invisible city or second world (that term having been established in *Reason and Other Women*) in which all of our unconsciousnesses/consciousnesses intermingle, those of all humans good and evil, dead and alive, but also all the unconsciousnesses/consciousnesses of animals, plants, rocks, whatever there is. *Benediction* tries to find this city, be in this ungeographical place, and of course it cannot do so by building a "city," as Christine de Pisan more literally did in *La Cité des Dames*: it can only do so by creating a changeable poem which keeps going after the impossible and occasionally realizes it (I think.) " . . . (W)hat things mean" in the above two lines—"Come with me amid this instability/ permit me not to know what things mean yet."—refers to more than the poem, it refers to the elements of what is taken for reality, it refers to the notion that we have created the world we perceive, by limiting how much we perceive and by defining how we perceive it. The lines hope for a poem with enough holes and slippery places in it for another way of perceiving or being to leak in, thus the poem is not terribly interested in keeping track of itself, because it doesn't want to be another system. Subjects are there, Themes are there, but they slip away due to the fact that they are "images." The ultimate—stated—frustration of the poem is its inability to keep new images from coming out of what's called the "hole of images"; the achievement of the poem would be its ability to lift the reader into the "city" (alas an image as stated) from time to time.

I don't think this is what Anselm would mean by instability, I think he would mean more of what we call keeping the poem open, letting it happen the way living does or should do, keeping the mind open to the freaky phrase which leads to the new poem place, the unexpected work or moment. That does not sound so dissimilar to what I've been describing, actually. But he doesn't want, and I have never wanted, as a poet, to know beforehand what a poem is going to do or say, although I have worked in strict forms occasionally and certainly taken on subjects. Everything is in the discovery, and the sense that one is getting somewhere; and unlike some poets I believe I am getting somewhere, I don't think I am constantly creating meaning, I think I am on a quest and am achieving it. I think I have suffered along the way, from being on the quest, and from what has happened to me by accident, or from fate, and from being a woman; I certainly haven't suffered more than many others. When someone close to me dies, I am drawn to the darkness of the world's genocides, wondering how people can endure so much and survive when they do—a commonplace thought process—but we are constantly creating these scenarios of many deaths by our limited and local perceptions of the world, our delusion that we need so much and need to make much more visible human world-structure, our inability to contact consciously the Crystal City, the city of my poems, our inability to know our interconnectedness and our literal creation of what is.

If my work is a quest, my knowledge has been and is being accumulated gradually, in time, though I sometimes know it all, all at once, past and future, that is, when I am consciously in that city. But I have been several selves or styles and I still am all of them or any of them when I wish. Recently I've thought of myself as being empty from loss, and full, since there's so much room, of only consciousness, pure self, but I can use a self or an old self whenever I want to, as I do throughout *Mysteries of Small Houses*, which is written in many styles. I think I'm supposed to be making jokes now, to lighten the gravity and possible pretentiousness (as if I could care) of what I'm saying, and I could do that if I wanted to, out of a style I used in the '70s, which I am very fond of and which allowed much instability but of a slightly different kind: it wanted to find out what people were actually saying now and not ten years ago, what said and how said. Therefore it let in the said while it was being said and hoped an artful shape would be present too. But it fought against the tendency of poetry to speak in just-previous manners or vocabularies, the ones older poets had made a success in.

A slightly earlier style, whose discoveries flowed into that style, wanted to find strength in what was and is my personal instability, a frequent shakiness which opens me up by first nearly breaking me: my sons and probably you yourselves as poets will recognize this instability. We aren't supposed to talk about it. Current academicians might call us something like "poets of the self" if we do, and our parents, still, will ask us to talk to the psychiatrist in the family. I am reminded of my son's, the poet Edmund Berrigan's, invention of a movement called Crackademics: it presumes to come from Harvard and its pronouncements are made in an accent only Edmund can achieve. Try saying "poets of the self" through the very top of the nose and you might get it. The Crackademics movement has produced three volumes of the magazine Crackademics, plus two poetry anthologies, all of which exist in one photocopyable copy each. It is a very subtle movement, since the Crackademy itself is one's, or Edmund's, mind. But back to my matter . . .

Here's the beginning of a long poem I wrote in 1973-4 when I was pregnant with Edmund, and very shaky, called *Songs for the Unborn Second Baby*:

Pregnant again involucre

(sounds gorgeous)

Pregnant

not the repast of news or psychological

though arithmetical

(stars, filth)

I ingeminate

I dream
of a compost

into whose composition paper
can go

and which itself
composes the paper
but literally,
how, do you suppose

the wonders
that would be facts,
from dreams,
get lost

reflex you refractor old saw you
thought
you'd got swisher,
craggy, from the Chinese, more masculinely
feminine, only refined
when wanting to be startling,
emeralds sacral putrid but
you're just cavernous
round a foetus
and true

A dream hole
in tower wall
to admit or
mirth music

the holes let issue

Mohaves coffins flowers jealousy

I'm struck by how much the compost dream is what one would call a poetics, and it illustrates one of mine surely, the idea of a piece of paper which is among and composed of the world's organic leavings, the poem as the shape of past taken into future, what really was alive, as one of my book titles from the '70s is *When I Was Alive*. The form of *Songs for the Unborn Second Baby* allows for a lot of slippage: alternating between long variable-foot-type lines, and short-lined vertical columns it would be Williamsesque but it's influenced by dictionary syntax and employs randomly selected words to keep going. And it wants holes in it, it says (I've just noticed this). It wants to be able to talk about postpartum depression, actually, which I was still experiencing during second pregnancy, and incorporate it into the passage of jeweled or coarse diction and external happenings, incorporate it into the whole apparatus of poetry, which is much larger than the depression and therefore can probably cure it. It is a composty poem in that it borrows language, uses all sorts of detritus, mixes and mashes living matter. It is like the collages I'd soon begin making, composed of glittery leftovers glued down and painted over into unity. What was on my mind could not be approached headfirst because then there was nothing to say except a stark sentence or clinical phrase, but the experience of the depression kept inventing itself in my living and so this sort of continuously invented poem embodied it.

Later when I wasn't depressed and was living in the spoken word as vividly and completely as possible, I wrote, among other works, those long poems composed of voices which I've previously alluded to. I had discovered that company was useful, that the spoken word was both transparent and mysterious, that my household was a community and if not precisely exemplary still human, American, and intelligent, in the sense that creatures have intelligence and communicate:

You might want to talk about it in terms of its difference.
It would be an act of generosity.
Generosity killed the cat.
But getting around the periphery of some similar kind of
thing. As I was moved toward trying it by these & by who I
am not. I don't want there to be any secrets told.
Instead how my shoulder feels when I turn this corner of
the left or whatever, finally to say that.
Pretty lavender plant, help me to make a go of it.
Me too.
Me too.
Right.
You can't pay me because you can't afford me, ever.
You may have to go down to Hades, I may stay on earth, but they can't
ever have either of us.
I am my own French translation.
So?
I want to be person in time, rather than personality.
It was not suitable for a newspaper. It was subject in a
formal way.
It was fantastic.
Don't be dumb now.
Allen said Exactly. Tell them why you have a stomach-ache.
Has this funny thing going on of this girl & it just goes on like
a quest a few bumps bruises & pains are the least of her
worries.
I do love the down on his cheek though.

How can she get through anything without something truly
awful happening?
This quest don't say beauty.

The woman on the quest is, literally, Kathy Acker, though she's never named. The words about her are used for their, her, sense of seriousness. I was attracted to the passage for inclusion here because of the lines about turning a corner—something Ted Berrigan said; then I noticed the Eurydice/Orpheus reference—something I wrote down as voice but didn't really say; then the "quest" allusion, already relevant to this talk, revealed itself. How everything finally works in together is part of the knowledge of instability. This passage is in a middle-period version of this voice-y style, being most of a section from "As You Like It," which was written in 1981, after Reagan was elected and two years before Ted, my first husband, died. This poem knows he's dying, though I didn't, but that poems know such things is something I now know and is perforce part of my esthetic or poetics. My poems by being unstable, open to whatever kind of language I'm using as it comes to me, do then operate from an unconscious level of selection, and the unconscious knows, because it isn't in time the same way as the surface, daily I is. It is in touch with the Crystal City which is above time, to speak in the language of my most recent poetry. But also, language shows you what you've said, thus what you know, once you're separate from it, objective. As dreams do. The dreamer floats above time too, as we all know from our occasional dreams about future events.

In the late '80s I began to use my dreams, and the dreaming process—visionary process, trancelike process—to write my poems. *The Descent of Alette* is all vision and dream: every bit of its story, anecdotal detail, and imagery comes directly from my imagination, and is either dreamed or visualized. To visualize I would concentrate on the first thing I "saw" beneath my eyelids, and then follow the next forms suggested until a story-shape had arrived. Or I would begin a visualization with a detail of a dream, but with the rule that it would be the first detail of the dream that came to mind, however disconnected it might seem from the poem. Dreams, of course, are immensely unstable, in imagery, progress, and emotional base. But their reality as experience, and as experienced, contributes to the suspicion that the everyday world is unstable too, that we have conspired to make it stable by inventing time, because the instability of a dream-like world can be so uncomfortable. (I was once subject to a period of déjà-vu after a trans-Atlantic flight and was unable to be "in time" with the city I'd landed in for about an hour: I kept thinking that everything happening to me had already happened.) But instability is also potential, full of the future and of the new. Thus, in *The Descent of Alette,* when Alette has committed the act which is about to result in the Tyrant's death, what is spoken of is change through dreams:

> "He spoke with difficulty,"
> "in fits:" "'I think . . . " "you have killed me . . . " "I am . . . " "really
> dying'" "He seemed so" "bewildered" "'How could you be" "this cruel?"
> "And do you not" "kill yourself?" "your own culture . . . " "soul's breath?'"
>
> "'I'm killing no one" "You are not real" "You said so" "yourself,' I
> said" "Forms in dreams . . . " "forms in dreams'" "I searched within"
> "for right words" "'I will change the" "forms in dreams'" "I lifted"
> "the dead plant" "& flung it" "across the grotto" "'Starting"
>
> "from dreams," "from dreams we" "can change," "will change" "In
> dreams," "in dreams, now" "you will die" "You will die'"

To change the forms in dreams has become an important idea for me, and I've repeated those words in other poems. *The Descent of Alette* is itself an attempt to change the forms in dreams, to provide a ground for a new kind of dreaming. If one can dream without the Tyrant present, one can dream new self and new relations, a new city, or even the real city. However, it has been necessary for me to kill the Tyrant various other times in poems; I am now, as usual, hoping he is finally dead in me. I know he isn't dead in the world, and much of my poetry since *Alette* has been directed towards telling the world that it is enslaved to him and that it is, as a consequence of all his policies, dying, as the end of the Holocene Era does sometimes seem near.

The style of *Alette* is obviously very different from the previous two styles exemplified. As explanation I can first offer the word "instability" again, my will or my inability not to stay the same. But the same style or self cannot handle everything that comes up, and so a poet of 'one style' sometimes sits out certain situations. Not being a poet of one style, I was forced by shock, as I often am, to change again: the death of my brother, who is alluded to, but remotely, in *Alette* whenever soldiers and war are mentioned, propelled me into the writing of the poem. He had been a sniper in Vietnam and had died of an accidental morphine overdose, in 1988, after years of post-traumatic stress disorder. *The Descent of Alette* is a descent into the misery of the used, the homeless, the tyrannized and mechanized. It proposes paradise, but is unsure of what it can be, since all previous descriptions of it belong to the Tyrant. *The Descent of Alette* is very much a poem for the public, despite the oddness of the quotation marks, which as ten or twelve years have gone by have begun to lose their oddness. They are for the public so that it can read the poem properly, aloud or slowly silently, with the right stresses and pauses, and be drawn into the story, which is its—the public's—story. The quotation-marked phrases are similar to each other in length and sound, but not the same, and the look of each page is similar: the formal variation of the earliest style discussed above is absent. The concept of voice remains in the very use of the quotation marks, which on one level signify "This is spoken"—this is a poem which should be read aloud or as if aloud. Above all, the whole poem is apart from me, and the quotation marks made that separation a continuous fact as I wrote.

After *The Descent of Alette*, I wrote two shorter long poems: *Close to me & Closer . . . (The Language of Heaven)* and *Désamère,* which are different from *Alette* and different from each other. *Close to me* is a dialogue, exclusively, between a dead father and a live daughter, the father speaking in colloquial "patterns," a metrical prose governed by ellipses and underlinings, and the daughter speaking in poems. The father tries to describe death and heaven to the daughter, so this is my first probe into paradise, my first go at the Crystal City. In the poem, the daughter tries to draw 'close and closer' to the father, in order to take on his knowledge, and at the poem's climax they merge, so she can know what death is, then draw apart. This is a "fiction," as *Alette* is, and I think of my long conversational poems of the '70s and '80s also as fictions involving characters and the boundaries of a story shape. But I also "experienced" the poem, and transcribed what seemed to be my dead father's voice in my head talking to me mornings, dictating the father's sections in his halting, Southwestern manner. The poem states that one must "stumble" in order to tell the truth, i.e. the truth is unstable; his voice stumbles, and her voice becomes more and more stumbling as well. The metrics are not smooth, as in *Alette*, and I hardly ever read aloud from the book, though it has had a lot of impact on some readers. It embarrasses me, but all of one's work can seem embarrassing at unexpected times; it embarrasses me rather consistently, though I love it. Even though it's a fiction, I can't find anywhere to hide in it, as I can in much more personal poetry: I'm addressing a forbidden subject, as sex for example isn't.

> (He speaks)
> There is nothing but magic anywhere . . .
>
> So . . . I guess that . . . what you have to find . . . you have to find your measure . . . by magic, or in . . . magic. Magic . . . is how the world, came about . . . Must be. Magic . . . I think, goes against . . . it goes against time. What the scientists . . well what people do now . . . they find out—try to find out . . . about the little bitty ways, of everything . . . how it works . . . in its tiniest . . . And they, you know . . . they seem to . . . put everything . . . in time . . . . More in time. They want it all to be . . . stretch-out-able! Like a . . . you know, formula. But it was started by . . . something . . . that wasn't . . . in time. They keep giving you . . . time, time . . . when what you need . . . is magic—not in time. Poetry . . . is magic . . . Or else . . . I mean . . . the words come from . . . nowhere, from no time. Like I do . . . talking . . . to you.

Like other women poets of my generation, writing long works on themes the world reserves for philosophy as such, I am often called ambitious. The word "desperate" would probably be more accurate: I can't accept the Tyrant's truths, I have a short lifespan, I need to find out everything for myself.

The poem *Désamère* is also a mixture of poetry and prose and is much more pessimistic than its predecessors, being about a global-warming-future world. It's divided into three sections, and I'm proud to say that the second section is an utterly invented piece of prose fiction. The poem as a whole marks my move to France: thus the first section is influenced by the metrics of the lais of Marie de France; and the French Surrealist poet Robert Desnos, who died in the concentration camp at Terezine, is a major character in the book. His is the oracular voice of the first section, and his style is the overt influence of the set of poems that make up the third section. I had floundered for some months before I started the poem, and when I got the beginning and showed it to my (late) husband, Doug Oliver, he said, "That's it! It's when you get that black voice that wells up from nowhere that you know you have the poem!" That statement has become my touchstone for when I'm finally writing "it," that a dark voice has welled up again, telling me what to say.

But to call that statement a touchstone is seemingly to contradict the surface of *Mysteries of Small Houses*, which I wrote next, since it is written in the first person singular and is ostensibly autobiographical: how can a mysterious "other" voice welling up, as Robert Desnos' seemed to in me, be the one to tell one's own story? *Mysteries* is meant to be an investigation of the self and not primarily autobiography, rather my self was the only one I had to investigate in the way I envisioned. I wanted to make the pronoun "I", the personal pronoun not the fictionalized "I" of *Alette* and *Désamère*, really personal in the sense that if I stood in it as closely as possible, stood in myself—which it seemed to me I had rarely done in poems—and said 'This moment am I? Who is it? What is it I am when nude?' I could terrify myself, shock myself, destabilize myself profoundly, and see if I were really there. In order to do this I meditated on all the events where I had most taken part in the givens "society" and "life": aspects of girlhood, marriage, childbirth, deaths, interactions with war, etc: society's idea of the self. I went into the past in a way which I gradually realized—again with Doug's help—was a sort of self-hypnosis: I used a trance state, which is not that different from the state poems are written in anyway, to focus on those events and who had experienced them. Was I there? Were those events I? My conclusions are best expressed in the final poem, "Lady Poverty" (and the she in this excerpt is Lady Poverty):

She's I

She should be

The shape of a life is impoverishment—what
can that mean
except that loss is both beauty and knowledge—
has no face no eyes for
seasons of future delivery—rake the dirt
like Mrs. Miller used to
down at the corner had a desert yard and raked her dirt.

Beginning in poverty as a baby there is nothing
for one but another's food and warmth
should there ever be more
than a sort of leaning against and trust a food for
another from out of one—that would be
poverty—we're taught not to count on
anyone, to be rich,
youthful, empowered
but now I seem to know that the name of a self is poverty
that the pronoun I means such and that starting so
poorly, I can live.

That is, there is a vast self, a real I, and that is almost all it is, I am. But I connect. I lean against and trust, I rake the dirt, and I address the reader: "Come with me amid this instability."

So I'm back at the beginning of the talk, and the word "instability" has succeeded. My most recent work, the three long books I mentioned first, are a compendium of these techniques and insights I've been discussing: they are variously and often in the same book, narrative, conversational, personal, public, fictional and as true as I the pronoun can be. They are in prose and poetry, they are long-lined and short-lined and sentenced. They are unstable, large and wobbly, all three of the books. I think as stance or procedure, they might appeal to the younger poets who seem to run with no "schools"—the movements of the '50s, '60s, and '70s having been too final in some way to generate more movements except one that uses them all but operates a willing blindness to doctrine entering the poem.

Sometimes it's so hard to be here in the right city   Can I see it?
I'm from each end of a spectrum   of I young and old, past and future
and it's so hard to get here   With no form but thought or dreams   With no
forms but the already seen   Already seen down there, but where do forms come
from?   I want to be in this high bare place   Allow it   Asking who
Ask me or you   How do you ask   Ask who?

Asking in the quick   broken phrases of thought. It's quick thought reaching out
and connecting   complexly needing only a few   A few wordlike things fan out
and curl   around other statements or expressions   How we talk here: We
think. telepathy, our true condition

Units of blue and red-yellow amorphous are seen against hills in a dream
units of two and three "things" combined into the amorphous tinted are seen
blue and red-yellow, along the hills   they could be anything or
us   they could be   us in

ourselves each and same

Same-looking not same

Could be anything. Could there have been anything What's anything?

Come with me amid this instability
permit me not to know what things mean yet.

I myself probably need to change again, having experienced another death of someone close to me, and having recently written so much. One of my most current esthetic procedures is, in fact, to give power, if I have access to any, to that younger generation and to learn from them. I have begun to teach the poetry of those under forty, and thirty, more frequently, in my workshop in Paris, than the poems of my own generation. I'm tired of what we say and even tired of what I say: their discoveries are not new—ours weren't either—but are so fresh, because they, the poets, are different. And their approach to relationships, to racial issues, to politics, to economic realities is new and knowledgeable, confronted by a completely battered world which I regret being among the bequeathers of. It is unstable and one is unstable in it. Here is a portion of a poem I wrote recently:

> my hair is mess, uncombed, pinned back and up, all brown. I'm wearing a denim skirt, and denim jacket. I help the young man with spiky hair position himself behind the microphone, then I leave the room, a cafe where a poetry reading will take place. To the side are two other young poets, with spiky hair, sitting in highchairs. I leave to the cave as always because I alone is free, the long blue dress is to see that blue is its choice of image but the meaning was forgotten. I has been selected because I couldn't simplify my direction. I knows everything next. I in blue, I with owl, I into light, I fly up or down. I the horse and I bleeds, that is just bleeding. I is secreting emotional

and intellectual

matter, soft and dark, I doesn't I don't need it any more.

2001, Talk given at Temple University

Benediction, Letter Machine Editions, Tucson AZ, 2015

Songs for the Unborn Second Baby, Distance No Object, London, 2021. First published by United Artists, Lexox MA, 1979

Margaret & Dusty, Coffee House Press, St. Paul, 1985

The Descent of Alette, Penguin Books, New York, 1996

Close to me & Closer . . . (The Language of Heaven) and *Désamère*, Two Books by Alice Notley, O Books, 1995

Mysteries of Small Houses, Penguin Books, New York 1998

Salvo

In talking about Douglas Oliver's *A Salvo For Africa* and certain questions it brings up—the writing of political poetry in general, expatriation on the part of a poet, and an intense cultivation of international sympathies—I will also be addressing aspects of my own life and work, explaining to you why I live and write in Paris. I have lived in Paris for the last ten years, eight of those years with Doug Oliver. Doug was British but spent three separate periods of his life in Paris, as well as four or five years in New York City with me and my sons. He had become the figure of the international consciousness, the politically involved writer—his blurb on *Salvo*, from the British *Guardian* newspaper calls him "One of the best political poets writing in English"—and it will probably be as a political poet that he is best known, though certain writers in Britain who are loyal to lyric or postmodern traditions, and therefore to those features, per se, of his oeuvre, might disagree.

I will give you a bit of Doug's background as a writer before I take up *A Salvo for Africa*, which was published a few weeks before his death in April, 2000. Doug spent ten years as a journalist, first working for a farm machinery journal, then for *The Cambridge Evening News*, Agence-France Presse in Paris, and finally a large-circulation Coventry newspaper. He then went to the University of Essex, in his 30s—he had left school at 16—and spent the rest of his life, for the most part, in university and educational environments. But he'd acquired interests and habits of research from journalism which he used to write all the poems and novels that I was witness to (he was a novelist as well as a poet; there are two unpublished novels, and two published ones, plus an unpublished memoir/biography, a dual take on himself and the French communard figure, Louise Michel.*) An early sequence of his, called *The Diagram Poems* (which is dedicated to Ted Berrigan and myself), is both a poem of grief for the death of his infant son, who had Downs Syndrome, and an account of an abortive attempt by the Tupamaros, a revolutionary group in Uruguay in the '70s, to take over a police station. Doug already believed that the personal and the political could not be separated, and this conviction began to drive most of his poetry.

Doug's milestone poem of the '80s—and the one that has received the most attention of all his work—is the long poem, *The Infant and the Pearl*, which is written exactly in the stanza of the medieval poem *The Pearl*. This is one of the most complex forms in the English language, involving a set stanza, and a set number of stanzas, with strict rules of rhyme, alliteration, and repetition of lines. Here is his email explanation of the stanza, for the benefit of the poet Marcella Durand:

> The number of stanzas is medieval-magical, being ten times ten plus one, that is perfection times perfection plus unity; the hundred and one resulting stanzas are divided into groups of five with one group of six; each stanza is twelve lines long and rhymed as closely as an Italian sonnet but there is a marriage with medieval alliteration so that every single line has to alliterate at least twice and up to four times; the first line of each stanza has to contain a key word, and this word is repeated in the last line of the stanza which is a refrain; the refrain changes every group of five stanzas and so does therefore the key word though in a slightly staggered manner from the refrain; you can add further refinements such as important plot changes at numerically significant stanza numbers; lastly the whole trick of it, of course, is to get the story told and rounded off ex-

actly within the one hundred and one stanzas. Practically no one who reviewed the poem ever mentioned that each of the one thousand and twelve lines alliterated though this is surely unusual in modern poetry.

The Infant and the Pearl is a satire of Thatcherite England. Doug figured that the best way to handle such material would be to dignify the poem through the use of this intricate, beautiful stanza, at the same time as providing a telling contrast between Thatcher's heartless policies and the beauty of a certain kind of poetry; between Thatcher's ruthlessness and the visionary light and sense of the good permeating *The Pearl*, a poem about a father's vision of his deceased daughter and of the heavenly landscape she inhabits, and, hopefully, Doug's own poem does.

Doug followed that poem with a different long satire, *Penniless Politics*, which takes place in New York City in the late '80s, is written in a rap-like loose stanza, and describes how a party named Spirit manages to form itself, rewrite the Constitution of the United States and elect as President of the U.S. a Haitian immigrant, a woman. The stanzas are interspersed with speech-like or incantatory poems, and documents, including a chain letter (via which the political party is initiated), press releases, and the new amendments to the Constitution. An ungendered pronoun is invented—esh—and a new species name, hooman. Voodoo and its deities permeate the doings of the plot; the poem is a plea for a sympathetic, multicultural New York in which the races not only are friends with each other but literally bed down with each other.

After *Penniless Politics*, *A Salvo for Africa* was Doug's next large-scale political work, begun in 1993 after we had moved to Paris. It was triggered by a statement he'd read, in which someone touting the new global free trade and going on about how beneficial to everyone it was then said, 'Of course, there will be basket cases such as Africa.' This line appears as follows in the poem "Our Family is Full of Problems" (p. 15):

And I read a Daily Mail economist forecasting great wealth
for all free market countries. 'Of course, there will be basket cases,
such as Africa.' And I grab you by the arm.
'Did you hear that? Africa! Not a Coventry suburb, a whole continent
written off in our free trade fanaticism.'

Doug had a long, difficult time getting the book published; he was constantly, therefore, in a position of updating material and rewriting the prose sections, which got cut and changed so many times that I see something of a palimpsest when I look at the book, for I was asked to read and reread it through its many versions. I sometimes look for poems that are no longer there. And it has taken me weeks to find this quote: I thought it was in the prose, but I thought I was looking intently at the poems: but I am looking away as fast as I look in case I become upset.

I notice I've already started to answer one of the questions I wanted to ask, that is the old, boring question: is it possible to write good political poetry? Should one try to write it? As I've hinted, one thing Doug would say is that anyone is being political at any time, that there is nothing but political poetry, but that political is not everything a poem might be. But *A Salvo for Africa* is not a poem placing an individual in her/his life which is by definition political: it takes on a subject for political journalists, a huge one—the present (1990s—though if anything, worse now) plight of the continent of Africa.

When I was a young poet everyone said that good political poetry could not be written, and I suspect this is still said in some places; or that political poetry is not of interest to one in X country though it might be okay for people in Poland (that was Communist Poland), or Northern Ireland, or South Africa; or that one is being political by changing the syntax of poetry and perhaps therefore of consciousness, and isn't that the only way to be effective? Then one might say, what about Allen Ginsberg? And then another person would say, but his best poem is "Kaddish" isn't it? All of this quite ignorant to my mind—in this world today, for example, exactly today, what business does one have not writing about politics? Yet my great friend Phil Whalen has renounced somewhere his poems on the Vietnam War, and they aren't his best work—but might not someone's poems on that war be among their best work? I think my elegy for my brother, who had been a sniper in Vietnam and died of a drug overdose in '88 after considerable post-traumatic stress disorder, is among my best poems, though I wish I hadn't had to write it. Certainly I couldn't help but write it—as Doug could not help but write *Salvo.* You might say then, but that was your brother, this is a continent Oliver never visited and anyway I don't believe he cared that much. Then I would say, a book worked on for years and he didn't care that much? It isn't personal? I lived it with him for years, after his death packing up box after box of newspaper clippings, to send to his new archive at the University of Essex. The many books on Africa are still on the shelves, and I cry when I read the poems aloud—for they are imbued with our time together but most of all with his voice, which is full of care . . . I must have a point to "come to": that this is what the phrase "international sympathies" means, and our—Doug's and mine—kind of expatriation can mean, a love or passion that arises after leaving one's country and, on the other hand, not really joining the culture of the new country. Because one doesn't do that—perhaps can't do that – unless one is young and literally marries into the country, marries a Frenchman say, and so the language, manners, literature, mind of it (as Doug posits in *Penniless Politics* romantic and sexual relations between members of all the races and cultures of the city of New York, in order to build a more inclusive social order . . .) Doug didn't do that; I didn't do that. But, British and American, we married each other and then finally lived in neither of our countries. We had fallen in love with the world's variety and also had both become deeply depressed by the economic brutalities, wars, mistreatments, genocides, famines, draughts, and environmental ravagings we became conscious of.

So it is 1993 and Doug wants to write about Africa. Period. There are several things to consider: can he afford to travel to Africa? No. But he knows everything about how to do research. Will he find out sufficient information about an entire continent to enable him to be called an expert? No. What is the point of his writing the book then? By making Africa's history and problems as vivid (a favorite word of his) as possible in his own mind, he can then transfer that vividness, that electricity, to the mind of the reader; this is the imagination, what it is and does. "Our greatest cruelties often arise from a failure to imagine," he says in the introduction. Who will these poems be for, what audience should he have in mind? He is angling for the attention of the ordinary British reader, of poetry; that narrows it down, but there is a somewhat dependable readership in Britain, which is most open to mainstream themes and clarities. Doug liked to change styles (as do I), to have several styles available, for different kinds of audiences; then this will not be an avant-garde book, and it will not be written to other poets. How will other poets feel about this? In Britain they will be pissed off, they will call him reactionary, retrograde etc etc—this is his fear and this happens. As some reviewers will chide him for never visiting Africa, and Africanists will chide him for writing about the already known! All of this is also anticipated, though Doug didn't live to see the reviews; but he did know what his poet friends thought about individual poems as they appeared. Will the readers read the book and think and care a little more about Africa from now on? That is the hope—who knows?—I still don't know. But he has his quote from Malcolm X as backup for the authenticity of the project: "Whites who are sincere should organise among themselves and figure out some strategy to break down the prejudice that exists in white communities. This is where they can function more intelligently and more effectively, in the white community itself, and this has never been done." For so much of the neglect of Africa is, still, simply racism.

The next problem, the delightful problem, is what form to use. Doug had a great regard for the mixing of prose and poetry: it is a procedure that goes back to Dante, and one that Doug had used before in an autobiographical sequence called *An Island That Is All the World*. If one thinks of *La Vita Nuova* one understands what Doug is about here: as Dante wrote his poems in strict forms describing the progress of his love for Beatrice, so Doug writes his poems in familiar-seeming forms describing what he is perceiving about Africa (and how he is coming to love it); and as Dante wrote prose passages explaining each poem to the reader, so Doug writes a kind of pared-down journalistic passage to go with each of his poems. Each poem deals with a different country, in general an Anglophone country; the prose passages deal with history, economics, plight. The prose passages at one point were very long; they evolved into their present form through several stages of cutting. The poems have a very subtle music—influenced by tapes of popular African music—which probably cannot be gotten without their being read aloud. Yet I think if you read the prose passages aloud, you will hear a gentle, personal voice speaking too.

Being convinced that this is a sequence that must be read aloud to be appreciated fully, I am now going to concentrate on a few of the poems, which I will read and then comment on.

First, I will a read a poem with a subject out of Zimbabwe's history, "The King's Garden."

[I read the poem.]

This poem is funny at the expense of the British, while telling a tragic story of the Matabele people, whose king, Lobengula, is tricked into giving up his country to Cecil Rhodes; but the picture of the 30 Englishmen squatting in Lobengula's dung-filled garden is irresistibly scathing. Lobengula's garden is contrasted with the militarily precise flower-garden of retired colonels, visited by children like the author, three generations later—in fact a real garden in Bournemouth, the city where Doug grew up. But now think about the sounds of the poem, the way the lines work. Using proper nouns such as Lobengula and Matabele, the writer is drawn into the field of a different language; and these words shake up the line, animate it, make pinpricks in staidness, underscore the hilarity of a scene in which unscrupulous men literally dip into shit courting a king. Doug immediately plays off the African sounds by paralleling "Lobengula" and "Matabele people" with "maggoty dung," "maggoty garden," but also lines like "The dapper London lawyer Maguire, / MP, Fellow of All Souls, stuck / out a leg to raise his buttocks from the mire."

The poem is alive down its length with this consonantal percussiveness. I recently refound an index card on which Doug had printed several key word clusters he used to get the sound of poems like "The King's Garden." One is the opening line of a song by Dindo Yogo (and I'm sorry here, I can't do country or language, because the tape doesn't say and I can't remember): ni poké a-molingo baas sumi la ta poinla té-o. I also don't remember if this is Doug's approximation of the sounds or a subsequent rendering he got from a man in a music shop. The point is that he listened to this word cluster and intonation shape over and over to get a line that would "go" throughout the book, a sort of background measure, not followed, but used as a haunt. Here is the opening sentence, five lines, of "The New Medicine," which follows the "ni poké a-molingo baas" sound more precisely. (This is a poem dealing with the scandalous decline of the English national health care system, and contrasting it along the way with witchcraft and traditional African medicine):

> Hospitals too productive, come to the end of their budgets for ops,
> routine surgery halted till the next budget, way of the world would mean
> some bag lady didn't get her op, the bishop got his
> with medical insurance like all higher-ups
> on the internal market for organ repair.

Another line on Doug's card, though, is not African but from a song of Dolly Parton's, called I think, "Potential New Boyfriend": Gotta keep your hands off my potential new boyfriend. I think this may have been misremembered—I remember it as "Better keep your hands off my . . ." But his version of the full chorus, which makes the line make sound sense, is:

> Gotta keep your hands off my
> Gotta keep your hands off my
> Gotta keep your hands off my potential new boyfriend

Doug had a Masters in Applied Linguistics and had done research which involved attaching electrodes to people's throats and getting them to read lines of poetry, then comparing the shapes made by the voices of the individual readers, that is comparing the machine traces made by the linguistic machinery the electrodes were attached to. Using this material, he wrote a book called *Poetry and Narrative in Performance*, which outlines a theory of stress in poetry, and also prose, and is replete with intonation patterns for single lines or several successive lines, in the form of raw data and simplified drawings of these contours. My point is, I suppose, that he was very sensitive to the individual line as an intonational shape. Here is his favorite line for discussion of stress, a line from "Backwater Blues," as sung by Bessie Smith, repeated twice and resulting in two contours and two differently stressed lines.

Back Wa- ter Blues done cause me to pack my things/&go
Back Wa- ter Blues done caused me to pack my things and go.

Do you hear the difference? During the years when Doug was writing *A Salvo for Africa*, he would occasionally give a lecture on stress, using "Backwater Blues" as a primary example, eliciting from the lecture audience a definition of poetic stress, which was close to a linguistic definition, but with an emphasis on Doug's favorite point, that the stress isn't anywhere in particular though it is there. But what part of the word "blues"—in the first line—is it found in? Here and gone and definite but not precisely placed: a paradox of time. This sort of very fine breakdown of the individual line and sound, which goes way beyond the iambs and trochees way of talking about measure, or syllabics or, say, the variable foot way of talking about measure, into an appreciation of the rise and fall of the real voice through sounded and unsounded consonants, pauses and clusters and the stress—the hearing of the intoned line of the line—informs *Salvo*. This is a very good ear, applied to the imagination, applied to the political.

I'd now like to read another kind of poem, with the prose this time: "Somalia Traditional Practices" (prose) and "The Infibulation Ceremony."

[I read the prose and poem.]

I must say this poem always makes me feel very quiet. It is a masterpiece of tact, but it makes one nonetheless feel it. I can't think of a subject more difficult to deal with in a poem; I feel that this poem holds unresolved all the contradictions of a situation in which young girls are being infibulated because their mothers as well as their fathers think it best for them, where Westerners are looking on and possibly judging, where there is without question a "hot, male wind" present, even if only women be present. There are many things one could say about this poem, its exquisite pacing, its tone so far from polemic as to be only full of care in the moment of physical wounding; but I'd especially like to say the obvious, that it would not work if the metaphor of the hut as vulva were not used—this metaphor explains the operation but it is a metaphor: it is quick and not clinical or violent. But it is explicit.

Now I'd like to read a poem, "The Mixed Marriage," which incarnates Doug's passion for the outer world of events and, truly, others. This is a poem about Botswana; the prose tells the story of Seretse Khama's mixed marriage to the white English woman Ruth Williams, Khama being the heir to the chiefdom of the country, situated on the border of South Africa, at the height of the apartheid years. The prose also speaks of Botswana's covetable (by other nations) wealth of diamonds.

[I read the poem.]

It is the suddenness and compression of the final images I'm most interested in: we are led through a description of the world as video game, to a search for "the real world's beauty"—an ordinary phrase (though note it is not 'the world's real beauty') for what should be ordinary but isn't, because it's buried, and the real world's beauty is figured as an "ordinary" woman, "not particular to me" who wears "different gowns in various seasons / of this tryst" but who now looks "pained, starved, flinching at bombs, or cackling with laughter . . ." Then she multiplies into millions, but also remaining one she, she waits for "any sincere person"—ordinary phrase again, but "sincere" is not a cheap word (remember how George Oppen uses it, speaking for a sincere poetry)—"to penetrate this strangeness we've created." Then, suddenly, she points her finger at the poet and onto her finger he slips "the black diamond, Africa, / which I found in a tiny country, Botswana." That is he marries her under the sign of Africa, as if to say, this is real, this is beautiful, this is ordinary, this Africa, whose suffering also distresses me so. This is marriage. That the black diamond is Africa is peculiarly satisfying—something about the color and size of a ring, one sees, feels it slipped on.

I'd like to say just a few words about the poem, "A Salvo for Malawi," which is too long to read, but is a masterpiece of narration, and also, as the title indicates, crucial to the meaning of the book as a whole. "A Salvo for Malawi" tells a story that Africanists, and obviously Africans, know well—it is, as the prose states, "a founding legend" of the country of Malawi, but one that people like myself might not know. It is the story of John Chilembwe, a Nyasaland preacher, a Seventh-Day Adventist who had gone to the States to be trained, and returned to build a church and prayer houses in the Shire Highlands, lands "stolen from Nyasa tribes illiterate / in our law" (the poem states in the voice of an Englishman). One land-owner was a Mr. Livingstone, a descendant of the famous missionary, whose estate was called the Bruce estate. Chilembwe

> Had the effrontery to build this huge church
> and prayer houses across the Bruce estate
> which Livingstone had to burn
> or the natives would think they had land rights.
> But all this was manageable until the war . . .

That is, World War I. Chilembwe called for his countrymen—badly treated by men such as Livingstone, made to work their hereditary lands for nothing or very little, "no pay, or money thrown on the ground"—to resist going to war for the whites:

Sheer need drives them
to recruit in our German war,
the Boche attacking by lake and land
from the North, long lines of porters
carrying munitions on their heads,
dying in a two-thirds majority
over the whites, their only democracy.

A letter written by Chilembwe, censored by the *Nyasaland Times*, is quoted from in the poem: "But in time of peace the Government failed to help the underdog. In time of peace everything for Europeans only. And instead of honour we suffer humiliation with names contemptible. But in time of war it has been found that we are needed to shed our blood in equality. It is true that we have no voice in this government . . . ."

Livingstone was stabbed and beheaded by Chilembwe's followers, in the presence of Mrs. Livingstone; his head was stuck on a pole in Chilembwe's church. Chilembwe was then chased down and shot by the whites. This is the story we are told, in detail, in the poem's nine pages. But the poem begins by abolishing ordinary notions of time (remember the poetic stress):

Yet as surely as my mother lived
on the tracer-path planet
left behind in our world's world line
so surely my memory discovers her
not in chemical coding but alive there still
and so surely John Chilembwe still gives off
that black light in his black preacher's suit
or is alive in all our pasts before our birth . . .

Out of this "fact" of time, this immortality in memory, Doug creates a story-shape that involves a continued confrontation between a white "I" of Chilembwe's time and a present-day, liberal Briton. The author splits like a novelist to become both people:

> Let me take you into the stolen land
> by the huge lake, and I'll come to greet you
> as some District Commissioner
> my tie round its stiff collar
> like a ribbon round a white plastic pot
> from your own days. I'm still alive
> in arm-creased jacket parted
> over tweaked waistcoat,
> topi going grey, white ducks
> flattened on my shins. You
> come back to me with old books:
> I come towards you with your modern
> news cuttings: racial attacks in England
> and Wales, doubled in five years,
> firebombings, knife attacks, killings.
> 'Many black Britons
> might eagerly return to their countries.'
> And we meet on a bush track
> marked with stone spikes.
> I doff my hat to the future
> as the natives doff their hats to me
> even at a thousand yards' distance.

As the story unfolds, these two consciousnesses keep meeting, past and future, in a terrible and from-the-inside reminder of that mind that colonized, patronized, brutalized, but being exactly of its time, how people thought.

Ethiopianism? you say from your future,
I thought that was Marcus Garvey,
rephrased by the Rastfarians.

Marcus who? I'm quoting the 68th psalm,
"Ethiopia shall soon stretch out her hands to God."
You see the brick-built church
rising before us over by Mbombwe, roofs
frosted with photographic light? Its towers
make it a unit of measurement
fit for your Bromley road but here lost
in the Nyasaland bush.
They've laid in the mortar crudely,
harsh lines stripe the entrance steps . . .

And later, after the murder of Livingstone:

We chased him across another hillside,
his Calvary,
recovered a pair of gold spectacles
and a pair of pince-nez, the right lens
missing in each case,
found next to his half-starved body.
Then we obliterated his memory
and dynamited his church.

Would oneself then have behaved differently? One is conscious that that mind is still alive in the present—the newspaper clippings after all; you are made terribly aware that even if you are liberal, well-informed, kindly, you are still conforming to the thought of your times, for you are participating in your economy. You aren't "getting something," seeing something, that the future will get and condemn you for. What am I ignoring? What am I doing to others today, unconsciously, that is the equivalent? For one thing, one is still involved in the exploitation of Africa, both as the past is still alive in consequences of its damage, and as present exploitation or neglect is a fact. . . The fifth-to-last line is: "And we imagine the First World War is over!" A few lines earlier:

> Not even Chilembwe's religious myths
> pass away, though in my own beliefs
> no man was resurrected
> after any Calvary except in the strange survivals
> of all this time as a haunting
> of our sadly avaricious, racist British lives,
> survivals as shadows outside a cosy house
> where we sit eating goats and chickens
> grabbed from Africa via foreign loans,
> money thrown on the ground.

I seem to have no final paragraph. As John Chilembwe is still alive, as Doug Oliver is still alive, as Africa is espoused now as cause by a few of the moneyed and famous and yet neglected by our (a very large our) imagination of these times—and if and when that neglect is overcome, these centuries will live on in their horror, because the time of a horror like the time of a stress, the time of a poem, a life, casts itself into the future pulling the past with it. For a full month, April, because of the

Mideast crisis, there was no news of Africa in the papers and magazines I read; and then, once the news begins to leak through again, one gets the saga of sub-Saharan wars—which have been called by themselves a World War—and a new Southern African famine, a terrible one. To talk about Doug's book is not to end with a reference to it, but to its subject. Please, let us change.

2002, Talk given at Bennington College

*Since published as *Whisper, Louise* by Reality Street, London, 2005.

A Salvo For Africa, Bloodaxe Books Ltd, Newcastle Upon Tyne, 2000.

The Iliad and Postmodern War

The Greeks in the ninth year of the war are attacked by plague, sent by Apollo, because "of the priest whom Agamemnon dishonored, and did not release his daughter nor accept the ransom. For this reason the god who strikes from afar has given woes, and will continue to give them, nor will he drive off from the Danaans loathsome destruction until we give back to her father the bright-eyed maiden, unbought, unransomed, and take a holy hecatomb to Chryse; then perhaps we might appease his wrath and persuade him." As far as women go, that's it page 4 of the Loeb Classics trans. Murray/Wyatt, women are over with, done.

As we all know Agamemnon doesn't want to give up the stolen Chryseis. However he says he will if he can have the stolen Briseis whom Achilles keeps. And then he takes her. This the origin of the quarrel between Agamemnon and Achilles, echoing the whole quarrel between the Greeks and the Trojans over the stolen Helen not necessarily stolen. It is a war about women as goods. Also an allegory of a war over power, territory, resources?

One purpose of war has always been to keep women from being fully functional beings/citizens. War is an assertion that only men are important. Only men can lead. Only men can liberate the women from their burqas. Sometimes a woman can assist, if she is of a requisite bloodthirstiness.

*

I've just read that Condoleezza Rice prays on her knees every night. Certainly nothing happens in the *Iliad* without the presence of a god—not one thing, as in the visitation of the plague in the opening. To quote Ms. Rice: "The prayers are more general than specific. It's not as if you ask God 'Should we try to take down the Taliban?'"

I never heard my brother, now dead, who had been a sniper in Vietnam, say the word 'God' ever. That, I realize, is a relief to me.

*

> 1/6/83 (excerpts from "Jimmy Valentine"):
> "Mom, who did you like best in the Trojan War?" Today I said
> Cassandra . . . he said he liked Patroclus . . . And the light is in the
> novel's page in the hand, some way that it's just yellowed enough
> old enough; as Anselm & I choose our funny favorites not at all by
> their fates: Didn't they both die?"

Patroclus is the character who receives the most intense affection, in the *Iliad*, from the author. It is perhaps only the affection of Homer for this character—coming about two-thirds of the way through—that mitigates the violence of the poem and the unpleasantness of most of the characters, though there are showy, marvelous effects on the level of the gods and goddesses to distract us from the fighting, but the gods and goddesses are despicable too. And Achilles loves Patroclus better than anyone, and grieves for him hard, conducting at his funeral, races and games and human sacrifice (12 Trojans of noble family are slaughtered in honor of Patroclus). Only a man is worth this kind of affection; Helen is property, and sex, and is hated by almost everyone at this point. But it is a softening in tone when Homer begins to address Patroclus in the second person. An effect that then spreads to other characters, but all that is so much later in the story, which I am not exactly going to tell because you know it as Anselm and I do, even if you have forgotten it. Even if you haven't read the book. It is what biologists really mean when they tell us war is built into the species. As if it were genetic and not literary: our very own invented story we think is our body of fate. The *Iliad* is the pattern for our civilization. It is war as we still conceive it, even though since 1991 we don't die in significant numbers, only our enemies do.

Cassandra barely appears in the *Iliad*. In Euripides' *The Trojan Women* she has been raped by Aias after being dragged by him from the sanctuary of the temple of Athene. She is then taken by Agamemnon (again!) as his prize, taken back to Greece. In Aeschuylus' *Agamemnon* she is murdered, along with Agamemnon, because she is Agamemnon's concubine. Of course I chose her for my favorite because she was a prophet and because she always prophesied the truth even though she was never believed. This was Apollo's curse on her when she refused to have sex with him.

*

Some words of Nestor the wise in Book 2: "So let no man make haste to depart homeward until each has lain with the wife of some Trojan, and has got requital for his strivings and groanings over Helen."

Some words of Agamemnon in Book 4: "Argives, do not relax your furious valor; for father Zeus will be no helper of lies; but they who were the first to work violence in defiance of their oaths, their tender flesh vultures will surely devour, and moreover we shall carry away in our ships their dear wives and little ones, when we have taken their citadel."

Americans are perhaps less overtly sexed. Or the superficial definition of the good soldier has changed. *Newsweek*, October 21, 2002: "A T shirt, popular among Special Forces troops passing to and from Afghanistan . . . shows the Statue of Liberty giving a one-finger salute, with the caption, WE'RE COMING, MOTHERFUCKERS!" Our mother, the unfucked statue obviously loves us.

Newsweek October 7, an account of Russian raids on Chechnyans (this war, never over, now called a "war on terrorism"): "Sometimes those who survive wish they were dead, as in Zernovodsk this summer, when townspeople say they were chased onto a field and made to watch women being raped. When their men tried to defend them, 68 of them were handcuffed to an armored truck and raped, too. After this episode, 45 of them joined the guerillas in the mountains."

*

In the *Iliad* the gods and goddesses are the real heads of state, the different kings being warriors who participate in hand-to-hand combat. The gods and goddesses manipulate individual soldiers, divided into the two sides themselves; though general fates for each important man have been decided long ago, and everyone knows how the war will turn out. The fates of women, though dire, aren't dealt with as divinely ordained events, even though everything is fated. I'm not sure if there's a reference anywhere in Greek literature to a woman's fate having been spoken or spun: the Moirae or Fates are women, with thread and a spindle and cutter for doing their fate job; but 'fate' means that which has been spoken. From the Latin "fatum" from the Greek esfaton: "godspoken," (Moira means "lot" or "portion.")

America became "she" in Bush's occasional sentences last summer. As he was speaking the world's fate into being, beginning to talk everyone towards an Iraqi war, making confrontation inevitable. Simply, unreasonably, fated. He has assumed the power of a god.

In the *Iliad*, on the level of the gods and goddesses gender distinctions don't always feel important. Behind the poem supposedly is a dumb female event, the judgment of Paris, which accounts for the fact that Aphrodite sides with the Trojans and Athene and Hera side with the Greeks. The *Iliad* never mentions the judgment of Paris. That story is too far removed from the brutality of war, which is human and essentially male. Homer knows this.

The gods and goddesses, intervening in battle, are rarely visible to mortals though they know they are there; they usually take the form of a known warrior and then make a speech to their favorite. Afterwards the favorite thinks Why that was Athena! In Bernard Knox's introduction to the recent Robert Fagels' translation of the *Iliad*, he speaks of how this divine intervention corresponds to the way it feels when the tide turns in battle. He is nostalgic for his war experiences and projects them wistfully onto the poem.

In Book V a number of gods and goddesses go into battle, and both Aphrodite and Ares, who have taken opposite sides, are wounded. Sexual parity is logical as a consequence of immortality; you can't really beat into submission someone who will never die. What is not particularly logical is Zeus's sovereignty, which feels based in social convention, though there is the occasional reference to his thunderbolt which must be some superior weapon, the nuclear bomb that keeps him daddy.

*

Some Americans will be aware of an exchange between Colin Powell and Hubert Védrine, the then French foreign minister, last autumn, in which Védrine characterized the American foreign policy as simplistic and Powell replied that Védrine must be getting the vapors. Védrine then had to be told what getting the vapors meant: he was informed that it was a hysterical condition of menopausal women. Védrine later said that this had been a virile exchange between friends.

*

Book V, of Phereklos: "Him Meriones pursued, and when he had caught up with him, struck him in the right buttock, and the spearpoint passed clean through to the bladder beneath the bone; and he fell to his knees with a groan, and death enfolded him." Book V is about where the gore commences, which is the essential poem except for, very importantly, the measure. (I can see that just past the Greek alphabet.) It is not the pride of Achilles, not the struggle exemplified by Achilles and Hector, but the bloodshed that is the *Iliad*'s story. From Book V through Book XXII there is little but combat—out of 24 books. Hand-to-hand combat between any number of characters.

From my notebook recounting my last conversation with my brother: "Another story . . . involves the accidental mortaring of a schoolhouse. Albert dropped the mortar shell, but was not responsible for the misaim; doesn't know if there were children in the building. He says his therapists have pretty much managed to convince him he wasn't responsible." And then I asked him wasn't there ever one, just one light moment there? He answered "No, never. It was just hideous." Everything he told us about Vietnam evokes a sense of airlessness. As does the *Iliad* once the poem becomes sheer battlefield.

Bobby Langdoc, who had also been in Vietnam, said to me of my brother: "You know, some people are just too sensitive to live." As if it could be a normal part of the human or male/human experience to be a sniper? Is war really normal?

*

Diomedes calling to Athene: "'Hear me, child of Zeus who bears the aegis, Atrytone! If ever with kindly thought you stood by my father's side in the fury of battle, so now again show your love to me, Athene. Grant that I may slay this man, and that he come within the cast of my spear, the man who has struck me unawares, and boasts over me, and declares that not for long shall I look on the bright light of the sun.'"

From a poem I wrote last winter:

. . . i bind Bush and Cheney and Rumsfeld, and their tongues and words and deeds; if they are planning war for today let it be in vain. Beloved earth restrain them, and make them powerless and useless . . . .

it's morning it's the same, i can't remember sleeping. i last remember walking in this corridor last night. i've forgotten the intervening time, it's as if i'm still walking from then. because nothing happens? can i forget you? "the U.S. servicemen are still at risk." *Newsweek.* "an unprecedented, real-time glimpse at an ongoing Green Beret mission." is it as dangerous as my love's cancer was? "the team spotted a campfire." etcetera. "Team leader Dean quotes Shakespeare from memory." yes but my love was a poet. "The men slowly made their way down the narrow road" etc. bloody accuracy of attacks. "Atta could see the bodies of Taliban soldiers blown into the air. 'We wanted to show him we could help him beyond boots and clothes,' says Dean." Beloved Earth restrain them all and make those fighting anywhere powerless and useless . . . .

*

Continuous reports on the Afghan women and how they still lack rights: they've always been, truly, a side issue, a non-issue, a used issue.

No one ever cared about them and it is an accident if their lot has been improved. The invasion of Afghanistan was not on their behalf, after all; and certainly the U.S. didn't care what the Taliban and Al Qaeda thought about women when it financed them in the '80s. It can even be argued that the U.S. helped make the condition of Afghan women worse before accidentally 'liberating' them.

> "So he spoke and hurled; and Athene guided the spear to his nose beside the eye, and it pierced his white teeth. So the stubborn bronze sheared off his tongue at its root, and the spear-point came out by the base of the chin."

*

Book V, Sarpedon says to Hector: " . . . but you stand there and do not even urge your men to defend their wives."

To defend American values, liberty, democracy. And Greece—Athens—is the origin-place of democracy, the first citizenry which votes. Except for women and slaves, of course. Usual birth of freedom.

Bush quoted: "America's security, he said, is 'challenged today by outlaw groups and regimes that accept no law of morality and have no limit to their violent ambitions.'" In this kind of language the words "America's security" seem to illuminate a vaguely feminine figure, another unfucked statue.

The *Iliad* is fought on a narrow ground, a war for a woman. Thus the spoils of the war are women: this is logical. Euripides' *The Trojan Women* portrays the fates of a handful of the women. "Each is assigned to a different man, not all to one," says Talthybius to Hecabe. Cassandra will go to Agamemnon, her sister Polyxena is killed as a sacrifice at Achilles' tomb, Hecabe is assigned to Odysseus. Andromache, who at one point says, "The Achaeans are carrying home their property," will go to Achilles' son. Helen is obliged to return to her original husband, Menelaus.

From the *International Herald Tribune* (from the *Washington Post*): "All five permanent members of the Security Council—the United States, Britain, France, Russia and China—have international oil companies with major stakes in a change of leadership in Baghdad."

"It's pretty straightforward," said James Woolsey, a former CIA director who has been one of the leading advocates of forcing Saddam from power. "France and Russia have oil companies and interests in Iraq. They should be told that if they are of assistance in moving Iraq toward decent government, we'll do the best we can to ensure that the new government and American companies work closely with them."

"But he added: 'If they throw in their lot with Saddam, it will be difficult to the point of impossible to persuade the new Iraqi government to work with them.'"

Five Trojan women, five permanent members of the Security Council with international oil companies. It's too perfect.

*

Blah blah the topless towers of Ilium: "Is this the face that launched a thousand ships/And burned the topless towers of Ilium?" Galway Kinnell's poem in the *New Yorker* September 11 anniversary issue: "The towers burn and fall, burn and fall."

> in the midst of all this
> I say an internal ceremony
> to kill my culture in me
> as far back as I can

and including all of now as
it is commonly understood.

*

In Book VI, Agamemnon says to Menelaus, on the verge of sparing some Trojan's life: "Soft-hearted Menelaus, why are you so caring for men? Has great kindness been done to your house by Trojans? Of them let not one escape sheer destruction and our hands, not even the boy whom his mother carries in her womb; let not even him escape, but let all perish together from Ilios unmourned and unseen.' So spoke the warrior, and turned his brother's mind, for he counselled rightly . . ."

*

I will now remind you that Astyanax, the small son of Hector and Andromache, is thrown from the battlements of Troy by Greek soldiers; his brains are dashed out. After the poem, though the future event is alluded to.

This space is for children abused and killed in modern warfare. The children killed by American bombs in Afghanistan (recall story of man who saw his several children and their friends disappear into a bomb's explosion—he picked up their body parts later); the 250 Palestinian schoolchildren and the 72 Israeli schoolchildren killed in the present Intifada as of September '02; the thousands of Iraqi children dead or malnourished in the '90s as a consequence of war or sanctions; should I mention the boys as young as five or six impressed into service in armies in Sierra Leone and Liberia (What does Africa have to do with us?). Recall the young Sri Lankan woman in Toronto who said to me, in a discussion of boy soldiers, I have no emotions left for this, I left Sri Lanka there was nothing I could do.

Plaque in my neighborhood in memory of the 500 Jewish schoolchildren sent to the German death camps from the 10th arrondissement alone. I dreamed of ghost children knocking at my door with candles, perhaps a week before the poster was hung on the door of my building telling us the names of two children, a brother and sister, who had lived here at 21 rue des Messageries and been deported to Auschwitz. This poster was an invitation to the unveiling of the plaque on the rue de Chabrol.

This is another useless plaque for you all including the schoolchildren my brother may have accidentally mortared.

*

Book 7, "And Athene and Apollo of the silver bow in the likeness of vultures sat on the lofty oak of father Zeus who bears the aegis, rejoicing in the warriors . . ."

Hector in action: " . . . and he himself leapt to the ground from his gleaming chariot crying a terrible cry, and seizing a stone in his hand went straight at Teucer, and his heart commanded him to strike him. Now Teucer had drawn from his quiver a bitter arrow, and laid it on the string, but just as he was drawing it back Hector of the flashing helmet struck him beside the shoulder where the collarbone parts the neck and the chest, where is the deadliest spot: it was there as he aimed eagerly at him that he struck him with the jagged stone, and he broke the bowstring; and his hand grew numb at the wrist and he fell on his knees and remained there, and the bow fell from his hand."

From my poem "White Phosphorus":

. . . "What's real" "is war" "they say" "some say" "some say,
war is" "the only" "reality" "The warriors mistake war for" "reality,

the reality" "Because they pierce" "the centers" "the physical centers"
"of each other" "Addicted to this" "Addicted" "& our government
of men" "organizes" "this addiction" "in the guise of, protecting us all"
"All of us part of it" "part of" "this addiction" "protector, protected"

*

The *Observer* 20 October 2002, British Troops 'Gang Raped Masai Women': ". . . Simon Ole Kaparo, a Masai community leader, believes the Masai women's allegations are just the tip of the iceberg in a part of Kenya where the British Army has trained for 50 years . . . . 'I was in my late twenties and had five children,' Nakarat Puiunoi, 45, says. 'I knew the British army was around and was trying to avoid them. When 'I saw the large group of soldiers I started to run. I don't know exactly how many raped me because I blacked out. They were like so many dogs at a bone.'"

Book 7: " . . . you are, it appears, no better than a woman . . ."

The *New York Times*, a special selection for *Le Monde* October 20 & 21: Soldiers for Hire Bolster U.S. *Forces*. " . . . these companies . . . need the government's permission to be in business . . . In Bosnia employees of DynCorp were found to be operating a sex-slave ring of young women who were held for prostitution after their passports were confiscated. In Croatia, local forces, trained by MPRI, used what they learned to conduct one of the worst episodes of 'ethnic cleansing' . . . No employee of either firm has ever been charged in these incidents."

From "White Phosphorus":

("we maimed" "another, a native land, we"
"helped maim another") "Please" "give it back" "Give us our heart,
whose" "heart might be lost"

*

"I loved Secretary of Defense Donald Rumsfeld's briefings during the Afghanistan war. They were no-nonsense tough, with a dose of American nationalism that resonated with me." Columnist Thomas L. Friedman. Oct. 3, '02 in the *IHT.* And elsewhere in paper photo of Bush flanked by 9 male heads—9 male heads!—after the House approved the language of a resolution authorizing use of military force against Iraq.

Where did the sick mind of war come from? Is there a myth of the first war? No one disapproves, on principle, of the mass killing of others of other nations. The *Iliad* is a sick book, the war against terrorism is our own sick poem. We will never have to read it, having gone far beyond reading. The *Iliad* is not redeemed by its sound and form which I love, just barely perceiving it. The United States is trying to tell itself a story and everyone wants to be in it, to be defended, to be frightened, to be vindicated, above all to hate. But we will win, our poem is and will remain in English as the *Iliad* is in Greek, the language of the victors. We must never lose again, as we did in Vietnam, and as the noble Trojans did. For in the *Iliad* we are invited to admire both Hector and Achilles, and possibly Hector more than Achilles. This means that if you lose, you can still win.

From "White Phosphorus":

"Homeric?" "he said it was hideous" " all of it" "hideous" "every
instant in Nam" "theatre of worsts" "now mantle of
white" "phosphorus & lilies?" "trees now lean down" "over our faces"
"Tell details of battle?" "As in an epic?" "As" "in lies?"

*

From Book 13: "Peisander struck Menelaus on the ridge of his helmet with crest of horsehair on the topmost part beneath the very plume; but Menelaus struck him as he came up against him on the forehead above the base of the nose; and the bones snapped loudly, and his eyeballs, all bloody, fell in front of his feet in the dust, and he doubled up and fell . . ."

Newsweek October 7: "At the same time, regular soldiers like those of the 82nd were, until August, mostly confined to their bases, just itching to get out and do the job for which they were trained . . . .They were trained to advance to contact and kill the enemy . . . . In the village of Marzak several witnesses say that 82nd troops chased down a mentally ill man, pushed him to the ground, handcuffed him and then took turns taking photos of themselves pointing a gun to his head . . . ." Later in the article: "Why do the Americans come here and search our women?"

*

It is all the same war from forever; it is not the same soldier, or the same woman.

*

Book 9, Agamemnon tries to persuade Achilles to rejoin the battle and offers him gifts. Achilles who is a petulant shit always moaning about the fact that he is fated—this is known—to die young, continues to refuse to fight until many more Greeks and Trojans, and finally Patroclus, have died. But in this unsuccessful attempt to cajole him back into the battle Agamemnon offers: "seven tripods that the fire has not touched, and ten talents of gold and twenty gleaming cauldrons, and twelve strong horses, winners in the race, that have won prizes by their fleetness . . . .

And I will give seven women skilled in noble handiwork, women of Lesbos, whom on the day when Achilles himself took well-built Lesbos I chose out for myself from the spoil, who in beauty surpassed all the tribes of women. These will I give him, and among them will be she whom then I took away, the daughter of Briseus . . ."

From today's *IHT*: "The operation focused on Bosnia because, since the war there ended seven years ago, the presence of thousands of NATO troops and civilian workers for the United Nations and aid agencies has made it a prime market for both prostitution and sexual slavery," officials said.

"Over the past two years, both NATO soldiers and UN officials, including some Americans, have been implicated in the exploitation of young women held in sexual bondage."

Book 9: "But Achilles slept in the innermost part of the well-built hut, and by his side lay a woman he had brought from Lesbos, the daughter of Phorbas, fair-cheeked Diomede. And Patroclus lay down on the opposite side, and by him likewise lay fair-belted Iphis, whom noble Achilles had given him when he took steep Scyrus, the city of Enyeus." Achilles and Patroclus love each other this much. And what intimacies do Bush and Cheney share, about oil-industry matters?

*

Wars are caused by the past. By the gods. By other depictions of war. By previous wars. By self-righteousness. By the existence of armies. By metrics. More than by economic and territorial interests wars are caused by the tradition of war.

I am interested in the pre-Greek sensibility, the literature of the Sumerians. It contains war but it also contains parity between the sexes, at times: see the epic *Inanna's Descent Into the Underworld* for example.

"However, excavations at Uruk are suspended for the time being as a result of the imposition of UN sanctions on Iraq, which makes all access to archeological sites very difficult." Gwendolyn Leick, *Mesopotamia*. Uruk was Inanna's city. It is over six thousand years old. Ms. Leick sees evidence for an earliest civilization, in Mesopotamia, with parity between the sexes and no rigid class system.

"Because it gathers the most serious dangers of our age in one place," Bush said, "Iraq is unique."

Ms. Leick again, of Nineveh, whose ruins are near the modern city of Mosul: "The looting of antiquities has become more common as clandestine markets have generated some form of undeclared income in an economy crippled by the UN sanctions against Iraq. A lack of finance and materials for the maintenance of the ruin sites has accelerated the deterioration of the monuments, creating a 'world heritage disaster' according to one American archaeologist who formerly worked at the site."

War is culture-destroying. That is almost its avowed purpose, isn't it? We propose to replace culture with Freedom, the female statue, carved in the West's best 19th century public style.

*

Thetis, the mother of Achilles, had pleaded with Zeus for the restoration of her son's honor after Briseis had been stolen from him at the beginning of the *Iliad*. The plan was devised that the Greeks would lose and lose and lose until Patroclus being killed Achilles would enter the battle and then, and only because of Achilles, the Greeks would win. This is Zeus's and Thetis's strategy. Conspiracy theory indeed! The other gods don't know and think there is a reasonably equitable battle being fought. Hera, who has sided with the Greeks, doesn't know this for example.

When she aids the Greeks so that the tide is in their favor, when they aren't supposed to win YET, Zeus chides her: "Hera, you are impossible; it is your crafty evil wiles that have stayed noble Hector from the fight and have driven the army in rout. I know not but that you may be the first to reap the fruits of your wretched ill-contriving, and I shall whip you with blows." He then reminds her of the time he suspended her by her ankles among the clouds.

Observer, Nov. 3: "Carve-up Of Oil Riches Begins. U.S. Plans To Ditch Industry Rivals And Force An End Of Opec . . . The leader of the London-based Iraqi National Congress, Ahmed Chalabi, has met executives of three U.S. oil multinationals to negotiate the carve-up of Iraq's oil reserves post-Saddam."

And an October *IHT* article had stated that most people in Washington didn't believe a war with Iraq would be over oil.

*

Book 17, Hector finally kills Patroclus, who has gone into battle wearing Achilles' armor, and he strips the armor from Patroclus and puts it on. Zeus "spoke to his own heart: 'Ah, poor wretch, not in your thoughts is death, that yet surely draws near you; but you are putting on the immortal armor of a preeminent man before whom others besides yourself also tremble. . . . But for now I will grant you great might, in recompense for this, that in no way shall you return from the battle and Andromache receive from you the glorious armor of the son of Peleus.'" One pukes at the idea of a "preeminent man."

And then they fight over a corpse: Aias defends Patroclus's body, which the Trojans want to drag around. Later Achilles will drag Hector's body around and then take it back to his "well-built hut" in order to mutilate it sullenly.

In Book 17 Zeus says: "For truly there is nothing, I think, more miserable than man among all things that breathe and move on earth."

At this point one sees that the poem is a hell. And that the wars we now inflict on others are airless and all-extinguishing. And the ones we ignore in Africa, sometimes spoken of as a "world war"—as we ignore the economic problems we create on that continent, parts of which we may suddenly be rediscovering because of its oil. For at least a century, all over the world, there has been relentless war—but always kept from our sacred borders. September 11 is nothing inside this fact. Acid between the breasts.

*

That the *Iliad* is about fate, that which is spoken into happening, becomes more and more explicit towards the end of the poem, as many individual fates are either witnessed or foreshadowed. Patroclus' and Hector's fates spoken of by Zeus before their deaths. Achilles' fate left to transpire just after the poem ends. A sense of fatedness is produced continuously in the Greek, throughout the poem, with its meter, its repeated epithets, its tight inflected syntax.

The poem ends with the retrieval by Priam, king of Troy, of his son Hector's body; the Trojans are allowed a few days' respite from battle in which to grieve. Andromache, Hecabe, and Helen line up to wail over Hector as the body is returned. They are good at this because it is a female ritual taught from childhood. (Isn't that almost still so, perhaps without the wailing? I know the stoic version.)

Earlier, in Book 18, Thetis had traveled to the home of Hephaestus to ask him to make new armor for Achilles: ". . . and there moved swiftly to support their lord handmaids made of gold in the semblance of living girls. In them is understanding in their minds, and in them speech and strength, and they know cunning handiwork by gift of the immortal gods." Gold robots.

After the poem the Trojans are defeated and the city is sacked and burned. It doesn't have to be in the poem; everyone knew what happened. Much of extant ancient Greek literature is about this war and its aftermath. It is the myth; they were always living it. We're always living it.

*

A story not covered in the *Iliad.* Before the war could begin, the Greek fleet could not set sail for Troy because there was no wind. It was determined that for the fleet to sail, Agamemnon had to sacrifice his daughter, Iphigenia, to Artemis, and he did. This is the story told in the play *Iphigenia in Aulis*, doubtfully attributed to Euripides. Iphigenia's sacrifice is the motivation for her mother's, Clytaemnestra's, murder of Agamemnon in the *Oresteia* of Aeschylus. You will remember that Electra, another daughter of the House of Atreus, then incites her brother Orestes to murder their mother Clytaemnestra. Orestes goes mad, pursued by the Erinyes, the Furies.

In Euripides' *Iphigenia in Tauris*, Euripides tells a different story: that Iphigenia was saved miraculously by Artemis from sacrifice, an animal having been substituted for her on the altar without the Greeks' perceiving it. Transported to the island of Tauris Iphigenia has been made by the Taureans to oversee the sacrifice to Artemis of any stranger who comes to the island. Any foreigner who comes to their land. One day her brother Orestes arrives with a friend. An oracle of Apollo has declared that if Orestes can transport the statue of Artemis from the island to Greece, he will be freed of the Erinyes and his madness. A new temple to Artemis must be built for the statue and a bloodless worship of Artemis installed to replace the former practice. This is accomplished and

Iphigenia also escapes, in order to perform the new rites in honor of the goddess.

In the spring of 2001 I dreamed of a steep hillside beside a harbor, covered with scrubby grass, in sunlight. I woke up and thought that I had literally just seen Tauris, that that was the hillside and harbor. I have never been to Greece and don't know if there is such an island now; I hadn't read the play in years. I then borrowed from a library a translation of *Iphigenia in Tauris.* As I read it I began sobbing without knowing why; I still don't fully understand this event. Except as it means that I don't want to be that woman. Any part of whose existence is sacrificed to war. Whose brother is made into a killer by historical tradition. Whose country slaughters foreigners. Who must always appease a stupid deity, follow the dictates of a benighted even stupid male leader. And survive. And take it, take it, take it.

*

From my poem "Iphigenia":

> I dreamed myself tatooed with all the history I had been, those stories, and the worst displayed where my vagina was torn and deformed, the worst story told, was where my sex was mangled, and I watched her then turned away. I couldn't bear to see the unveiling of the lower part of her torso; not precisely Iphigenia, she was more native to me
>
> CHANGE THE ORDER NOW
> of her unhealed
> body.
>
> She I was revealing herself so END IT AND CHANGE ORDER. All because in sex, you tatooed of Iphigenia the story. Was written on myself.

My poem states that the effigy of the goddess must be destroyed, not transported and used in different worship. My brother and I destroy her, the statue. The gods and goddesses must be destroyed. All of them.

*

Fate is created by groups of human beings living in the past. They say it. Fate is created by language. One becomes the body of Fate before one is able to think much: then it is too late.

The poet's job is to unsay Fate. The body's job as a spiritual entity is to resist Fate. The scientist should recognize that Fate is a linguistic invention imposed on the body; the scientist should not reinforce Fate by believing in a version of it. We need to reinvent this species.

Our leaders and our systems of government enforce Fate in our bodies. We must declare our leaders and institutions dead as they obviously are. We will not do this but I do.

Our president is dead; he is a spiritual vacuity. Our president and his company are all dead.

I refuse to live in the ancient world.

Sept.-Nov. '02

(Written to be a talk at Poets House, New York, in December 2002.)

All citations from the Iliad are from Homer, *Iliad*, Loeb Classical Library, translated by A.J. Murray and William F. Wyatt, Cambridge MA, London, 1999. I also quote from myself, from poems that may now be found in the books *Manhattan Luck* (Hearts Desire, Oakland, 2014), *Grave of Light, Selected Poems 1970-2005* (Wesleyan University Press, Middletown Connecticut, 2006), and *Alma, or The Dead Women* (Granary Books, New York City, 2006).

Intersections with Edwin's Lines

I know Edwin Denby's poems well; his isn't a large body of work and his poems lend themselves, by their form and by his character, to being remembered and meditated on. I was introduced to Edwin's work, and Edwin, by Ted Berrigan, and at the beginning of our relationship observed Ted's obsession with certain lines, phrases, mannerisms of Edwin's before I myself became involved with the poetry. Recently, after not having looked at the work for awhile, I glanced through it again and started remembering and also seeing newly, as I was a little older since the last time.

So what I'm going to do is look at some specific poems and lines, and say things about them, in a somewhat notational fashion, because it seems this will give me pleasure. I'm going to presume some familiarity with the poems on the part of my reader. I will sometimes tell what Ted said; but with the *Later Sonnets* I will probably only reflect my own attention, because they are special to me, I imitated them, and also listened for what they could tell me about staying alive despite the suffering and shame of being human. I will be working with *The Complete Poems*, ed. by Ron Padgett (Random House, 1986).

From *In Public, In Private*

"The Shoulder":

The shoulder of a man is shaped like a baby pig.
It terrifies and it bores the observer, the shoulder.

and later

The shoulder, hung from his neck (half orchid, half tumor)

Those are the lines that have stayed with me. I was too young for this poem for years, and I think it terrified (though didn't bore) me. It echoes a celebrated de Kooning painting, from the '30s, of a man with such a shoulder. I suppose I was unable to think of a part of the human body as a thing by itself that might repel a moralist (Edwin), and fascinate an artist (de Kooning become Edwin.) I say repel because the shoulder, in this poem, seems so arbitrary, used (by its person but also by others—"It takes the . . . shape of . . . money, that connects with a government somewhere"), and then all its own to the eye.

"The Silence at Night" (*The designs on the sidewalk Bill pointed out*):

Edwin with de Kooning, again in the '30s, looking. I don't usually remember the lines so much as what happens—that slime and cracks and stains on the sidewalk are seen to take on new shapes and become fantastic pictures, and that later there are three lines in which the word "honey" is used beautifully. Here are the first two lines:

The sidewalk cracks, gumspots, the water, the bits of refuse,
They reach out and bloom under arclight, neonlight

And here are the "honey" lines:

So honey, it's lucky how we keep throwing away

Honey, it's lucky how it's no use anyway
Oh honey, it's lucky no one knows the way

I—we, can I say?—have been working with the problem of garbage, refuse, human stain in cities for years. And mediating between acceptance of what is, even having an "eye" for it, and at the same time loathing it. William Carlos Williams never quite loathes it. Edwin can. Frank O'Hara picked up (I think) an appropriate sense of disgust from Edwin, which is never quite absent from his poems that love New York.

"First Warm Days":

We had this on tape but I can't find the tape now.

April, up on a twig a leaftuft stands
And heaven lifts a hundred miles mildly
Comes and fondles our faces, playing friends—
Such a one day often concludes coldly—

I have a precise aural memory of Edwin saying "mildly" and "coldly" in his even way, so that "coldly" feels pretty cold, and the rhyme is an intense mental event, a piece of dead-on logic. There are also the lines

And human faces—hardly changed after
Millennia—the separate single face
Placid, it turns towards friendly laughing
Or makes an iridescence, being at peace.

This is the other side of "The Shoulder"—but places the human in a larger, lonelier context, at the same time as admitting to the possibility of a lovelike intimacy, even among strangers. Because this is a poem about New Yorkers drawn outside together into warm weather, a yearly event I remember very well:

> We all are pleased by an air like of loving
> Going home quiet in the subway-shoving.

From *A Sonnet Sequence: Dishonor,* no. 17:

> Thin air I breathe and birds use for flying
> Over and through trees standing and breathing in air
> Air insects drop through in insect dying

and at the end

> When with it I give up the insanely hid
>
> The airless secret I strangle not to share
> With all the others as others share the air.

Ted was caught by the notion of "thin air" and what it meant to breathe thin air. He assured me that certain people breathed thin air, and other people didn't; that air itself was not thin but could be breathed thinly. He wrote a poem, which he later destroyed, that catalogued all of his friends at the time in terms of how each breathed and the quality of the air breathed: viz, "Anne gulps air," "Lewis breathes thin air richly." Edwin's poems can lead you into this kind of thinking, since they are so spare and each word is so meant.

The last lines, again, frightened me, and I wasn't sure what the "airless secret" was. I suppose it is the fact of oneself known only to oneself. But I used to think it might be something more melodramatic, Edwin's own secret.

From *Mediterranean Cities*

"Trastevere: A Dedication"

The first and last two lines of this poem were important ones for Ted. They are respectively

> Dear head to one side, in summer dusk, Olga

and

> As laughing Olga, feeding through the window cat-shadows
> Then reading, then sinking into slumber, too does

These lines contain small effects that Ted tried to achieve over and over in the early '70s: the delay of Olga's name until the end of the first line, and the delay of "too does" till the end, in the closing lines, but with the inversion of the two words from normal speech order.

In the first line Edwin is following a precise order of perception: one sees, then names, but cannot see her without affection, so though she, Olga, is seen first as unnamed she is still "dear."

Allen Ginsberg was also interested in the accurate ordering of perceptions, having gotten the obsession through Cézanne's work. Edwin loved certain Cézannes in the Metropolitan Museum of Art, and also loved Stein, who of course owed a debt to Cézanne. These influences can lead one to a notational kind of diction, and Edwin leaves out a lot of articles in his later sonnets, as Allen did in his poems. They were not influenced by each other.

Mediterranean Cities was published as a beautiful book, a collaboration with the photos of Rudy Burckhardt. The influence of Rudy's eye on Edwin's must be mentioned, though one sometimes suspects they had the same eyes. When I see Rudy's photos of people in the subway or walking on 14th Street, I know I am also seeing as Edwin saw. People are not glamorous, or stark, or interpreted: they are there, in motion or in a moment. I always believe Rudy's camera about people, but I don't know why. It allows them, maybe.

I went once or twice to the New York City Ballet with Edwin. We rode there on the subway, because, he said, he loved the subway, it was the last place where you were allowed to stare at people.

"Ciampino: Envoi"

The last two lines of this poem were important to Ted for what they said:

> For with regret I leave the lovely world men made
> Despite their bad character, their art is mild

For Ted, these two lines said everything about Edwin and what he was like. The absoluteness of the declaration of humanity's "bad character" amazed Ted. It is hard to think of another poet who would say such a thing. The line brings to mind Edwin's rather famous sentence "I am assuming that one knows what it is to be ashamed." But then there is also the characterization of human art as "mild," as if that were the best of qualities. So is it? One might think about that for a thousand years.

Ted had several conversations with Edwin in which Edwin said something in passing that Ted had to think about hard. So they became part of his lore. In one conversation Edwin said that Melville was right, the night sky in New York was not black but purple. Then Ted studied it and saw that it was in fact purple. (I looked at it and discovered it was navy blue.) And once Edwin said of someone, "He just wants to be loved." Then Edwin paused and added, "Despicable, of course." Ted was horrified, because he was sure he himself just wanted to be loved. So he went home and worked on that one for forever.

I should add that for Ted (and many others) Edwin's relationship with Rudy Burckhardt was a moral touchstone for what human relations should be and was often referred to: "Edwin and Rudy". . . Also Ted found it funny to say "Edwin and Rudy," as he did in his poem "Things to Do in Providence": what could those names mean to anyone? Which reminds me of Edwin's poem "A Postcard," a birthday poem for Rudy which is a list of names of people who supposedly wish Rudy a happy birthday:

> And then Victor, and Bill, and Walter the mild,
> And Frank, David, John, Aaron, Paul, Harry and
> Virgil, the Photoleague, Oliver, Ebbie wild,
> I and Gankie and the Shoe-man shake your hand.

Snoring in New York—An Elegy

This is a remarkable longer poem which I ignored for a long time. Then one year —it was in the late '70s—Edmund Leites taught a workshop at St. Marks on "Poetry and Philosophy," and he asked me to read the poem aloud to the class. I was asked to read it again, a few months later, at a reading; I think it really got into my system, since I had to keep "rehearsing" it. It contains some very Steinian lines, such as in the following stanza:

> Mythically slow or slow United States
> Slow is not owned, slow mythically is like dearer
> Two slowly come to hear, one indoors awaits
> Mere fright at night, bright dismay by day, fear is
> Nearer, merer and slower, fear is before
> Always, dear always is, fear increases more

As far as I know, Edwin's major influences were Dante and Stein. His favorite book of *The Divine Comedy* was the *Paradiso*, and like Doug Oliver he kept a copy of it in Italian in his jacket pocket. And he read Stein constantly and told others to do so too. (He had known Alice Toklas, but not, I think, Stein. There are anecdotes.) I'm pretty sure he told O'Hara to read Stein; he certainly told Ted to. A key text seems to have been the very difficult *Stanzas in Meditation*. Once Anne Waldman told me she had been discussing her recent work with Edwin, and "he told me to keep on reading Stein."

Anyway one hears the layering and punning—"Always, dear always is, fear increases more"; the sound of definitions—"Slow is not owned"; the ordinary? rhyme—"Mere fright at night"; etc. All of which one associates with Stein.

Later Sonnets

In 1970 Ted stayed for a few days at Rudy Burckhardt's and Yvonne Jacquette's loft and found a full version of the *Later Sonnets* in a closet. Many had been published before, but he had never seen them altogether or seen them all. He made a copy and gave it to me. I proceeded to imitate them, in my way, in 1971, writing my first sonnet sequence, *165 Meeting House Lane*. I was twenty-five years old. I learned a number of things about writing poetry from imitating these sonnets: that a form can make you say the unexpected thing that turns out to be true; that form or metrics and the order of perceptions can unite in a most pleasureable way; that I might be much more my poems than myself living, socially observed. I learned a great deal about how poetry is artifice and artifice is closer to the real than one's sense of everyday life lived is. That was a lot to learn, and I wouldn't have known how to say all of that then. What I would say then was, the form—this particular sonnet form—dredges things up from myself I would never have anticipated.

Of course the form, this peculiarly Edwinesque sonnet form, was very different for Edwin: it suited his speech and his way of seeing (it had very little to do with the way I spoke.) And in its compression and drive for clarity it reflected a lifetime's experience of form in dance, painting, poetry, and living.

"Born in my loft, dancer untame"

What a beautiful line that is, and its successor line, and then the two subsequent lines, what are they and where do they take us? Here are those first four lines:

> Born in my loft, dancer untame
> A wilderness imagined, small
> Cat, which we reached for real by plane
> You stalked on the roof up the hall

The word "Cat" is a deliberate flatness and descent of tone, if you believe a cat is less worthy than a human. ". . . small" and then that flat funny word for a specific creature which this poem celebrates and elegizes quite passionately. "Cat, which we reached for real by plane": that is the sort of line that taught me I certainly didn't have to explain everything—"for real by plane"? What was that?

The last three lines of the poem are magnificent

> Cat-heart that knew me gone, I cried
> It stopped beating drugged in a cage
> Dear, mine will too, and let go rage

"Dancer untame" as contrasted with the dancers of Balanchine's company whom Edwin certainly adored too. But I have always been struck by how completely this poem is about one cat and Edwin's feeling for her. The middle of the poem tells the story of the cat's life in seven lines that condense narrative into the shortest of phrases and the most event-filled octosyllabic lines:

> You stalked on the roof up the hall
> Heart nursing six kittens, that grew
> With them, long-tailed splendid-eyed cat
> A disease struck the womb, left you
> Savage fighter, playful at night
> Lamed, ireful you prowled then; vet cut
> Out the womb, so rage might subside
> Telephone rings, speaks, I hang up
> Cat-heart that knew me gone, I cried

How much is compressed into the lines between "A disease" and "subside," and is that a sentence, does it matter, and the shift into present tense with "Telephone rings" just for that line. Sometimes I didn't want this poem to be about a cat, that fact made me uncomfortable.

"Writing poems, an employee"

This is a poem I wore as an amulet:

> Writing poems, an employee
> I lived here at nineteen, who I?
> Current boys nineteen, their beauty
> Of skin, all I can recognize
> On this passport, soft vague boy's smile
> Recalls few facts, does, his horror
> Scale's abyss, void becoming real
> A heart's force, he was going mad
> Which I?—surviving forty years
> Schizophrenia of a goof
> I remember his savage tears
> The kind reproof, the kind reproof
> Vague-faced boy, he faced what was it?
> A white old man, approved, I sit

This poem helped me to know that I would get through certain life passages (mental events, anguish—as in another sonnet beginning "Disorder, mental, strikes me . . ."); it also taught me its techniques, such as that of identifying a former self as almost a stranger, thus creating two characters out of oneself—the device that drives the poem.

I think I remember a version of this poem in which the third-to-last line read "The kind reproof, kind reproof."

"Small paintings seen, I cross the Park"

This poem exemplifies a kind of progression of action—recalled later but written as if in the present, as in an O'Hara poem—that I tried to get into my own sonnet sequence. These are the first eight lines:

> Small paintings seen, I cross the Park
> Toward six, end of March, pellucid
> Close boulder, black velvet so dark,
> Glare, one or two lithe descend it
> Grass March-green, in air the hard buds
> Flushed barely the buildings' vista
> Up Fifth, downtown is where I head
> Scraps of Park speech, blown scraps of paper

Ted worked on this sort of description as well but leaving out anything pretty or obviously natural (of nature) because he thought he had no talent for that. And so he arrived at his own technique that involved leaving out almost all of the description but including the "scraps of Park speech" that are left out here. He would have been most influenced by the first and seventh lines above.

"The grand republic's poet is"

This is a visionary poem by a poet seemingly not given to visions. It puzzled me because I didn't understand that Edwin could "see" Whitman pointing at the moon or inhabiting his, Edwin's, own room in underwear, and also write a poem like "Small paintings seen, I cross the Park."

The grand republic's poet is
Brooklyn Whitman, commuter Walt
Nobody else believes all of it
Not Harvard, that finds him at fault
I have, but first he broke my heart
He points to the moon but breaks it
I look for him, Twenty-first Street
Sleep against the push of a cat
Waking stumble to start coffee
At my back Walt in underwear
His head slants from unaltered day
Strokes my cat, the cheeks streaming tears
Sits on the bed, quietly cries
While I delay turning round, dies

I would wonder if Whitman dies because Edwin has found him at fault. This was an interesting thing to wonder about, even though I also knew that Whitman dies because his America only lasts an instant, in the imagination, and has been betrayed, as much by himself, his blindness, as by subsequent history. Harvard, which Edwin attended for two years, doesn't seem worth thinking about here in delineation of cause and effect. It's one's own complicity that matters most, and Whitman is certainly more like Edwin than Harvard is.

"Awakening, look into sweet"

I have finally come to believe the last few lines, though I don't believe the fourth line, and don't believe Edwin did, except in the context of the optimistic day, the specific day, of the specific poem:

Chance roommates, you cats and roaches
You have cultures purer than mine
Of yours I shelter the success
And at mine's failure don't repine

Anne Waldman, who was very close to Edwin and visited him often, told me that he refused to kill roaches and that she had seen them walking in and out of his sugar bowl. She was horrified. And she was the Buddhist not he. I think she persuaded him to get rid of the ones in the sugar, at least.

"Inattentively fortunate"

This was another talismanic poem for me, for its even-keel joy in living in New York among artists, for its first four lines especially, their syntax and floatingness and how the whole poem floats grammatically launched by this beginning:

Inattentively fortunate
Have been pausing at lunchcounters
While what I most like, art that's great
Has been being painted upstairs

But I remember a variant here too; I think the second line was once "Having been pausing at lunchcounters."

"Roar drowns the reproach, facing him"

I will close with this poem, a masterpiece, which integrates the gestures of a lovers' quarrel observed, and the poet's rush to a ballet "foreknowing" its "games," into one sequence of motion. I will simply quote it in full, but want to say the line "Quarrels I believed riders win" has stayed with me out of its context as an instance of the inexplicability of poetry's use: I never quite have to think about what it means but I can't forget it.

Roar drowns the reproach, facing him
Quite near, subway platform, she heeds
Head tossing slow like a pony's
In the wrong, the pinto I rode
A boy of twelve, that lovely head
Quarrels I believed riders win
White-haired pass these lovers in luck
Hurry to ballet, its invention
Where there's no quarrel, but there's fate
A scream unhurried of music's choice
And we recognize the games played
Like in heaven, foreknowing they cease
The move, the pitch arrive, turn to air
Here, as if love had said forever

I learned, from Edwin, that each phrase was an object and that word order was plastic; that each word used all of its space and so had to fill it, that each line floated as well as connected; and that where a sentence stopped and another began was ambiguous, like in speech. I learned that one could place personal suffering in a context that might be communal as of persons or communal as of objects and actions and words—either one worked as community. I thus learned a scale one was being along that began with oneself and the others in one's apartment and proceeded out onto the street and into the imaginary space of painting and ballet on up into the sky above tall buildings, all inside one and one inside it. I learned not to fear the sound of personal peculiarities in poetry, personal "music," that that's what the poems would finally be made of. I learned that any sequence of actions I had performed might be interesting if embodied in words that at the same time made their own sequence and assumed their own shapes: this is not the quotidian, it is not autobiography. It is motion and event purified of self and then laid next to self as a different kind of shape. I couldn't stay with my version of Edwin's style because I needed to use a lot of words, but I never forget about these poems for very long.

Aug, 2002
for Yvonne

First published in *Jacket,* 2002.

All quotations are from Edwin Denby, *The Complete Poems*, ed. Ron Padgett, Random House, New York, 1986

Noir Talk

I will refer to detective or crime fiction written mostly during the '80s, '90s, and zeros. Salient names: Michael Connelly, James Lee Burke, Dennis Lehane, Robert B. Parker, Harlan Coben, the French author Fred Vargas, the genius James Ellroy. Basically I read all of certain authors between April of last year and March of this year (2004), because I couldn't do much else but read, being often in a state of physical incapability. I would discover an author and read most of his/her oeuvre in two or three weeks. Besides the above-mentioned, I read all of the Swede Henning Mankell, certain books by the two hideous Kellermans, Faye and Jonathan, a book each by Sara Paretsky and Sue Grafton. A few by John Lescroart. One by Walter Mosely. A couple by George Pelecanos. A couple by Peter May. Three by Sarah Dars, who writes in French of an Ayurvedic Indian physician called "Doc" (her books are not very noir.) Lawrence Block, Laurie King, Peter Robinson, Robert Crais, many others.

I've been reading crime fiction since I was twelve, starting with all the Perry Masons (Erle Stanley Gardner.) In order to read the Perry Masons I had to become both Mason and Della Street in my reading consciousness; but detective fiction has not progressed much further than that of "chief"—Perry's nickname as chief protagonist male—and secretary (female—Della), the femme detectives notwithstanding.

I'm not going to be very organized; I'm going to be fragmentary and circular. These books pretend to be coherent but mostly they aren't, being both violent and, usually, not well written. They don't inspire coherent exegesis. Also I've already forgotten everything about most of them; what lingers of this genre is always a mood, which is how it slides over into "poem."

*

A poem is more than a word machine: it is the experience of reading it and having it in one's head, thus an ambiance, a sensory-intellectual passage, a fluid room. Unstrictly speaking, this whole group of books is a poem, however badly or cynically most of the books are written. The books are haunted by readers' demands for emotional release after a standard difficult experience—the crime that is local to the book. Story-wise the demand is to repeat the old story. (I must have wanted this myself.) A story repeated becomes a poem. You already know what the salient moments will be like, so you skip much of the book and search for certain words, the ones evoking a city or locale and a protagonist's character traits, the crime, the anguish, the name of the murderer, the confrontation; some of these books I seem hardly to have read a word of. "Page-turner" actually refers to not reading but literally turning pages. As a consequence of reading all these books, I began to write some Noir poems. (At the same time as I was studying this genre, I was studying Bob Dylan's performances of his songs: I could also call crime fiction a type of folk song—a bloody ballad maybe.)

*

The poem's in the preoccupations of the genre. The solution of the puzzle as to who is the murderer now seems a little secondary, since the form's so padded with words. (As I've indicated above, the reader must edit on her own.) I'm not sure if this wordiness is due to the existence of the computer, the pathetic need for many of the crime writers to assert that they are novelists, some equation of number of words with price: how much the author is paid, how much one pays for a—what I've always called "trash book." I'm old-school and want to know who the murderer is, that must be one reason why I do so much skimming—but often the writing is really bad (it takes Jonathan Kellerman umpteen pages for any passage of time: he has to record every word of every conversation; and he can only write in the first person—the mark of the inept crime novelist.) Other major preoccupations have always included violence against women; the need to penetrate and dissect the human body; the existence of the mob, conspiracy, and corruption; and the location of the point in the story where the protagonist himself may kill with impunity. There are also urgencies about race embedded in the genre. All of these themes have intensified, and many of the books simmer with cruelty, I'm not sure whose: the reader's as well as the author's?

*

Feature a heroic protagonist or protagonists coupled with a sort of killer/psychopath sidekick who is a Vietnam vet: when the hero has compunctions about killing, the sidekick literally begs to kill. This is the case, complicatedly, in Lehane's Kenzie/Gennaro mysteries. Patrick Kenzie's is the consciousness we identify with, and Angie Gennaro, his partner—our new Della—too, carries a gun. But there is a third, Bubba, who is a vet and thus (oh logically) a source of weaponry, munitions, etc., also a source of hits. The idea seems to be that the protagonists need to be able to stage hits just like the mob. Coben's Myron Bolitar has a partner named Win, not a vet but a martial arts expert, who begs to kill in every book. In Robert Crais's Elvis Cole novels, there is a sidekick named Joe Pike, who is a vet and a martial arts expert but who doesn't beg to pop people—

he is a gentler variant of the character. In Burke's Dave Robicheaux series, Dave is a cop and a vet who can be violent when he drinks; his friend Clete Purcel, also a vet, kills much more readily than Dave and appears when Dave gets squeamish about offing the lowlife. (Mosely, in *Fearless Jones*, takes the convention back in time to the post-WWII era, in the Watts section of L.A.; the protagonist, Paris Minton, is a wimpy bookseller; his friend, Fearless, is a decorated WWII vet. They exemplify brains and pure-minded brawn, rather than heroic scruples and an executioner mentality.)

We are obviously involved here in the poem of how we must have war, how violent conflict is unavoidable. Though one doubts that any of these authors were anywhere near Vietnam. And no one among them (so far as I know) is against capital punishment (the genre would be out of a job.) But we get to have the separation between hero and hit-man that is so necessary for the folks at home from whatever war, from among whose ranks the rather unsuspecting soldiers come. One might argue that this aspect of the genre, in its current state, began as a disillusioned elegy for Vietnam and became a justification for Afghanistan/Iraq.

*

In *A Drink Before the War*, Kenzie and Gennaro, Patrick and Angie, do execute someone themselves, a black man named Socia, who is a gang leader, murderer, and pedophile (how could you be worse?):

> I said, 'How many more will it take, Socia?'
>
> He said, 'What?' shuffling the edges of the photocopies into a neat stack.
>
> 'How many more people are you going to chew up before it's finally enough? Before even you get sick of it?'

Angie said, 'Do it, Patrick. Now.'

Socia glanced at her, then over to me, his eyes a blank. I don't think he understood the concept of my question. He stared at me, waiting for me to elaborate. After a minute or so, he held up the photocopies. His thumb rose up the front one, pressing between Roland's bare thighs. He said, 'Kenzie, is this all of it or not?'

'Yeah, Socia,' I said, 'this is all of it.' I raised the gun and shot him in the chest.

He dropped the photocopies and raised a hand to the hole, stumbling back but staying on his feet. He looked at the hole, at the blood on his hand. He seemed surprised, and for a brief moment, terribly afraid. 'The fuck you do that for?' He coughed.

I pulled back on the hammer again.

He stared at me, and the fear left his eyes. The irises peppered over with a cold satisfaction, a dark knowledge. He smiled.

I shot him in the head and Angie's gun went off at the same time. The bullets hammered him back into the salt pile, and he rolled onto his back and slid to the cement.

*

(Poem by myself:)

HEMOSTATIC

He wanted to know what blood was for.

Who is of interest when the water gets low? Or,
Does blood wish to be in a seaport town?

Would it have to be another he?

Is it interesting when the older ones shed theirs?

I once found a city for several years.
Perhaps we founded it, down where it pumped.

And I was sure of my worth.

Someone could die. Before they
Anyone, left me here facing your walls.
Each minute where nothing seems to circulate.

This is a red ride without
And maybe you can't know me now.

Maybe I'm just blood.
Whatever that's for.

*

Of all the characters created by the inferior writers (inferior to Ellroy) I only really respect Connelly's LAPD Detective, Harry (Hieronymus) Bosch. I "respect" the attempt, in the context I'm outlining, to create "decency" (but what is that?) coupled with the "flaw" that he can only work alone at the most crucial moments of a "case": nearly a rogue cop, as the U.S. is nearly a rogue state? Does decency plus flaw plus case create a story trajectory? Yes. Decency, like respect, is a word that screams out social conditioning, and has mostly to do with male comportment. ("Indecency" has to do with female comportment.) Decency has no place in a poem: neither a poet nor a poem should be describable as "decent." Does a poem have a "flaw"?—eye of beholder; many poems are "cases" though, and it is the geometry of case-solving that soothes me, as I've indicated. Meanwhile I suspect Bosch's creator of at least residual decency. You can tell things from author photos, can you? Connelly looks as if he wants to be Ellroy but knows it comes with a lot more karmic overload and ruination than he's really up for. (Dennis Lehane, on the other hand, looks slimy in his photo.)

In *The Last Coyote* (1995) Connelly takes on the theme that Ellroy established as his own the subsequent year (though there was earlier essay material) in *My Dark Places*: the many-years old, unsolved murder of the mother, who is a loose woman. As Ellroy's real mother was such a woman and victim, the fictional character of Harry Bosch's mother, a prostitute, is the victim of a murder, which Bosch undertakes to solve. Ellroy in real life pursued his mother's case, never discovering the killer. The theme occurs also in Burke's Dave Robicheaux series.

Early on Bosch leafs through the murder book, "The surprise was in the official cause of death. It was listed as blunt-force trauma to the head. The report described a deep contusion over the right ear with swelling but no laceration that caused fatal bleeding of the brain. The report said the killer might have believed he strangled the victim after knocking her unconscious but it was the coroner's conclusion that she was already dead when the killer wrapped Marjorie Lowe's own belt around her neck and tied it off. The report stated further that while semen was recovered from the vagina there were no other injuries commonly associated with rape." This is serviceable writing; Connelly has been a crime journalist.

Do note once again —this is one of my major points—that these writers all copy each other; it's hall of mirrors stuff. (Don't poets do that too? But not for monetary reasons.)

*

Some Title Groups According to Key Words (i.e. poetic buzzwords):

LAST

The Last Coyote—Connelly
The Last Detective—Crais
Last Car to Elysian Fields—Burke

WHITE

White Jazz—Ellroy
The White Lioness—Mankell
A Stained White Radiance—Burke

BLACK

The Black Dahlia—Ellroy
Black Cherry Blues—Burke
Blacklist—Paretsky
The Black Echo—Connelly
The Black Ice—Connelly

BONES

City of Bones—Connelly
(there were many other Bones titles about, which I didn't buy.)

RAIN

The Neon Rain—Burke
Prayers for Rain—Lehane

LIGHT & DARK

Lost Light—Connelly
Darkest Fear—Coben
Darkness, Take My Hand—Lehane
My Dark Places—Ellroy

BLOOD

Blood Work—Connelly
Flesh and Blood—J. Kellerman

MISC. POETIC WORDS

Heartwood—Burke
Stone Kiss—F. Kellerman
Sacred—Lehane
Mystic River—Lehane
Trunk Music—Connelly
Sunset Limited—Burke

*

There is also a somewhat fluid "in the know" vocabulary in most of the books. I was surprised to see "snitch" still used so much. Then there are words like "perp," "murder book," "body dump," "civilian," "pop" (for kill) as well as "cap"—"I capped him," "made" (Angie Gennaro is Mafia-connected, she's "made.") Many others, but these are the ones I seem to like the most and so remember. I've been meditating on the word "snitch" for several months now, and have used it at least twice in my poetry. It takes on heavy psychological and philosophical connotations if you consider that everyone needs to have someone to snitch to; I live in relative isolation, a widow, and can hardly ever snitch. Husbands and wives, and best friends, snitch to each other all the time.

*

The idea of the murder, the primal murder, and the need to know the identity of the murderer are basic materials of mythology, i.e. poetry. Who murdered her? Who murdered oneself? Was there an event in your past, is there one in your present, that feels like a murder? Why are women murdered in a good two-thirds of the books I read—or stalked and threatened? Why the obsession with the serial killing of women, with pedophiliac abuse particularly of girls?

I began sometime ago to ask seriously the question: Have I been murdered? and might conclude from this year's reading that I have. That all women have—were murdered a long time ago—that that is the earliest murder, not the murder of Abel, for example. My response to recent crime fiction, as a poet who is supposedly a woman, has been to turn the form around, use it against the murderer whose name is You. Since I did this particular spate of reading during an eleven-month hepatitis-C treatment, I read these books in a state of despair, suspense, and physical weakness; I identified with the atmosphere as well as the hidden primal story. I have perhaps a hundred of these books, sitting behind my brown chair; I bought most of them myself, at two stores in Paris, paying probably a thousand dollars all told. I'm almost ashamed.

*

Examination notes by the coroner in the case of James Ellroy's mother (*My Dark Places*):

> There is a double tightly occlusive ligature about the neck, producing deep grooving of the soft tissues. This ligature is comprised of both a length of apparent clothesline cord, which has apparently been placed first about the neck and knotted tightly in the left posterior region. The ends of the cord are, one extremely short and apparently having been broken loose at the knot, while the other one is of moderate length and extends inferiorly. Apparently applied over the first ligature is a tightly knotted nylon stocking, the knot likewise located in the left posterior lateral surface. The nylon ligature overlies the long limb of the clothesline ligature at that point. The nylon stocking appears to have been tightly affixed by the usual overhand knot first and in the formation of the second knot, one limb of the free end has been looped under a partial slip knot, which is quite tightly drawn up.

There is some beauty in this passage, by a certain Dr. Gerald K. Ridge, though at least one of the sentences is structure-faulty. The latinate language, the detail and gravity of the description make for a writing superior to Connelly's in the description from *The Last Coyote.* Ellroy goes on to write (his own words now):

> Dr. Ridge removed the ligatures and noted the "deep pallid groove" around the neck. He shaved the victim bald and described her head tissues as "Intensely cyanotic and suffused with dark bluish-purple discolorations." He cut the scalp down to the skull and pulled the flaps back. He diagrammed eleven wounds and labeled them "intense red deep scalp ecchymoses."

A boy's mother. The boy's own wounds seem to have shocked him into an original and righteous use of language in his later crime writing. Here is a passage from *L.A. Confidential* (1990):

> Jack killed time—thinking about Karen. Ten days since the party; life was mostly aces. He had to apologize to Spade Cooley; Welton Morrow was pissed over him and Karen—but the lukewarm Joanie/Ellis Loew deal almost made it up for him. Hotel shacks were a strain—Karen lived at home, his place was a dive, he'd been neglecting his payments to the Scoggins kids to make the freight at the Ambassador. Karen loved the illicit romance; he loved her loving it. Aces. But Sid Hudgens hadn't called and L.A. was heroin dry—no Narco jollies. A year at Ad Vice loomed like the gas chamber.
>
> He felt like a fighter ready to dive. The Christmas geeks kept staring; the punk he'd thumped had on a nose splint—probably a phony some Jew lawyer told him to wear. The grand jury room door stood ajar; Jack walked over, looked in.

This is fiction, and language, coded into music, bop-you-once reference hits; you have to be in the story to know. Ellroy's work often comes close to narrative poetry, particularly in the story *Hush Hush* and in the two big conspiracy novels, *American Tabloid* and *The Cool Six Thousand*. Ellroy seems to find everything rotten—corrupt, bleeding, unredeemable. Jack's love for Karen (above) is embedded in murders, deals, drugs, racism. The release (for both reader and author) is in the writing, never in the story. When I discovered Ellroy I wondered why I'd bothered with that other shit, but after I'd read most of him I went back to it.

*

(poem by myself)

THE MAIN OFFENSE

It could be in one's flesh, probably is.

Whatever you are, as born; as well as
the disease you might carry.

String me along, anyway, in case.
You might get something out of me
I could be like your bag man,
if you use my words right. Poetry
can justify you too.

I went up to him and put my hand
on his chest. Why bother healing
such a huge abscess? Do we have
anything in common? You are a
mean bastard; I just write things down.
They made me up for the part
But I grew both into and away from it.
            If there's
something you can't reach, I used to try
to do it. Now I don't know where my
primal loyalty lies. I think it
can't lie. I kind of wish you were dead,
but that's death, isn't it?

*

He moved her sodden hair and pointed with a pencil. "Bullet went in here, I think," Jesse said.

"A bullet?"

"Yep, went out the other side. No need to look. Let's roll her in the bag."

Death in Paradise, Parker

A woman was sprawled on one of the stepped seats about midway through the car. She was wearing gray leggings and a white thigh-length T-shirt. A large flower of blood had blossomed on her chest where she had been hit dead center with a single bullet. Her head was snapped back against the sill of the window behind her seat. She had dark hair and features, her lineage obviously stretching somewhere south of the border. On the seat next to her body was a plastic bag filled with many items Bosch couldn't see. A folded newspaper protruded from the top of it.

Angels Flight, Connelly

He stopped to take another gulp of beer.

'I went out there—just a block from Harris's place. She was pretty much decomposed, the young ones go fast. But I remember how she looked. Like a little angel, her arms stretched out like she was flying . . . '

Angels Flight, Connelly

'. . .Then two guys roar up out of nowhere, come up the sidewalk real fast, and push her inside.

'What they done, I don't like remembering it, I closed my eyes, that's the truth, she was whimpering, I'm not kidding you, man, I wanted to stop it. What was I gonna do?'

'Call for help.'

'I was strung out, I got a serious meth problem, it's easy to say what you ought to do when you're not there. Look, what's-your-name, I've been down twice but I never hurt anybody. Those guys, they were tearing her apart, I was scared, I never saw anything like that before.

Burning Angel, Burke

When he and Wu arrived, Pathologist Wang had finished with the body and was breadloafing the brain. It was routine stuff. He had already examined the organs the killer had left him. Shortly he would start dictating his notes, and his assistants would reassemble the body as best they could, stitch it up with coarse twine and deliver it to the morgue for cold storage. There was no doubt about the cause of death.

Li looked at the young girl's horribly slashed features. Her nose was almost completely severed. 'Can't you do anything about the face?' he asked.

Wang looked up and raised an eyebrow. 'Why?'

'She'll have to be formally identified.' He could not imagine how it must feel for a parent to look upon their own child in such a state. He did not want to imagine it.

'Not a lot,' Wang said, and he turned to slice through another half-inch of brain.

Chinese Whispers, May

*

I could quote from many more descriptions of dead females, but I've already gotten bored and weary typing these, though they're not all bad. The best noir writers can't tolerate the stasis of corpse-description passages. The earlier description of Ellroy's mother is probably a unique instance in his oeuvre. I'm also thumbing through the works of Fred Vargas, a French woman who is both a crime novelist and an archaeologist; but the horrific won't stay fixed in her work: I can't seem to find much of a description of a body in situ. Rather the force of the crime, its visual force even, is distributed throughout the book.

Vargas's *L'homme aux cercles bleus* features a murderer who pretends to be a serial killer in order finally to kill his wife. He is an historian, an expert on a narrow period of Byzantine history, whose wife—secretly the real author of all of his books—is threatening to leave him. He constructs a persona who draws blue circles on the streets of Paris, with thrown away articles in them—e.g. a cork, a dead pigeon, finally a corpse, then a second, and a third corpse, the third being his wife. Around the circle in each instance is written the sentence, *Victor, mauvais sort, que fais-tu dehors?* Victor, you poor boy, what are you doing outside? In another of Vargas's books, *Debout les morts*, a woman wakes up and finds that a tree has been planted in her yard during the night. She disappears, and in the workings-out of the story first her corpse is not under the tree, when the ground beneath is dug up, and then, the second time the ground is dug up, it is. Vargas's stories are poetic, and one associates these two books respectively with the image of the circle with objects inside and the image of the suddenly appearing tree. The images themselves seem to have generated the books.

In another of Vargas's books, *Sans feu ni lieu*, there is an old man who makes table-high wooden statues of women (my translation):

> "Tens of small women in wood, nude, in postures seated, kneeling, thinking or vaguely imploring . . . Minutely detailed and realistic, they were not, frankly speaking, works of art. They were small women very well made, much too weak and prostrate for (Marc's) taste. . ."
>
> "You only make women?" asked Marc.
>
> "Because something else exists? . . ."

"What else?" repeated the old man forever scratching his torso. "Boats? Churches? Trees? Fruit? Cloth? Clouds? Deer and woods? That's women, all of that, in any case, you would not say the contrary if you were just a little smarter. Symbols bore me. It's better to make women straightaway."

The old man is actually sculpting women who were victims of crimes: his son-in-law, Merlin, is the book's serial killer.

*

(Excerpt from "The Black Trailor," a short story/poem by myself)

You enter the lives of people who don't exist. You want some of them to die in the course of the story. The face is blown away, the fingerprints are decaying.

But first two people become lovers. I now watch them make love. He is both a man and a literary character. In her own room she keeps her artist's things, though she's fictional too. Enclosed in a circle I watch her with sadness; will I never be that person again? My fingerprints are almost gone from that scene.

It's a beautiful hit if your identity is the story. Are you identifying with death, in anticipation because death's you? But it isn't necessarily me, I say; so I may look for you later. I will confront you somewhere where you aren't the order, aren't in order, I say to you.

She is Catherine, a martyr who never lived. They will have no evidence of her existence. She will be robbed of her sanctity. They won't be alive at the same time as she, trembling crumbling lightning. I don't know if it's lightning or lightening.

His name is Mark; it will stay in place. For that really is the past when I was broken. When only a Mark would do fine.

I said, I like this play. You said, it's no good. You placed the corpse onstage, and it became the good. Was it mine? If I am, say, the ocean; the earth; whatever dies for you.

I will search for you after your death, to confront you. I will pose to you your timelessness and lack of fixity. I will say you have now never won.

I will search for you across heaven, for you marked me when I was indistinct, when I was loving, I say. When the drama still had its humor, and the ocean was unjudged by you. Before you thought it worth destroying like the sky the earth, in what order name those three spiraling? When I didn't have to be either a woman or a bird. When the bloody wheel wasn't tatooed into decaying flesh. When we didn't love the murder.

I will search for you across light to undo the murder. How can I let go, I say, just because there's no time now?

*

The opening sentences of the entry for "elegy" in the Princeton Encyclopedia of Poetry and Poetics are as follows: "ELEGY (from Gr. elegeia, "lament"). A lyric, usually formal in tone and diction, suggested either by the death of an actual person or by the poet's contemplation of the tragic aspects of life. In either case, the emotion, originally expressed as a lament, finds consolation in the contemplation of some permanent principle." I'm not sure that last sentence is true, unless 'permanent principle' may be expanded to include the notion of form itself. It is the form of the elegy, and the emotion invested in it, that give release and consolation to the reader.

The detective novel is a form that is in one aspect an elegy. The genre provides an emotional expanse for grief and anger; and it doesn't seem to matter what the reader's politics, class, profession are—the form works, emotionally. The question is whether another form does this adequately at this time. I couldn't get what I needed elsewhere, except in the act of writing my own poems; and there was something in a handful of Dylan's songs (and in some blues songs and folksongs. Also, I began to pay attention to opera again.) People would say to me, Why don't you read something better? Why are you reading such depressing, bloody books? Well I needed to read these, though I certainly welcomed the better written of them.

I believe there has been a murder. I believe the "murder must be undone," as I say above in "The Black Trailor." I see that living requires me to face the fact of the murder over and over. This is what I know, and this is a knowledge I share with crime fiction. Perhaps contemporary poetry has become too reticent for my taste.

Paris, May 2004

"Noir Talk" was first published in *The Encyclopedia Project, Volume 1*, Encyclomedia, 2006.

All works of mine quoted from were subsequently published in *In the Pines*, Penguin USA, 2007.

Musical Influences

One has always used music for company. Poetry isn't as companionable, nowadays: it demands things. That you not be so social; that your force, or intelligence, work alone at the words; that they stop being words. They are a kind of music, which no one defines well.

Poetry splits off from music, returns to music, depending where you are. The thrust of the 20th century made poetry hive off, not be music. Was this a good thing or a bad thing? You can think about that, if that's how you think.

I have an experience very occasionally, that I'm not supposed to have, where I dream while I'm awake. I don't hallucinate, I have quick dreams, open-eyed, while I'm doing something, about what I'm doing and who I'm doing it with. I hate this experience.

So I am teaching a private workshop in a friend's apartment. I am reading a passage from *Beowulf*, the Frederick Rebsamen translation, which follows the original closely, retaining the double-line with caesura, the alliteration, the cadence as it is possible, etc. I have read it aloud alone and it's dead; I read it here with others and it comes to life: this is a poetry, I realize, that depends on a live audience, not just an oral performance but the presence of others. It is now a fully electric poetry: the brunette woman next to me rocks back and forth slightly, as I do while reading. During the break in the workshop, the dreaming-while-awake experience is triggered in me, and I have split-second dreams about this woman as I chat with her in the gold-lit room (I then go into the bathroom and take a tranquilizer.) I realize that the chantlike reading is the triggering factor this time, and that's interesting: something very old is happening. When the walls in your mind collapse, you might realize that you aren't a single body or time or way of thinking. Your poetry doesn't have to be just rational words in position—the 20th, possibly the 21st century, way. By rational, I mean clicking into the line, the sentence, the pattern, the presentation of poetics that everyone thinks is so special. Poetry also has a sort of cry, a real cry not theorized—it has a curve, simultaneous curves, the sound-shapes mean as much as the words. And the best of contemporary poetry likes its sound—and not in a corny way. Nor in the way of *Beowulf*:

> Then an alien creature   cold wanderer
> could not longer endure   from his dark exile
> bright bench-laughter   born to the rafters
> each night in that hall.   The harp sounded
> the poet's clear song.   He sang what he knew
> of Man's Creation   the Measurer's work

I always write as a sort of Measurer, and I am evidently indebted to Williams and his variable foot, which looks as strange as *Beowulf* on the page. I think of Williams as an unmusical reader. And yet the music is all there for me on the tapes of him reading; as, when I listen obsessively to different performances in concert by Bob Dylan of my favorite songs of his like "The Man in the Long Black Coat" and "Blind Willie McTell," I still wonder if Dylan is singing well at all. It just doesn't seem to matter, and I can't figure out what matters.

In 2000, 2001 I listened quite a bit to a flamenco singer named La Niña de los Peinas—the little girl with the combs—who has been dead for a long time. She was recorded in the '30s and '40s. A famous singer (and a friend of García Lorca.) I see her always on a flamenco stage (was she really there?) sitting in a line of chairs with the others, the guitarists, the singers, the dancers. I would put the CD on and then sit at my computer and type while she sang:

mi marido
mi marido no esta aqui
qui esta a la guerra de Francia
al gurugurugu al gurugurugu al gurugurugu

my husband isn't here
my husband's left me all alone, he's gone to the war in France.

There was no way I could duplicate the flamenco rhythms on the keyboard and have any fluidity while writing, and I didn't want to reproduce the patterns—I would have to play the song for you, if you really wanted to know what I was listening to, "Al Gurugu," a flamenco tango, a highly stylized form for singing, playing, dancing. I typed in whatever pattern came into my head:

look at their diaries and change them.   dead woman may i change your
diary?   covered with silver and gemstones   i have no diary i had no, did
i have   a diary? my husband is not here, he has gone into France to the
war.   is literally what   i greet her and she sang no diary for them
no   diary   for a man   to witness, sell or   an antiques store   your
precisions   swollen am swollen with flight   have you seen gem
what does it say   short   black dress   diary aiy   aiy aiy the days
were not mine in the almanac so i took the discredited beads   so i
accepted the discredited vision   so i
rejected aiy   the diary

(from "Necklace"—*Alma, or The Dead Women*)

There is, or was, an argument, as to which came first, music, poetry (drama), dancing—OR did one of them come first, were they one thing at the beginning? Likewise there is the controversy, did the myth or the ritual come first; the myth or the dream? If I dream while awake, am I letting in a form of thought—for I believe dream to be partly a form of thought—which was tidily relegated to its night-time mental room at the so-called dawn of time? But an old poem like *Beowulf* lets it out of that room.

We have time partly so we can make music and poetry. I use Dylan to talk to, make music back to, as if we were in chairs on the stage like flamenco artists waiting our turn.

> I've gone with the jaguar in the blood-red coat through the soul-hell transformation.
>
> In that old dance hall, where only neurons or songs or tears float, someone is chanting, in order to cross over.
>
> As I had said, there must be other ways of leaving. Of returning.
>
> This song lifts you. Way above the black coat. Way above your self-identification of the night high golden moon, an image.
>
> (from *In the Pines*)

And on and off during my career as a poet I've gotten poetic stimulation from Dylan's long line influenced by Woody Guthrie, the Surrealist poets, and my friend Allen Ginsberg among others. We are all in this together.

I need to talk about Maria Callas now, and the art of performing someone else's work: for I've avidly taken something from her recently, though I'm not sure how to define it. I know that she reshaped—her intelligence being like no one else's—the arias the scenes written by others into, not their Platonic original but: if it's going to be right this time, she'll make it right. I listened to her recording of *Mad Scenes* in 2003-4.

Can there be such a thing in reality as a mad scene? No. This is a poem for a terrible experience—I have to use the word poem for the total shape of event and content, and as Lucia follows the flute, in her blood-spattered wedding gown, we might be in Rwanda in 1994; or is one singing as Lyndie England who married the Service and did "as she was told"? Donizetti and Cherubini are pleasing the opera audiences of their times: Callas makes the poem of the mad scene so intelligent that you figure you can go on living even though the world is mad and bloody and you are shattered. I was haunted all of the spring of 2004 by Callas's photo, an ad for the newly restored Passolini movie *Medea*, in which she plays the title role but this time doesn't sing. Passolini figured she had become the role and didn't even need to sing it: I didn't see the film, I would have been terrified without the music.

Callas said some very important things:

1) That when you sing you should aim for the center of the note. I take this, for my poetic practice, as meaning that one should aim for the center of the issue, or technique.

2) That the opera *Medea* is practically all recitativo and the singer must keep that going above all else. This is a very energetic and dramatic process. I take the statement as vindication both of my writing of narrative poetry and the way I perform it when I read. A lot of my own work seems to be a combination, in one flow, of recitative and aria. But that is also the way of Dante and Chaucer, though without the confrontation of live bodies on stage.

3) Callas also says that "Vissi d'Arte," the famous aria from Tosca, and perhaps its most famous moment, stops the action of the opera and therefore she hates it. I love this. Though she was unable to erase the aria for subsequent tradition, I am willing to erase like moments in my own work before they are born.

Here is a poem of mine influenced by Maria Callas, spoken by a sort of character, in an unpublished book called *Songs and Stories of the Ghouls*:

I stand here in whose eyes
the name of light is audience
burning into my forehead
waitresses' voices along the spine
if what was once light
            isn't
            my audience
what are you doing to me?
who was I broken for
was it worth it to be?

If I'm a shade
            acting
what once will occur
it must be for the song I wore
hear what they all said to you
a gesture or tone: someone lies
in the intentional tongue
betraying you again and again
            the one
            or the many
whose thoughts I stand here before

Because there's no light, what an
            outrage
was made of the science
of definitions

like what happened to me
performing here in a mad scene
    not
    and never mad
I hadn't seen clearly until I enacted her

I always write poems; I have always imagined them, while writing, as performed live, for a long time even in a specific room—the Parish Hall of the St. Mark's Poetry Project, which isn't a large room but can sit almost 200 and has good acoustics. I had/have an interested audience there, a people or tribe who love to listen to poetry. Not having lived in New York for a long time, I now concentrate on a sort of room-in-the-air, not so concrete; but it seems more crucial than ever that my work be performed live and by myself. I am aware that Dylan drives himself ceaselessly to perform his work all around the world, to large and small audiences, in his Neverending Tour—because he works in one of the performing arts: and something will be lost from the performance of his songs when he dies; but also the songs must be sung, they can't be read on the page. And the studio recordings don't get it. The primary artistic experience, finally, is with the live audience; the recordings of his songs in the studio are rather score-like.

My poems can be read on the page, but I try to invest them there, as much as I can, with my voice in performance. I know that they are poems. I still believe that poetry is in some sense the highest of arts. I still can't explain ...this, and I still don't know what a poem is exactly. I know what a song is but not a poem. Or do I? It is, like a song, a stylized sound experience, but it partakes of more levels of language than song does. Is that it? The walls in the mind can better topple, and the poem can layer and condense many more kinds of thought and experience, bear more of history, refer to much more, all while going on, consciously, in time. It is for you, though, and I perform it for you. I read my poetry aloud to myself often: I do all my editing from reading aloud; I keep track of the shapes of my narratives by reading aloud almost daily. But the voice of it is more than the vocal voice: a voice in my brain rolled up on skeins in cells, which can be taken out and read through. I possess the voice/poem in both the rolled-up and extended form. A poem is about knowing something both all at once and in its unrolling in time. A song is more about being in time.

2006

(Georgetown University workshop)

Songs and Stories of the Ghouls, Wesleyan University Press, Middletown Connecticut, 2011.

In the Pines, Penguin Books, New York, 2007.

Alma, or The Dead Women, Granary Books, New York City, 2006.

Beowulf, An Updated Verse Translation, by Frederick Rebsamen, Perennial Classics, New York, 2004.

"Where'd You Get It?"

Where do/did the words come from? I ask. And open my 1975 edition of *Slinger* at random, to:

> his head is a spasm
> of presyntactic metalinguistic urgency
>
> What What What
> Where Where Where
> Who What Where
> What Where Who

I imagine this to be a good description of how Ed began writing *Slinger*—and how he felt each time he went back to it after a lapse in the writing. However, one thing I notice rereading it, is that I find some of my own words and sounds therein (Where'd I get them? *Slinger*):

> Dear lengthening Day
> I have loved your apparencies since you created me

I wrote a poem called "Dear Dark Continent" in what had been Ed and Jenny's house in Chicago, at (I think this is the number) 911 West Diversey Street; and a year later, in England, a poem addressed to "Your Dailiness." I wonder if there was a broadside, on the wall of the Diversey

Street house, of "The Lawg," which serves as a preface to *Book III, The Winterbook*. How have I forgotten where my words came from?

In my twenties I seem to have heard Ed read from *Slinger* in a number of cities: I know I remember New York and San Francisco, but it seems as if there were Chicago and London, I dunno, doano—which spelling suits this ambiance? *Slinger* is the most physical of poems, despite its purely oxygenated (but knee-slapping) cerebrality; and I associate it with Ed's voice and his reading stance, very straight and tall. There was a lectern in Ed's study, and he wrote standing up. But I can't get this chronology of thirty-some years ago right. Everyone was waiting for what would happen next in the Story; there was an especial suspense as to how it might end—Book IIII: what would it be like? Or rather, would it be as good as its predecessor books? (The pundits finally judged No, but also Yes—Ed had become another person; it was nice that the Slinger said Goodbye, Hasta la Vista—see you later.) It wasn't that there really was a Story—what the hell happens in *Slinger*? People ride around in a stagecoach or whatever and talk; but there were changes of consciousness between the books, as there were relatively long periods of time between, and there were fabulous word-generated entities talking in the poem, in slant-wise relation to everything that concerned us. The revelation of the new sections was the Story, and the straight-ahead thrust of the line, what it was like when Ed appeared somewhere and read new passages.

Ed's reading style for the poem seemed like a very hip take on the then-current Black poetry style: he was so Kool, and his Whiteness remained cool. He acknowledges Black & White in Book I, in the "Hi! Digger" and thereabouts passages (there were a lot of people who had named themselves Digger in the '60s, though Heidegger hadn't), but the Bombed Horse is also the Oblique Horse and the question "Where's my dark ace?" is as ambiguous as allegory might be (at least one Ed expert thought the line was about black holes.) When Ted and I moved to Chicago and rented what had been Ed and Jenny's house, Ted taking Ed's job at Northeastern Illinois University, we found that some young white poets emulated Ed's reading style, but there was this pervasive, real, black sound, out of Chicago and of course New York and Newark (Roi/Amiri Baraka), that had inspired Ed. You may not hear it coming off the pages of *Slinger* now, unless you remember it. Along with the inescapable politics of the times.

The poem isn't character driven; single stony words often become characters: Slinger/Zinger himself, but also I, Everything, Sllab, the Barrel, and the two-worded (how Baroque) Taco Desoxin. I was present for the germ of the generation of the latter character. Ted and I came to Chicago just before the inception of 1972, as Ed and Jenny and Kid and Maya prepared to travel to Mexico. Ted and I and Ed and Jenny "did" some desoxyn, on New Year's Eve '71; some time later Ed informed Ted that there was now a character in the poem named Taco Desoxyn. This is how the poem worked; the words come out of the air, out of currency, is the answer to Where do the words come from? On New Year's Day night Ted and Jenny were completely wiped out, but Ed and I went to find some dinner, and the only place open in Old Town—our neighborhood, which is several times named in Slinger—was a rather poor-grade so-called Mexican restaurant. Is this how "Taco" came into it? I was a young woman from the Southwest and took my Mexican food seriously; I think I complained about the meal but I had a great time. This was my first real conversation with Ed, who focused it on me. He was delighted to discover I was a Westerner, had been born in Bisbee, Arizona—see the wife of the mayor of Bisbee passage in Book IIII—had connections in Prescott (I had lived there too as a small child), and had grown up in the Mohave Desert town of Needles. I remember describing Prescott's Whiskey Row to him, and the whiskey-and-stained-wood smell of the bars. God, he loved it! I think he gave me credence as a poet, thereafter, because I was a true Westerner; he was the only person, later, who seemed really to get and savor the melancholic last three words of my poem "At Night the States": "Montana. Illinois. Escondido."

Northeastern Illinois University was a commuter's U, with a lot of working-class students. Ted inherited from Ed as students—and we inherited as friends—the Stone Wind guys (they edited the poetry mag *Stone Wind*): Al Simmons, Terry Jacobus, Steve Pantos, Hank Kanabus. They adored Ed—they were like his knights—and constantly referred to the Greek philosopher Parmenides, some of them being Greeks and Ed having just been in process with *Book III, The Winterbook*, with its character the Secretary to Parmenides. I think Al helped generate the character "Al" in the poem, didn't he? This group was also sometimes called 'the new Barbarians'; and their names were the answer to the question posed in Ed's off-to-the-side-of-Slinger poem "The Poet Lets His Tongue Hang Down": "WHO ARE THE BARBARIANS?" "Parmenides" and "Barbarians" were thus words—concrete entities of import, code words—that greeted us right away in Chicago; though my personal favorite squib of Ed's, of that time, is to be found in *The Day & Night Book* (a diary with weird entries published in Tom Clark's fabulous anthology ALL★STARS): "There's some bad vibes / at Goldblatts." Goldblatt's was a Chicago department store; I myself had occasion to go there and feel horrible.

Effie Mihopoulos, another student of Ed/Ted, was sort of a Stone Wind guy, but she was a girl so constituted her own category. Her interview with Ed in *Letter Ex*, in 1991, on the occasion of his returning to read in Chicago, elicits a very clear reflection on *Slinger*. Her questions are direct and come from a past when Ed was God, the teacher and poet, who also let you in, to His conversation and heady air. Ed says of the poem, "I just let it be its own thread and what people are saying to each other, the kind of, sort of vague, abstract sort of irrepressible mindlessness at times, and the vocabulary that generates all that, were natural to the time. That's what I was hearing around me. When I look at that poem now, I don't see it as anything but an empiricism of the language that I was hearing at the time." I take this as Ed letting us know we can have the poem at face value as its language—our delight in it, the fact of it, is what it sounds like it says, though the compressed reading/knowledge therein be so considerable. Despite the erudition, the poem's obvious, and it's for us. Ed goes on to say, of the quality of the obvious: "Because except for things that are extremely esoteric and only a few scientists know about, everything IS obvious. So if we couldn't constantly claim a new connection for the obvious, we'd be in bad trouble real quick."

In the interview Effie asks Ed whether *Slinger* is really a narrative poem—a good question and probably not answerable, though Ed answers: "Sure. Maybe that's a bit gratuitous. I suppose. It tells a story. It's not much of a story; it's a thinnish excuse." Effie's own argument against the poem's categorization as narrative is its extreme concision and the discreteness of its sections. Ed obviously thought he was writing a narrative poem while he was writing it—one thinks like that while writing—but maybe that isn't strictly what he did. The spaces between the sections are an important aspect of the poem, time-caused, as I said before; if you look at the poem without being conditioned (I am) to think of it as narration, what you might see is a collection of incredible pieces which add up to something quite different from a story, more like *The Waste Land* than the *Iliad*. Ed calls *The Waste Land* "the great poem of the twentieth century" in his interview with John Wright, a judgment only very obtuse people would argue with: *The Waste Land* created twentieth century poetry. Maybe he was unconsciously emulating it, many people of his generation must have been, in order to get past it. Ed also evokes Kerouac's *On the Road* in the interview with Effie, and addresses "Jack" in Slinger,

Jack being one of those ineffable slidey words/names—Get out of my way, Jack!—that won't stay fixed, but look carved in granite. Certainly Slinger feels like the period of the mid-60s to mid-70s, where one was always in a vehicle, in an unfixed life, high and talking to some others. Shooting out bullets. The line "Bullets are not necessarily specific" may be more pertinent to discussion of the poem than the oft-quoted "Speed is not necessarily fast."

Another of Ed's influences, though, was the lowly television series, a very narrative form. Ted and I moved to England for awhile, in 1973, Ted again taking a job Ed had held, at the University of Essex. One day we saw an episode of the British sci-fi program *Dr. Who* and were astonished at the physical resemblance between the leading actor (can't remember his name; he was, I think, the third man to play the doctor) and Ed. Yes, we were told by others and then Ed himself, everyone sees this, and Ed has modeled the character Dr. Flamboyant on Dr. Who. Dr. Flamboyant is the science-fiction aspect of this supposed western; he has an uncertain space ship which causes his dimension-shattering body to arrive bit by bit at salient locations in the West. Ed was also influenced by another TV series, *The Wild Wild West*, though I only remember this dimly and don't know if Ed or Jenny or one of the Stone Wind Guys—Steve Pantos?—told me so. I found *The Wild Wild West* incredibly tacky and rarely watched it; I've had to look up the website to refresh my memory of it. The following is the official description of the series: "James West and Artemus Gordon are two agents of President Grant who take their splendidly appointed private train through the west to fight evil. Half science fiction and half western, the Artemus designs a series of interesting gadgets for James that would make Inspector Gadget proud. A light-hearted adventure series." I remember the show in terms of the train, and have a vague image of Robert Conrad (West) in a cowboy hat; there were episodes with vampires and Martians, appearing out of nowhere in the western landscape, along with characters from Washington D.C., like President Ulysses S. Grant and his Attorney General. This is pure Ed land if you think about it for about two seconds. You also start to wonder if Slinger doesn't consist of "episodes".

If the poem seems episodic, it's still constructed in a tightly designed way, with Books I and II, then its cosmic center *The Cycle*, flanked on its other side by Books III and IIII (the "IIII" as opposed to "IV" is not mere conceit, it refers to design). *The Cycle* with its numbered quatrains, as opposed to the continuous style of the other sections, is like a mock-creation myth; in spite of its mockingness it scares me plenty. It really does feel like a creation myth, or an anti-creation myth, and it does feel like it knows what creation is:

14 The Grand Car with the Superior Interior
Moves with a basal shift So Large
It would be a dream to feel time curve
For no masses so locked serve straight time

15 Thus rhythm has a duty to de-tour the Vast
Contra Naturum? Baby you ain't heard nothin yet
Like this is a day in the life
Of The Man who grabbed the crack

16 And wrapped it around the Antho-space
From the Eye of the U on out
Displacement is never felt
If that's where you're at, uh,
It looks like that's that

(from "The Interior Decorator Runs the Scenario of the Wingéd Car")

This pre-Socratic, Platonic, Plotinean, Blakean section seems to me the most on-cocaine one, with its very extreme compression and its feel of standing in the room where the primal gears move. I've been in that room while not writing, and it made me want to get out; it's different to be in while writing, it's under control, it's yours. There's a term I've recently picked up, "phosphenes," which refers to "the images perceived by the human brain as visual images in the absence of visual stimuli . . ." (*A Field Guide to Rock Art Symbols of the Greater Southwest*, Alex Patterson, Johnson Books: Boulder: 1992). Phosphenes can be perceived when the eyes are closed, during physical stress, meditation, or when one is on drugs. They are highly geometric, with lots of checkerboards, triangles, grids, crosses, parallel lines etc; and are found in Southwestern Indian rock art all over the place. Sometimes these patterns are used to construct a human figure. *The Cycle* reminds me vividly of this kind of image (Ed would love this reference), coming so purely out of the imagination and its most basic geometries. It's a real first-things place.

The point of being in such a place is to be in it. One has been influenced, has read widely, been instructed in various ways in order to stand there; but when there the influences are beside the point. They (and the drugs) have simply been used; they are not authoritative—oneself is. As the Slinger says in Book III:

> To a poet all authority
> except his own
> is an expression of Evil
> and it is all external authority
> that he expiates
> this is the culmination of his traits

Poetry concerns itself with what it leaves out; it gets its effects by omissions. It renews by finding new aspects of explanation to omit; the difference between twentieth and nineteenth century poetries is where the spaces are. Nineteenth century poetry waivered between leaving out the story and telling it; it lost interest in the discourse and treatise. Twentieth century poetry created omissions on the physical page itself, put more white space in front of the readers' eyes, tried to leave out the story pretty much entirely, and dispersed the discourse and treatise here and there. Contemporary mainstream poetry professes no idea that any of this is happening: it has kept syntax rigidly tight, shrunk the story to anecdote, and made an utterly boring poetry. Orthodox innovative practice, on the other hand, supposes a lot of spaces, but places them all on the surface, and that can get a little old and didactic-feeling. Space isn't always visual, or perceptible as disjunction; in a highly compressed poetry, like Ed's, it's inside the line and thought pattern. It's how the poet's mind works. Ed put the story back in (Olson left it out), and he isn't ever disjunctive, but he NEVER explains, or demonstrates, his reasoning. This is how *Slinger* is fast.

But now
            A weak-minded mammal stands
on the corner of his head
and fort Phil Korny avenue
you can catch him
as the Driverless Horses pull in
this must be Everything's connection
whos haranguing the perspicacious crowd
'But why is he so loud' Lil asked
'perhaps he can use some help
before he gets boxed up and sent North

This poetry entertains and pushes one ever forward, without one necessarily knowing what's going on, because it is possible to be funny, fast, and linguistically brilliant without elucidating. Everything—Everything is a character, after all, a unity—is right there as you read it. The words are as concrete as it gets. This is a poetry with a consistently hard surface; although the words may mean a lot of things, they never float loose, and you aren't permitted to stop and contemplate the layering. Any word might become a character, but then it is. Period. You're in the story the same way you're in a dream: situations and events are taken for granted and you keep going through it. The surface tells you not to stop and meditate on references; it tells you you're being pulled ahead by the driverless horses. The poem gives you everything you need for it, by existing the way it does. I certainly accepted it as it was.

Ed did a lot between the sections of *Slinger*—including write other poetry: *Hello La Jolla*, *Yellow Lola*, *A Day & Night Book*, the two sequences for Jenny, *Love Songs* and *Songs: Set Two: A Short Count*, *Recollections of Gran Apacheria*, some individual poems. This is an amazing amount of work; but certainly living got done too. It's just that the living and the poetry are so interconnected. Ed sometimes talked as if poetry wasn't everything—Everything!—did he really believe this? In Boulder in 1980 I once saw him in a state of total exhilaration. It turned out he'd been playing golf. I think I must have looked astonished when he told me he'd been playing golf, in fact I really didn't know what to think. He looked at me with defiance and said, "Don't you ever want just to live?" I didn't say anything, I wasn't sure if I did; I'm still thinking about it.

2007, published in *Big BridgeSlinger,*
Wingbow Press, Berkeley, 1975

“To do exactly that, right now”

The Collected Poems of Philip Whalen, Wesleyan University Press, 2007, edited by Michael Rothenberg

It is thrilling to have a huge collection of Philip Whalen’s poetry in hand; the poems as always seem the most readable ever written—and why would anyone not want to write like this? You just fall into the work; whereas so much poetry at the moment seems to be more about thinking about it than reading it, this poetry is all tactile and grabbing and natural. Everyone used to say, That Phil Whalen is too self-indulgent!, by which was meant the work wasn’t constantly high-minded—and we’re all soooooo high-minded, who can bother with actual reading pleasure what with all the panels to go to? The brow screws up at this very moment, thoughtfully.

A key to getting what he’s up to, if that’s what you want, really is the famous SINCE YOU ASK ME, subtitled “(A Press Release, October 1959)”:

> This poetry is a picture or graph of a mind moving, which is a world body being here and now which is history . . . and you. Or think about the Wilson Cloud-chamber, not ideogram, not poetic beauty: bald-faced didacticism moving as Dr. Johnson commands all poetry should, from the particular to the general. (Not that Johnson was right . . .)

Whalen wrote down everything he thought about, drawing conclusions too, but within the same poetic fabric, and he thought about toilet paper as well as philosophy, masturbation ("THE WARS OF ONAN") as well as the life of Nikola Tesla, etc etc. He thought about every tiny and big thing and how to describe it without boring himself or the reader. The mystery is how he managed to unify so much detail so pleasantly and musically; the biggest mystery is how he managed to be himself illuminating words, but who would want to take on the reality of personality in an age of denial?

Quoting from SINCE YOU ASK ME brings up the major strategy of this edition, which one is not sure one is in favor of: judgment is reserved by this writer, though people who are reading Whalen for the first time may not care a bit. That is, the editor, Michael Rothenberg, has decided to present the poems in chronological order, as one continuous entity, without any indication, as one reads, of how they were previously collected in books, and making no other divisions in the collection, for example by decade, form, or place of composition (How can one find anything?). Rothenberg pays lip service to Whalen's original books as published, in his initial note, but writes: " . . . sometimes Philip Whalen's 'creative process' was simply to allow a publisher or editor to make their own organizational choices. For example, when I asked PW why the poems in *On Bear's Head* were not organized chronologically, he told me he had no idea,'It just came from the publisher that way.'" Well I don't believe any of that for a minute. Phil worked hard on the organization of his books, and the selection and arrangement really counted. SINCE YOU ASK ME was the second-to-final piece of the book *MEMOIRS OF AN INTERGLACIAL AGE*; the final piece being the tiny poem *Awake a moment / Mind dreams again / Red roses black-edged petals* (entire poem). Obviously quite a lot of deliberation went into this exit—a press release followed by a three-line evanescence in italics? Only the author would have done that.

I sense, throughout this edition, the invisible covers of the books I loved; I grasp at movements from poem to poem that aren't there. When I was young, the publication of a volume by Philip Whalen was a huge event; the copies got worn out, and I have memorized his layouts and transitions. Whalen made something new when he made a book, the same way he often made the poems themselves, out of pre-existing pieces. But it is one convention to demonstrate the chronology of a life's work in a collected poems: another poem has been created here in this collected poems, and it must in some sense be PW's. I do keep wanting the books back. But new entities seem to arise from these pages, because it's the nature of the poetry to force chunks of time and space to realign themselves into new shapes. Whalen dated everything in order to underscore not so much chronology as connections. Consider the following short extract:

> Songs to induce prophetic dreams
>   sold only for the prevention of disease
>
> *
>
> We are happy when we are slightly uncomfortable
>   for a long time & can complain about it
>   afterwards
>
> *
>
> Choose again, choose as often as you like
>   you never get your money back
> Money is never the same as you've got or as you've had
> You must get more. Get a new batch as often as you can.

That's from the long poem, MY SONGS INDUCE PROPHETIC DREAMS, dated 15:x:63-19:i:65, and first printed in the *BRAIN-CANDY* section of *ON BEAR'S HEAD*. Within the same time frame he wrote the lyric GODDESS, dated 14:ix:64:

Where I walk is with her
In fire between the ocean waves
Towards that Lady I stand beside
Center of the earth in the center of the air
Stand moving star cloud
Roar music silence
Waves break over our muddy heads
Dash against our sunny feet

GODDESS found its way into a different book (also collected in *ON BEAR'S HEAD*), *EVERY DAY*, along with, e.g. THE ODE TO MUSIC and THE BEST OF IT, quite important poems, dated respectively 2:iii:64, 2:v:64 (it has two dates) and 3:x.64,7:xi:64 (it also has two dates.) THE BEST OF IT is a longish, garbage-heap (glittering garbage) poem like MY SONGS INDUCE PROPHETIC DREAMS. But it's different: its pieces are less diaristic—there's less tracking (see MONDAY IN THE EVENING: "There was an animal / It left a set of tracks / The animal was I / & the tracks also & the mud ") My point is, the poetry becomes a universe of simultaneity and synchronicity that includes chronology. The poet describes himself and his world, but in parallel poems, written virtually at the same time; there are parallel concerns. The reader will figure this out despite the chronological order of discrete poems.

Whalen's secret for unity—his ability to collage, meander and observe, and leap from low-brow to high-brow in an instant—lies largely in his metrics, at least according to his own assessment. I don't think this information has been written down anywhere, but in conversation he often avowed using one particular musical pattern: he tried to tell me, but I didn't get it then but have remembered the gist; I get it now. (In the '70s he credited John Paul, a young Chicago poet, with being the only person who really understood his poetry.) He always, and he meant ALWAYS, used the same underlying rhythm for his poetry: an 18th-century-type bass, almost a basso ostinato, of continuous eighth notes. If you think about this—it helps if you know a little about 18th century music—but if you consider that sound and then read some of the poems, you'll see this is right. There are eighth-notes underneath, and they seem to continue right across the page, even in the white spaces, pulling together just about all the poetry and, one might say, this whole collected poems:

Alas dainty Belshazar! Divine Exogamite!
            Perished!

    Folie de grandeur: horror & degradation is my name

Another damned lie, my name is I
Which is a habit of dreaming & carelessness
            no nearer the real truth of any matter
In any direction myself bound & divided by notions

            ACT!   MOVE!   SPEAK!

(from SELF-PORTRAIT SAD 22:1X:58)

Fred Merkel,
What are you doing
Fred Merkel is my name

And I'm just a little drunk
But I'm soberer than I was this time yesterday evening

(from THE REVOLUTIONARIES, 15:viii-7:x: 61)

Morganatic marriage is the answer to an otherwise ruined life.
Let's rebuild Hadrian's villa.

(from THE GRAND DESIGN, 9:x-27:x:66)

"I TOLD MYSELF THAT I WASN'T GOING TO GET HIGH TODAY
AND I TOLD MYSELF THAT IF I *DID* GET HIGH
IT WASN'T GOING TO BE ON ACID—

(from "I TOLD MYSELF": BOBBIE SPONTANTEOUSLY, 16:viii:71)

Gibbon says " . . . the wisdom and authority of the
Legislator are seldom victorious in a contest
With the vigilant dexterity of private interest."

(from LA CONDITION HUMAINE, 6:i:79)

It's not at all that the poetry sounds the same, or that each syllable is attached to an eighth-note, it's that underneath, there is a ghostly bass setting the pace; and Whalen does ride the same pace, even though the figuration above is various. This quasi eighteenth-century sound is most obvious, of course, in the quote from Edward Gibbon, the great eighteenth-century (take note, L. Scalapino) historian. Gibbon's is a syllable-perfect prose reflective of its times' taste. The same rhythm, though, might be said to underpin much of 20th century jazz; Whalen always managed to sound perfectly contemporary.

The ground bass technique runs the show in Whalen's longest poem, SCENES OF LIFE AT THE CAPITOL, written in Kyoto and first published in 1971. Whalen's earlier method for achieving length, which involved the accumulation of clearly separate pieces often separated by asterisks or other symbols, has evolved into a capacity to get everything into an ongoing and similar continuum:

> Vegetable nerves
> Cold noodle time in the Capital
> I got to kick my coffee habit.
> Anybody seen my tranks? Remind me
> How is Steve Carey?
>
> Haloes
> Which the angels left behind
> Empty niches where holy saints once
> Hand-hewn bases for noble columns: garden decorations
> Wintermin (Chlorpromazine hydrochloride, 12.5 mg tabs)
>   "Motion sickness, vomiting of pregnancy, potentiating
>   effects on hypnotics and analgesics, psychoneurosis
>   such as anxiety neurosis, bed-wetting, Pollakiuria."
>
>   did you say "Bum trip"
>   or "dumb trip"?

There are no breaks in this poem, which states near its conclusion:

Japan is a civilization based upon
An inarticulate response to cherry blossoms.
So much for Western Civilization.

SCENES OF LIFE AT THE CAPITOL is indeed long—over sixty pages in this edition, a heroic feat of edgelessness. I once heard Phil read it *all*, in a dual reading with Allen Ginsberg, in San Francisco in 1971. After we, the audience, had seated ourselves the two poets entered the room from the back, Phil blowing on a huge conch shell. Allen read first for a mere 45 minutes, there was a break, and then Phil read the whole thing. It took a couple of hours. This was still, as I say, the heroic age of both writing and reading. People actually let you read your work! At length! They liked it! Then they ran away and wrote their own. The poetry, with its sound and vitality getting into your nerves and thoughts and memories, was the thing. (I wasn't there in New York the time John Ashbery read all of "The Skaters" and had forgotten to bring the last page, but I've obviously heard the anecdote: 'By that time it didn't make any difference.' I remember him reading all of "The New Spirit" in 1970.)

After SCENES OF LIFE AT THE CAPITOL the poems become shorter and more condensed, partly because PW has absorbed the lessons of SCENES, and partly because Phil became a Zen monk in 1972 and devoted the majority of his time to his new practice. I first met him in Bolinas a year before he became a monk—he still had the red hair and beard—and then we reconnected again in Chicago when he was about to lose his hair and had just sewn his ordination robes. He said he was partly joining up because he needed community and sustenance, room and board: very hard to come by if you're a committed poet. But afterwards he spoke increasingly of the need "to get this thing right"—the

Zen thing. Still, there were a lot of poems to come, and the Zen thing wasn't necessarily what they were about. The Buddhist angle isn't something the reader is obliged to take on: as a friend of Phil's, I rarely discussed Buddhism with him; I noted the references in the poetry, but the poetry remained Phil's poetry. If you're a Buddhist, Buddhism is everywhere, but everywhere remains specific details, everywhere being both concrete and imaginary. I'm now trying to find the poem about the dentist who looks like Kenneth Koch, but instead I come upon the one with Hasleton Brasler, from 1974:

> I was falling asleep in my chair
> Now I lie on the floor, ruminating ideas of life's brevity
> The feeble intensity of enormous ambition
> Hasleton Brasler said he'd be over
> He had to pick up his car and take a haircut
> You understand what I'm talking about . . .
> "including the power tools"
> There's no excuse for an imitation of Billie Holiday.
>
> (HOW TO BE SUCCESSFUL & HAPPY
> WITHOUT ANYBODY ELSE FINDING OUT ABOUT IT)

I'm reasonably sure that there was no Hasleton Brasler, as there was no Fred Merkel, or Margaret Gridley. Whalen wrote two wonderful novels, *YOU DIDN'T EVEN TRY* and *IMAGINARY SPEECHES FOR A BRAZEN HEAD*, and was an inveterate inventor, in his poems, of characters and scenarios. One of my favorite moments in the the oeuvre of PW is the invention of Margaret Gridley, which takes place in a poem called WAITING FOR CLAUDE, written in Kyoto in 1966:

Margaret Gridley is logical.
How can evil spring from a virtue?
Margaret Gridley is clinically sane.
Margaret Gridley is ambitious and industrious.
Margaret Gridley grieves . . . .
The willows mourn for Margaret Gridley.
She was a Radcliffe girl.

If you've read *IMAGINARY SPEECHES FOR A BRAZEN HEAD,* published in 1972, you will know that Margaret Gridley is one of its main characters, a woman from Whalen's own smalltown Northwest, who goes away to college, becomes a brilliant and famous assemblage artist, takes up with the black jazz musician Beefy Johnson who dies, shoots a lot of meth, marries briefly the poet Roy Aherne (some combination of Whalen, and, by his own admission, Robert Duncan—whom he always called Dunky Poo), and goes back to the Northwest to marry her childhood sweetheart and best lay, Herbert Wackernagel. God how I love this novel—my worn copy is inscribed "for Alice Notley with vast admiration & thanks for wearing out the first copy, Philip Whalen, San Francisco 26:VI:81." *IMAGINARY SPEECHES* may sound from this description purely comic or even silly, but no discussion of Whalen's thoughts on time, including Buddhist time, would be complete without reference to this book, which destroys chronology as well as making it pretty clear. The story is told in sections taking place at various points in time, all out of order, falling around the reader circularly: Time is. Time was. Time is Past. All at once. The epigrams to the book are from Robert Greene's play *The Honorable History of Friar Bacon and Friar Bungay* and from *The Famous History of Fryer Bacon* (you will recall these works from your Elizabethan play studies—a devilish mechanical head is invented, & etc.); the book itself is held together by the pompous sayings of The Grand Mahatma, a brazen, quasi-wise head who simply wants out of the world of the novel by its end—but who can understand the workings of time, which is never over, haunting one in disordered scenes?

It's possible that PW was trying to leave that world, or the world, when he became a Zen monk, but it never felt like that. And, like I say, he kept writing, though not as much or at length in the same way. He did tell me, at least once, that he was going to come out, at some point, with a "big blastola," that would knock everyone over and, it would seem, reestablish some of his previous writerly identity as an extravaganza-maker. I of course liked everything he wrote. I heard him read some of the last works in the collected poems, written, it felt, after a long hiatus, at the Poetry Project circa 1985-86 and begged him to publish them. They were finally published in *SOME OF THESE DAYS,* in 1999, dedicated to me (Why can't I say that? It feels good.) But there just wasn't much poetry after the mid-80s, the reason being that Phil's eyesight failed him drastically. He told me he had "vacant nerve syndrome," though others have told me other things—glaucoma, David Schneider says; but Phil said vacant nerve syndrome—"the nerves vacate themselves." The last time he visited New York, circa 1990, he couldn't walk from Allen Ginsberg's apartment to our apartment on St. Mark's Place without being guided. People began to read aloud to him, and he dictated his correspondence. I received letters from him in someone else's handwriting—a strange thing, since his calligraphy was, as the reader will see from the collected poems, so much a part of him.

Thus I come to the problem, in the collected poems, of the calligraphic pages. They are delightful, but it should be pointed out that they are not poems and are not equal in weight to the poems; they really are more like doodles. And there are probably plenty more of them out in the world. Phil habitually scratched with his pen while he talked to people, writing down things being said and illustrating what was being talked about. (This is also, of course, how he often wrote his poems.) He might then give you a doodle or drawing; I have had a few in my possession. *Highgrade*, a collection of such works, which are distributed chronologically in the collected poems, is a rather puzzling book to own: you can look through it but you can't do much else with it. You certainly don't read it, but it isn't art: you can think about Phil in relation to it, and you can just have it.

Furthermore, MONDAY IN THE EVENING, a long poem presented here in its handwritten form as first published in a small edition in Milan, would have been better off in its typed version (see *ON BEAR'S HEAD*). The poem has been quite influential—along with MY SONGS INDUCE PROPHETIC DREAMS, THE BEST OF IT, and THE EDUCATION CONTINUES ALONG, it taught the second generation New York School half of its tricks—and it should be treated as if it really exists. (The Milano edition was, I think, larger than this one and easier to read.) On the other hand, I don't know why *THE INVENTION OF THE ALPHABET* and *WINNING HIS WAY or THE RISE OF WILLIAM JOHNSON*, two works that exist only in calligraphic form, aren't included. *WINNING HIS WAY* is a little dirty: I don't own it any more but remember it as featuring a lot of homosexual sex and a man with three penises; but *THE INVENTION OF THE ALPHABET* is perfectly polite and intrinsically apt as calligraphy (note title).

Finally, I am sad to have to close now, but I am glad this book exists. It is lovely to be thinking about PW. The last time I saw him, he was in the hospital he was to die in and couldn't walk anymore. Still being interested in stories, he was "watching" television with his blind eyes: there was a daytime soap opera he said all the Zennies were interested in, and he was following it. He said he could still see movement and now considered—possibly, he said (very carefully), because that was all he could see—the world to be motion. Like his mind, I would think. Mentality is a continuum that doesn't necessarily follow, of and on its own, but you do things to it: for example, proceed from the particular to the general, in that 18th century moralistic way he loved. One imposes order, including the order of being out of order, and it is nice to do so as long as one isn't ordering others. This was a gentle and luminous and musical spirit that I still feel in touch with, particularly through the poems.

I urge anyone with what Phil used to call "a serious reading habit" to buy and read this book.

2007, *The Poetry Project Newsletter*

The Martyrology, Book V by bpnichol

The proposition, by David Rosenberg as editor of a special issue of *Open Letter,* was that I read *The Martyrology, Book V* by bpnichol (other poets being assigned other books of *The Matyrology*) and react as a first-time reader. The subtext, or not so sub, to the proposition was that *The Martyrology* is a great unfinished 20th century epic, largely unknown outside Canada. I would hopefully find my assigned volume to be great.

I have ended up reading the book twice, once as a reader sans sex or profession, once as a poet who is a woman and who knows and writes "epics." The first time through the book was mostly a gas, because it's friendly and readable. There was a hook for me in remembering the style and tone of the '70s, when the volume is set, and in the fact that I had known, in the late '60s, some of the people initially referred to in Book V. When I reread the book from a more judgmental aspect, things shifted, somewhat, not hugely. I should say here that I believe criticism—critical writing on poetry—has become more and more destructive of the art (for the time being), supplanting it, demeaning it, making it either an art complicit to its demands, or one taken as a sort of infant that has to be babysitted, indulged, and patronized. I am not a critic.

As a reader I am schizophrenic or negatively capable: I can judge or not judge, or both at the same time. As I say, when I'm not-judge the book is a delight for me: a journal mutating into other forms, quasi-personal, influenced by some of my own influences, particularly my friend Philip Whalen. The mind of the book is nice. The man is rather Blakeian, a bit like oneself is said to be. Above all, the book has a great sound, being given up to a net of rhyme which is even more than aural: "eyes rhyme the landscape," a world of streets and roads taken inside a squeezed-up life that poetry liberates you from. So the book can be a lullaby, and I read it in bed.

David Rosenberg suggested I contrast the book with my own practice at the time of its composition. In the '70s I was beginning to carve out a place for myself, as a woman, in a literature almost exclusively male for thousands of years throughout all the cultures I know about. I tried to master the male genres (lyric, epic, narrative, etc) at the same time as creating my own forms; I sought an athletic excellence of accomplishment at the same time as I had to write poems corresponding to my life's circumstances and influenced by the poems of those around me in New York. I was ultimately to come to the conclusion that the depth and extent of the exclusion of women poets from previous literature was an unfathomable void that no man was ever going to be capable of understanding. The suppression of women from poetry was an incomparable loss, a tragedy for me and everyone else. By the mid-80s I was plainly articulating this black dilemma. Our poetic record is the male face, consciousness, force. If I read to judge, I must think about this awesome and overwhelming circumstance. I don't mean to set a test, but then I do: almost every male poet, until after my generation, fails it. nichol does.

The poem is lovely. It contains no women: it contains no people except the poet's consciousness, which is all the words and letters chosen, all the rhymes, puns, and silliness (a point of praise). You are asked constantly to be inside him, though he isn't self-centered in the usual meaning of the term. He gives you playfulness and depth and soothingness. Do I identify with him in any way except as a poet? No. But it is a gentle consciousness and the only one he has, especially now that he's dead: it's the one he's given to us as a present. No, he never addresses my problem or me; he doesn't address the reader, despite the considerable intimacy of the writing. He addresses god, God is his You, and though this God is not your usual one, he is pretty Male. The particulars of the poem are taken largely from givens of map and grid. There's a map of a quarter in Toronto at the beginning of the volume (though the poet also travels), and the map is the site of transcendence; it is a poem—its lines; it is where Sts, streets or saints, are located and God is talked to.

> spoke to you Lord . . .
> Maker who spawned makers
> raised these temples for you gestures of their awe
> i name the places for you . . .
> i make these glyphs for you

There is a sort of Mrs. God who is referred to once or twice, but she doesn't really take:

> Mother
>   White Lady
>   Goddess
> the less is known of You
> the less is sung
> You grow old & lonely when Your children leave You
> vindictive it's said
> rain Your rage upon our worlds

Well, this is kind of ridiculous. nichol sounds slightly Whalenesque here, but Phil had an actual relationship with the Goddess, come through Buddhism and his personal loves, which isn't even corny. See his poem

"Goddess": "Where I walk is with her . . ." The Goddess is shown as half of existence, and thus half of him, inside and out, intermixed: the two of them together are the whole sphere of the earth.

As long as I'm talking about bp and Phil, I should bring in the visual and pictorial angle, which is of some relevance. I suspect nichol of getting a lot of his permissions for drawing on the page, for layout and visual glyphs—and this is all delightful, and taken to a different place—from Phil. Phil's visual imagination, though, comes first from the outer world through the eye, then down to the page. Or from the visual imagination, as worldly, through the mind's eye to the page. nichol's eye relates most strongly, for much of the book almost exclusively, to the page:

> picture a man (31) narrating this poem
>
> picture a man (36) typing this final draft
>
> picture the man they speak of
> who is almost them
>
> picture the man who writes
> (myself)
>   a pose or the real thing?
>
> & picture me
> spoken of by the man telling
> telling in my turn.

One will have noticed that there are, in fact, no pictures here, there is nothing to visualize whatsoever, no literal detail for the eye. It is an idea, a quite interesting train of thought, that the reader is probably satisfied by, seeing nothing particular. Here is an excerpt from Whalen's "All About Art & Life," surely nichol's model:

PICTURE: a wood-engraving by Bewick
GIANT WOOLY COW

PICTURE: children, their faces concealed
by their hats which are heads which are
flowers

PICTURE: Leonardo: Madonna & Child, with
S. Giovanbattista . . .

PICTURE: 2 Bedouins praying in sand/ocean a camel
with square quizzing-glass on head

PICTURE: All of us when we were young before you
were born

This is a mix of literal "pictures"—paintings, imaginary pictures like paintings, and then the headbuster koan of the final one I quote (there are several others). nichol's poem binds one deliberately to the page, being written in a style I associate with the '60s and '70s that employs the lower case i and little punctuation, and in doing so makes the physical poem its room and/or landscape. nichol is perhaps apotheosizing his manner here, and I'm willing to go there, into the apotheosis, with him. This style in general used to drive me nuts, but now it doesn't.

As the poems or sections (demarcated along the sides of the pages by numbers, in the way that dictionaries sometimes are by letters) become less journal-like the book achieves its form not through subject—though subject is always simmering underneath—but through change of shape, a release of emotion and tension into new forms on the page. I found this movement gratifying, because I didn't have to keep track of anything—information, people, events. Section 4 is particularly beautiful, it feels like the ending in the middle and probably is the true climax of the volume. This is where "St Reat," having evolved from "St Reet" in the previous section, becomes the hero of the book, the straight road, the saint who is going to some sort of heaven somewhere! The words come apart, to become more and more contorted:

> bridge d i s
> carded
>   vo ices
> l i e
> no after   no ons
> blow n conscious
> dif f
> idence
>
> how clou
> dwha tso
> c i a lwa   sHali
> fax

As reader I was fascinated but became tenser and tenser working out the "sense" of the words (I couldn't always do that), and so I was incredibly relieved when the poem finally became staves of music with words following the shapes of actual notated tunes.

It should probably be mentioned that section 7 is a play, with characters, stage directions, dialogue, the characters being saints, and so one is presumably being referred to Stein. But actually we are being shown that a play is the appropriate form for the drama of life, which the poet is living offstage and which isn't finally what "it" is all about, especially if one is part of the company of saints. "It" is the poem and poetry, it isn't specific events, because no one really knows what they are: one moves through them as one moves through this book. They—events—are defined by definers, and one asks do we need the definers after all? This is a satisfying meaning that I picked up the second time through (and so got to stow some more meaning in the meaning place—why not?)

Essentially, I find the construction of the book of great interest. Placing the section numbers to the side is a good invention—the book doesn't really contain sections, it contains twelve poems; but there's more than that. A verticality is emphasized that's part of the work's flow. This is difficult to articulate—the book's shape seems to be exactly the way it's published here by Coach House Press. I know I'm being asked to call the work an epic, but I don't find that word correct. I'm often asked to call books or series of books epics—there is a certain pressure on one when great length is involved. This is a book. I don't know what the other books of *The Martyrology* are like, I admit. But the 20th century long poem is not veering towards the epic, so much as redefining the nature of the relation of the poem to the book. And why shouldn't it be? A book as mass-produced (and now virtual, perhaps) is a radically changing form; the poem's relation to it changes too. A collection of poems is still possible: yes: but if you envision a book when writing a poem, because it has become less and less of a big deal, through the ages, to publish one, the occasion of a poem changes. The poem presses towards the book it will be in, and the individual poems start to stick together in different ways. Once you begin to ask, What book am I working on? not What poem am I writing? everything changes.

Finally, *The Martyrology, Book V* leaves me thinking, once again, about how boring the standard novel has become. It simply doesn't know what to leave out anymore. This book is an indicator of how much can be left out without one's feeling that anything has been omitted. Sound is an integral part of character, setting, and story: you don't need all that exposition. You need literal poetic overtones, the music of the speaking voice that the poet puts within and between the words: it's almost everything.

November 19, 2007

Published in *Open Letter* (Fourteenth Series, Number 1, Fall 2009) "The Martyrology Survivor's Retrospective" guest-edited by David Rosenberg

How to Break Through: An Homage

Ted's speech was layered with accents: as he explained himself to me in 1969, I gradually heard New England, Tulsa, and New York. But it was the Tulsa I was taken by, it didn't belong next to the Eastern sounds, containing a slight drawl, a softness, though his consonants were clipped and he said 'aunt' not 'ant' as I did. It was a version of me, my sound, with its Westness and Manhattan, but it was, just, different. I identified right away with the other Tulsa people too: Ron and Pat, Dick, Joe. I understood something about where they came from, the part of the country, and how it clashed with New York, in which one wanted to be lost and changed forever—and that one was, lost and changed forever. It's in this clash, that the Tulsa School gets made, isn't it? In it find Ted, after an immense struggle to let go of all his Rhode Island insularity, educating himself at the University of Tulsa and in the Village, with the help of and despite his teachers, and initiating the slow destruction of his health that all that transformation seemed to entail. And Ron with his bootlegger Dad, his hypnogogic cartoon imagination, his naïvété to get work from Kerouac and Ginsberg for *The White Dove Review*, published when in high school, his get-into-Columbia smarts, and *his* drawl. Joe, of course, stuttered a lot, so it was hard to hear his accent—I'm not sure I ever caught it: Joe, with the eye/hand coordination of a genius, who came out of the closet in Boston, but chastely shared the same bed with the amazingly straight-butch (though inwardly delicate and subtle) Ted in some awful room somewhere in downtown New York: "And you were never attracted to me?" he asked Joe, desperately trying to understand human sexuality (fat chance). And Dick who wrote phrases in Greek, on his letters from Tulane, attributed to Woody Guthrie; who pasted squiggly plastic eyeballs on his high-school graduation portrait and gave it to Ted as a present; who sounded like he was from Tulsa and used the same phrases and intonations of special words that they all did and taught to everyone: "Totally great!," "Okay, Boss," etc.—but that was in '69 too, and I want to concentrate in this piece on the earlier time, before I met them and of which I have no right to speak. Dick who invented the "hinge tree," widely alluded to among die Tulsa Lyriche (probably wrong German rendering, from memory, courtesy of poet Rolf Dieter Brinkmann), Dick who wrote "Joe can fix this one" on a collaboration with Ted and Joe featuring Bobby Vee's face and some blue green beans. But there was Pat, the intense and the adored—by Ted, Ron, and Joe, and I think, Dick; Pat is a member of the Tulsa School too. No poems by her, though there are some watercolors and crayola drawings (I possess a few of the latter) and certainly a legend. There are also Marge Kepler, Anne Kepler, Lauren Owen, Dave Bearden, and some others Ted talked about incessantly—maybe Tessie (Mitchell) is a member, Tony Powers, John Luwendyck; but chiefly there are Ted, Ron, Dick, and Joe, and Pat.

*

From *Summer Balloons* by Ron Padgett:

only
yesterday
and the pansy
of your eyes
only

that I may
love you with
out my lies
                    only
today
my stumbling promise
nothing dies.

★★

drop fears
          into
                    tears
your head
          on my
                         shoulder.

That's two of the six parts, written and published when Ron was a teen in Tulsa. I no longer possess a copy of Ted's corresponding Tulsa chapbook, *A Lily for My Love,* though Ted was in his early twenties, just out of the army. But here we have a realization, a manifestation of the dogma Ron later formulated as "First came Patchen, / then Ferlinghetti" (from a poem called "Poem" in *Triangles in the Afternoon.*) Ron and Ted *loved* Kenneth Patchen in Tulsa ("The apples are red again in Chandler's Valley / redder for what happened there / Never did know what it was / never did care"—TB, "Tambourine Life", 1965.) Whenever I read "Summer Balloons" I look for a line Ted insisted Ron wrote in it, "A pansy told me what love is." That line isn't there, but the poem contains the word "pansy" twice: "pansy / of your eyes" and also "pansy for your hair"—the poem having for its dedication-like epigraph, *pour une pensée.*

This, I think, some years before Joe's manifold painted pansies—I have an exquisite pansy paperweight made by Joe and given to Ted; mostly black inside the glass, with yellow crinkled pansy rim and yellow single pansy eye. The pansy—*pensée* in French—being really all face, black outlined in the yellow, against the black background.

This poem of Ron's is pretty good, though I expect he worked on the line breaks for months. Early works are always better than anyone thinks they are: they genuinely tremble, and they loom with futurity. Ron wasn't going to rhyme much ever again; Ted fascinated by the vulnerability of doing just that that way (Ron's poem's way) tried it out in a spate of poems circa 1970. Though first he wrote "A Personal Memoir of Tulsa Oklahoma / 1955-60" which contains the words "there" and "where" and "air", rhyming humorously about a hundred times. Ron has kept the pansy/*pensée* place intact inside himself to reappear in certain unrhymed love and sorrow poems, though that place can be obscured for years by the pleasureable drilling of the Woody Woodpecker beak on one's head.

*

Here's another pretty early work, this one by Tulsa lyricher Dick Gallup:

SONNET: To Pat and Anne

The girl that wears tight socks
In bright colours, and long,
Delights my eyes like rocks
In their bright, angled song.
And the girl dressed up in black
With sensuous lips and new-

Found hair, bids me step back
To watch her grow. And now
The cold wet rains which fall
Along this windy world
Reflect my thoughts which bow,
Here in, there out, and whirl.
Such sorrow bespeaks my life,
As willows drawn to strife.

Richard Gallup
15 January 1962
New Orleans

One rather adores this dopey poem because of the "eyes like rocks," but also the short spare-for-a-sonnet lines. The rocks, in fact, call everything else in the poem into question, as if that line—line three—is the real point of the poem. Which was sent in an envelope postmarked 22 Jan 1962—a 7 cent stamp with a jet on it—from 1036 Robert St., New Orleans, La., to Ted Berrigan, 81 Horatio St., Apt. 1F, New York, New York, No zips. Ted has carefully stapled the poem to its envelope and placed it in a folder containing letters by both of them—one of several voluminous early correspondences among these folk. (And this is folklore, isn't it?)

From an all-in-lower-case letter, from Dick, "march 27, 1961, monday 9:05 am, to ted—"

> i've been reading some montaigne—tell you about it sometime. started to read a book called the classical tradition in poetry by gilbert murray—but i disagree with his basic thesis (that the ancients

have essentially the same relation to nature that we do.) i may read it anyway for the more substantial correspondances—like tracing the metre of a line by milton to greek and roman models. about the relation to nature: the ancients mostly worshipped nature, their poetry about nature does not make a distinction between themselves and nature (i'm using absolute terms when actually, I think, it is a matter of emphasis) modern man is more removed from nature—in a sense he is more free from nature (this line of reasoning leads to the prediction or wish for a korzybskian (essentially) position. read *escape from freedom* by fromm skipping the section on fascism. both fromm here and korzybski i consider to be much too optimistic about the status of modern man. modern man is on the verge of a complete mental crackup, and i am not so sure he has the sense to avoid the catastrophe *now*— maybe later (if there is a later) he will arrive at the realistic (the word isn't sufficient) position. look for a correspondance between the manhood of humanity and mann's humanity in *snow* and the steppenwolfe final position and what goodman seems to be striving for in the empire city . . .

You must admit these are heavy dudes; all the letters are like that circa '61. Everyone else is arriving in the Village around now: Ted there starving, and Joe, Ron at Columbia, Pat on her way. The break from Tulsa is occurring, fueled by drugs sure, but mostly by ambition. But it's an ambition towards truth, knowledge, and poetry—"and the promise never to truckle." Great poets are idealists, that's what we are, and will remain, in the adolescent as well as the mature sense, openly and correctly.

*

Week of Mar. 24, '58: This is a KODACHROME PRINT/Made only by/Kodak.

Pat, slender, in an outfit for still cool weather in Tulsa: long-sleeved, high-necked w/ long midcalf sheath skirt, red belt in middle around ultra-slim waist. But it's possible she's wearing a dress, or shell top and skirt with bolero jacket. I think, in fact, it's a bolero jacket (like the toreadors, you know): it's black-and-white-checked but with a slightly quilted look, or puffed texture, and there are six small black buttons down the chest. A line of black, which may be the under top, shows around the neck and above the belt. The belt is the masterpiece-making touch though. It is several inches wide like a cummerbund—or is it even a belt, is it part of the dress? Oh, and toreadors wear sashes, don't they? But it appears to be leather, if it fastens it's in back, and it's scarlet red. Pat's lipstick is a slightly deeper red. She's smiling; she's very pretty; her dark hair disappears into black shadows cast by the house in back of her to right. She's wearing black pumps, not a very high heel. A black shadow of her is thrown on the ground behind her, connected to her feet.

Here are two black-and-white snaps of Joe, undated, but in one he looks terribly young. Each is near a house—the same house, maybe. He's on the ground in one, on a step in another, a bike is visible in the first, a ladder in the second. In each he's with a painting: in the one in which he looks younger a faux Bernard Buffet, carafe, wine glass, water glasses, grapes, other fruit, outlined in black, both casually and studiedly naive (Joe's later persona). The other photo features a nude woman, a sort of Picasso blue period figure or maybe Matisse-ish. She's standing, small-breasted and small-nippled, angled toward one side, one arm shows in front of what would be the crotch, but the lower body's covered by cloth or just abstract brush strokes. Her mouth is pursed and not quite where it should be—off to the side. Her hair is long and brunette, pulled back, but with a high crown as in mode of late '40s, early '50s. In New York, Ted told me, Joe would turn these out by the score, selling them on the sidewalk in Greenwich Village in an open-air art festival I vaguely remember. Joe paid the rent this way; he had creepy patrons.

*

Ted Berrigan
210 E. 6th St.
NYC

THE DAY I READ *THE WHITE PONY*
(after Frank O'Hara)

It is 9:30 Wednesday morning in
Providence and I am waiting for the
Mailman. Half an hour to wait I
Decide to go to Cole's for a cup of
Coffee. I am thinking about Chris who
Hasn't answered my letter.

On
The way to Cole's I stop
In Bessie's and buy a Morning
Journal and a copy of THE WHITE
PONY though I consider THE ORWELL
READER and a novel by Isak Dinesen:

At
Cole's I read the paper over
Coffee (the Red Sox lost again, but

Williams hit a homer), and joke
With Red Brennan about
His hangover. Then I go
back home

And the mail has come. Nothing
from Chris. A bill from the
Readers Subscription for $13.00 and
an ad for THE ENCYCLOPEDIA OF
SEXOLOGY. I open a letter from
Dave Bearden in Tulsa

Which says Martin Cochran
Is dead Dear Berrigan. He died
In Hillcrest Medical Center
At 5 A.M. today.

I think of Chris. And of Martin's
Curly hair, which I thought
Beautiful. Carefully I put my mail
Away in my desk; and
Settle down to read my new anthology.
In Providence it is 10:23.

This poem, written in early '61, or maybe late '60 when Ted was in Providence getting ready for the move to New York City, is laid out quite differently from O'Hara's "The Day Lady Died." It's largely, though not entirely in six-line stanzas—the form can't contain what Ted's doing, and he drops it after stanza four. He tries for a ten-syllable line and capitalizes the first letter of most lines. Alas to keep the six-line concept going he indulges in two one-syllable lines, “On” and “At.” The poem looks a little Rexrothian—another early influence being Rexroth and “natural numbers,” though Ted suggests Stevens in a letter to Dick:

> After, means an imitation of his O’Hara’s methods, but as me. If you read his poem, the Day Lady died, you will see I have done something totally different than he did, although I used the same devices. But I used anti-climax, he didn’t. (among other things.) : And, I think each stanza is self-contained but leads to the next: The whole poem is hermetic in the same manner as Idea of Order or Voltaire at Ferney. And, for you to ponder, only in relation to your paper on Stevens, what is the relation of the title to the poem?

It is most of all important that O’Hara wrote his poem in July of 1959—it was first published in Don Allen’s *New American Poetry* in 1960, and later in *Lunch Poems* in ’64. Ted picked up on it, imitated it *immediately*; O’Hara was *not* a well-known poet everyone was watching. Ted, the working-class guy from Providence and Tulsa, was one of the ones who *found* Frank, the brilliant, Harvard-educated, scene-galvanizing, heroic guy from upper-middle-class Massachusetts. Ted was often put down for idolizing him, daring to say “Frank.” But my real point here is the Radar! It took Ted one second to find, as soon as it was published, and imitate what became one of the most famous poems of the second half of the twentieth century.

*

I’m going to try to remember the Asthmador anecdote, not because it’s officially important, but because, as with describing Pat’s toreador outfit, I want to. Asthmador rhymes with toreador.

This transpires in Tulsa when Ron is still in high school, living at home, knowing Dick and Joe for forever, but Ted is now his friend. Everyone's trying out drugs—didn't all great poets mess with their own minds in order to be able to mess with other people's? One night at home, with Ted present, Ron takes a large dose of something called Asthmador, an over-the-counter asthma drug, containing the ancient, powerful, don't-mess-with-me substance, belladonna, that transmogrifies the subject, certainly, and bizarrely. Ron gets very "high"—if that's what you'd call it—and indulges in somewhat obscure antics in the kitchen, mumbling. He takes a nickel out of his pocket, stares at it, declares, "This is broken" and washes it down the drain of the sink. A few minutes later he has the coffeepot—presumably an old-style percolator, turns it upsidedown directly under the tap and watches the water splash and wash over the edges of the bottom surface awhile, then proclaims, "This one doesn't work!" Then. Then Ron's mother haplessly enters the room, and Ron says to her, "Kiss me, baby!" Ted soon decides he'd better leave, he returns to his room in the locked boarding house where he lives, goes to bed, turning out the light. Lies there, thinking. Soon there's a noise at the window: Ron's father, Wayne Padgett, pops through—I can't remember if he has to climb up a fire escape or if Ted's on the first floor. Anyway. Wayne, whom Ted is rather in awe of, just pops through the window. Then Wayne says, with his slow Tulsa voice, "Ted, whut's wrong with Ronny?" Ted tells him what's wrong with Ronny, in a nervous but matter-of-fact way, assuring Wayne that the Athsmador will wear off pretty soon. Wayne is cool with this. Wayne is always cool. And that's pretty much the anecdote, except that Ron later reported having spent the rest of the night whirling around and around on an immense roulette wheel. I heard Ted tell the story a couple of times—it could be quite endless, if told with Tulsa pacing, and hysterically funny. He told it to Ed and Jenny Dorn in late 1971, and it wound up being referred to in

Book IIII of Ed's epic *Gunslinger*:

> La belladonna was abroad. She's the one
> who turned the coffeepot upsidedown in Tulsa
> who maintains the madness of mumbling.

*

And now, to quote from Joe: I want to excerpt from FROM JOE'S SECRET JOURNALS, 1961 (written in New York when he was nineteen)—but can't figure out how to do it, it's too embarrassing a work, and *that* it's supposed to be. So I'm going to pick a single page at random, like a Tarot card, and deal with it.

> . . . Beethoven's 7th Symphony; people who know what they know and want to know more; people who appreciate the shape and purity of an egg, plus its organic satisfaction); people who love red, dance to Elvis Presly, offer you a cigarette, listen for hours to *Don Giovanni*, people who need you; who play in the snow and are excited by the sensation of their frozen toes, hands, and ears; people who (like myself) like long hair or just feel they must let it grow absurdly for the sake of being absurd; people who realize the actual value of a rectangle with a sterile portrait of George Washington, and all kinds of frills, and detailed ornament so it will be hard to counterfeit; people who know it's a piece of paper and if they hurry some fool will give them a book, a tube of oil paint, great food, or a taxi cab in exchange. But we are the ones that don't really labor away time and energy for our money; we sell blood occasionally, borrow here and there, paint signs on some guy's truck which logic tells us is O.K. but that we know is, if nothing else, is a symbol of decline and defeat and that we must keep up the phony guard until it's no longer phony; we sponge off friends who know *why* you are sponging, and

understand and even some that don't and are resentful. We are takers, but we also know the value of giving. We work in antique shops at night where we can read (especially when we unfortunately no longer have electricity because "Old George" came in too handy to trade for Spenser's *The Faerie Queene* in two volumes bound in dirty dark blue with plain faded gold lettering giving the general effect . . .

Well I got off easy: no references to beating off, pills, the selfishness of women, Joe's tears, or the flaw of homosexuality (Joe has not yet come out.) One is struck by the fact that Joe was on top of the list form way predating *I Remember*—the "people who" passage begins on the previous page and is lengthy—and also on top of the sharp verbal image and sensation. The passage doesn't feel like Joe's breakthrough art that would soon appear—the assemblages—except maybe in its considerable lavishness and effusion. Nowhere in this particular excerpt are the large number of phrases that Ted stole from the journal for *The Sonnets* (as he likewise stole from Dick); nor on this page appears the sentence underlined by Ted in my manuscript copy: "Ted is the only person that I think has learned something from me, and used me."

*

A bit later (oh I don't know when) Joe and Dick collaborate, with input from Ted. why do *I* possess this slightly unsuccessful, playful, slightly worn collaboration?

Joe begins, I would say, with the blue rectangular solids heaped in the middle like logs, on scarlet-red fire and there are erupting firecracker-like or rocket-like shapes too, but the blue things are labeled, by Joe, GREEN BEANS. Black-ink chaos there, blue pen scribbles, and Dick has printed diagonally in that same space "Two sensation-seeking hipsters / And their jet-propelled search / FOR / (. . . segues into) GREEN BEANS." Below, Dick writes "Joe can fix this one!" Then "OK." Then Ted writes in black "The End." Along the far left border is written, I think by Dick, "An RKO Albee Picture"—Albee as in Edward Albee. Below is a photo of minor teen idol Bobby Vee with cutout black cardboard rectangles X-ing out his mouth. The photo contains the reproduced signature—in not Bobby Vee's Palmer method script—"Bobby Vee." Below the photo Dick has printed "Guillaume Apollinaire." And, finally, to the right, in the remaining white space, Ted has put '"One of the years 10 best!"—Time.'

Well they couldn't get it to be serious enough; I guess that's why I have it, still; I really like it—it has a fine, happy spirit, and contains Ted's idiosyncratic handwriting, and Dick's spontaneous, slanted printing, and the block letters of Joe—those personality traces, soul traces, now obliterated by the computer. Is that why we value the collaborations so much? The presence of the naked, several hand.

*

15 Mar 61

Dear Marge,

hello. Do any birds sing in Texas? Last Sunday in Greenwich Village a big sun was shining. All roads there are paved with cobblestones. Did you know that? And all the shops are little. And on Sunday, closed, except for restaurants. sidewalk cafés. In the center of the village is Washington Square, where Tom Wolfe used to stride wild haired in the rain, chanting "I wrote ten thousand words today . . . ."

Joe goes to Mexico on April ten. I work on obscure theories concerning Bernard Shaw. I write poems, letters, postcards to my creditors, sarcastic notes to friends. Joe paints tangerines, and powerful driving flames erupting from bottles of seven up. A fat lady tries to rape him every day. Ron reads all books, writes sentimental poems to lost schoolgirls . . . . systematically works on his senses. Gallup writes from New Orleans that sex impedes his intellectual progress . . . . He writes poems, too. Amazingly good. (I say.) Sample: (last stanza of his latest):

But the force has turned within again
To gnaw upon the blood.
To suck my life, waste my gold,
Opulent, sinister, and cold.

All heroines of movies look and talk like you! Have you seen *The Entertainer*! *The Misfits*? Hollywood movies have discovered you (or the you of aeons ago).

I write arty letters full of elaborate theories on art and self development and send them to Joe's wealthy artsy craftsy patroness. Signed Joe Brainard. Some day the collected letters of Joe Brainard will be published in thirty seven volumes and you can expose the hoax. So save this otherwise inane letter and it will be worth something.

And from another letter to Marge:

The folk festival was great, and Odetta signed my program, "To Ted, Go well, Stay well, Odetta."

*

When Ted moved to New York, he was still working on his masters for the University of Tulsa, which he eventually completed, writing his thesis on G.B. Shaw: "The Problem of How to Live As Dealt with in Four Plays by George Bernard Shaw." There is extant an essay circa 1961 (the paper bears the 210 E. 6th St. address) entitled "On George Bernard Shaw's *Candida*." Ted still doesn't know how to write prose or a paper: something he famously learned how to do just a little later writing papers for Columbia students. The breakthrough paper—when he *saw how to do it*—being on the rise and fall of the Tokagawa Regime in Japan. But in this little essay on Shaw's *Candida*, Ted refers to—invents?—the concept of "levelling off." *Candida* mainly concerns three characters: Morell, a socialist clergyman, Candida, his wife, and Eugene Marchbanks, an eighteen-year-old poet. Eugene wants Candida, who is fifteen years older than he, to leave Morell for himself, Candida ultimately declining to. Ted's short essay contains references to Ibsen, Colin Wilson, and Whitehead, discussing in Shavian terms the ways in which the characters show themselves to be both realistic and idealistic—Shaw's categories. But Ted uses the clunky but admirably to-the-point phrase "levelling off" two or three times. Morell has levelled off, and Candida has too, in their shared life situation, despite their politics: the poet, on the other hand, never levels off:

> Eugene's education culminates in realizing that the kind of ideal relation he thought he wanted with Candida, the kind she does have with Morell, is not for him. There are higher things, he realizes, and he must go on, even though he does not know what they are yet. His idealism, which was a block preventing him from going on, has been cured through the educational experience of *seeing* for himself.
>
> At the end Eugene tells Candida that he must go. She tells him to remember over and over that she is fifteen years older than he is. His reply is that he has a secret better than that. Shaw's last comment, as the Morells embrace, is that they do not know the secret in the poet's heart.

Part of the secret has already been expressed. Eugene, says Candida to Morell, has learned to live without happiness. There is something higher than happiness. They do not know what it is. But the poet, although he does not know where "on" is, knows that to go on is superior to levelling off at happiness.

Ted wrote these sentences about happiness before he ever read Frank O'Hara's "Poem Read at Joan Mitchell's," with its last line "happiness / the least and best of human attainments". This ending constituted one of Ted's O'Hara touchstones; he quoted it often and emphasized "least" when he did, though still pondering the paradox.

*

Here is a photo of Joe post Mexican-Madonna breakthrough, embracing, physically, an assemblage, a madonna in a birdcage with necklaces and other accompaniment, the cage on a slab with a line of plastic birds and adorned on top with roses, beads, and plumes. The photo itself is influenced by Warhol, with Joe's face bleached out and his glasses predominant. As he himself represented Sandy Berrigan in paintings and assemblages, in terms of her glasses and the shape of her face.

Here are lines from a poem by Dick, still from the '60s but after *his* breakthrough, called "The Sharpest Knives in the World":

Sea Night Sand
            Innumerable scratches on the shore
   Like an old alley shot toward the stars

The door is new and creaks
The room within is fine

For days and days

And finally it is like falling in love with no one
Busting through the bursts and gusts of life
To where I sit
At a desk
looking into the grain

Here is the opening of Ron's now classic poem from the '60s "Wonderful Things":

Anne, who are dead and whom I loved in a rather asinine fashion
I think of you often

buveur d l'opium chaste et doux

Yes I think of you

with very little in mind

as if I had become a helpless moron

Watching zany chirping birds

That inhabit the air

And often ride our radio waves

And here are some lines from Ted's Sonnet II:

Dear Margie, hello. It is 5:15 a.m.
dear Berrigan. He died
Back to books. I read
It's 8:30 p.m. in New York and I've been running all day
old come-all-ye's streel into the streets. Yes, it is now,
How Much Longer Shall I Be Able To Inhabit The Divine
and the day is bright gray turning green
feminine marvelous and tough

So, then, they made it. They all broke through. The Tulsa-New York transition happening over and over, in poems of the '60s and, too, later, where suddenly one is operating on a new level, incorporating the past one into the present one, or sometimes willfully stripping away the present ones, and presumed future ones, to reveal the past one. I will always be like that, but I can never go back. *And I'll never go there again.*

I meet Ted in 1969. I had already read most of Shaw, though not at Barnard College: there was a shelf of Shaw's prefaces and plays, in separate little volumes, in the one-room Needles Library that I read most of the books belonging to, in junior high and high school. I took the Shaw prefaces home first, until I discovered that the plays too were readable, despite their play-script format, with their long descriptions of character and scene and their amazing feminism; so sometimes I'd check out some prefaces, sometimes some plays. I particularly liked the preface to *St. Joan* and waited months before checking out the play itself. I gave no thought to what must have been the absolute novelty of what Shaw was doing with the form: I just accepted it. And. When I met Ted I was also familiar with the works of Odetta and Woody Guthrie. I guess I was ready. I guess I already knew the "secret in the poet's heart," that which is finally never spoken or written down, except perhaps in every word.

I have nothing further to say, except I must leave you with one final point, the final final point, what you need to know to be a poet, and to continue to be a poet:

Never
Level
Off.

August—October, 2009

Presented as keynote at conference at the University of Tulsa on the Tulsa Poets of the Second Generation New York School. Later published in *Denver Quarterly.*

Before Babel

> (And yet—the lingo of Babel was the single language that all humanity understood, that a jealous commander-in-chief then got rid of as punishment for the early humans' communality; "divide et regna" already the essence of YHWH's political science. So that Nimrod either remembers the first, unified language of the human race which we no longer know, or he speaks in one of the post-Babelian lingos, which are what makes translation possible.)

This aside from Joris's impressive "Nimrod in Hell" (*Aljibar II*), referring to the inexplicable language the hunter speaks in a verse of Dante's *Inferno,* contains also hints of one of Joris's central tenets: that all writing is a translation, a trying to get at what can't be got at because we speak so many languages, having strayed from the primal one Nimrod's utterance would be. That one believes must still be somewhere within one. That maybe flows like a crystal river, rather than being rough or strange—as I am now veering away from Pierre-land into Alice-land, but I believe they are both of the ur-land, of the ur-language. Pierre and I both believe in that place and tongue. Some years ago we attended together a panel hosted by Michel Deguy—I forget on what subject—during the course of which Pierre commented, in one or another of his languages, that all writing is a translation. Or perhaps Michel said so and Pierre took up the theme. Later, at dinner, I told Pierre that this was not my experience of language or poetry, that I never felt I was translating anything. You should have said that, he said. I was too busy thinking it, I said. I mean I was very struck by this exchange, and I still am—it affected me deeply. I believe Pierre translates—he grew up with so many languages—and besides he wouldn't lie; I believe that I don't translate anything, I am wedded to English, speaking bad French, a little Spanish, and less Latin. I still believe we are doing the same thing, as poets. How can that be?

The answer would lie in what poetry itself is, a riding of ur (I will not do an Ur riff here, you can do it, the city, the sense of early, of first, the lowest level etc), a harnessing of the magic horse of sound, rhythm, *magic*: it's magic, it's grace, even inspiration, it's all those words we're not allowed to use at the moment, it's a magic animal-self chakra rakish kral feature that might be everything. So what? It's the *real* intellect, *un*plodding, unbelievable. Poetry's written in the language of music and "get-it," without music's tendency towards the big wordless or lyrical-blur swoon, who needs that? Well, sometimes. But we animals like to think with our vocal chords, we vibrate not just like tympana, receptors, but like the *émitteurs* of the world's details, sprung from our own brain/tongues: for we have defined our and the world's natures, and will continue to do so with whatever words come to us in whatever langue or accent from wherever:

youreappian Kulchur hang   the big O
l'outre l'autre now becomes au-tonomia   another alphabeta
begins   towards mania   l'altera ô becomes au   begins
towards dawn drawn with your fingers   in shellacked snows
of old   we have learned nothing from millenia   your
defense the great meltdown   domination domination of the
planets Uranus   hello   Mario Tronti Tony Negri Sergio
Bologna Franco Piperno Oreste Scalzone   hello & good-bye
you too the night of Europe   the workers no longer the edge

will lift the whole   construiamo una vita no longer
the definite article

(*Winnetou Old*)

The clue for me lies precisely where Pierre mixes the languages he knows most intimately, adding from a few others, why not? As in "Canto Diurno #2 à/to Jack Kerouac Ode Bilangue." Does it seriously bother anyone that this poem is in two languages, is there really anyone who doesn't understand it? Particularly if it's read aloud—as all poetry should be, and all of Kerouac's work should be. But what I like about this poem, aside from its considerable tenderness—Pierre is a master of *tendresse*, that quality that Europeans writing in English seem to get better than, say, Americans—is its ability to enable the reader-aloud's tongue to accommodate itself to both languages, even though they change back and forth so quickly:

tu écrivais (235 Chorus)
"Je sais que je suis mort.
Je ne camperai pas. Je suis mort maintenant.
Qu'est-ce que j'attends pour disparaître? . . ."
30 years ago—& aujourd'hui
ici aux chiottes
c'est écrit:
"Colfax Driver Sucks"
(dans la bouche, oui,
dans le cul, non,
la sexpol de Jack)
graffiti & café
une carte dé-
roule la route
drive to Lowell

dark shades in bright
a.m. rising
sun, in the house,
  of,
    mon teenage dream
of America
    mon truckstop blues
un blues for Jack
gone these thirty years now
& Allen gone
& William gone
mais reste Gregorio
in Nueva Yorkio . . .

Pierre chooses to quote from *Mexico City Blues* in French, again why not? He *translated* it ("mon teenage dream")—but this passage alludes secretly to another of Pierre's influences, that of Ted Berrigan, poetry *frère* mixed with *père*. Pierre spent a lot of weekends in Ted's and my house in Wivenhoe, Essex, in 1973-4, and he imbibed Ted's lore, Ted being the Interviewer in the irreplaceable *Paris Review* interview of Jack Kerouac conducted in 1968 in the aforesaid Lowell. There was the interview as published, but first there was the famously-lost, entire and untampered-with interview, in which—or maybe it was an aside—Ted asked Jack if he had ever made it with any guys, and Jack replied: Blow jobs yes, ass jobs no. Here translated into French, "dans le bouche, oui / dans le cul, non": in the mouth, yes, in the ass, no. This whole passage is, well, fun, culminating in "in Nueva Yorkio" (calling to mind, in my mind, Ted's "I may have been in a state, but it was my state, / I even gave it a name: New York. Most people are in other / York, they aren't even in Old York yet, let alone York." ("Thin Breast Doom") It's a kind of playfulness that comes from Beat goofing, but it's a Jack's/Gregorio's/Ted's streetcorner goofing. The pretend tough, maybe, of extremely sensitive workingclass Americans or one hypereducated European.

But as I was saying. If you read Pierre's poem aloud, you come to passages like

> vertes forêts & collines
> du Massachusetts
> plis sur plis tout autour
> de la voiture,
>   open as I ride
> sweet tender light
> green,
>   gobbles us up,
> in intimations of
> la même vielle
> mortality.

Pierre's quickness, deftness—so light with these short lines—intertwines, plays the French and the American, making the American voice come up not flat like a midwestern or western accent, but flat like a jazz trumpet can be. When you say "open as I ride" you sound like a damn singer (or I do). This is a very very good ear. And I'm thinking now it is the Ear that is Ur, that's before Babel. It doesn't really matter what the words are, though of course everything matters desperately to us poets, but the metrics allow any word, if it's the exact right word, if you get what I mean. Before Babel is the same as after Babel, all the languages mixed together, and understood properly. Or maybe that's good Babel, bad Babel being the politico/radio collage we have ever within range, in our heads, as exemplied in Pierre's "Aegean Shortwave":

news in french from Jerusalem parse the value of
the gold napoleon in relation to the shekel radio
mediterranean emits in english a flying hospital
soon to be put into service in Italy carried by regu-
lar plane the voice of america tamil insurrections
in sir lanka a concert of baroque music held in as-
pen colorado tent sip çay & codis

In another poem ("Short Wave Radio #2") Pierre addresses another Jack (Spicer): "Jack you were wrong (or not / the radio is not from Mars / it is sitting here it has / the world / by its short / wavy hairs, home." We are exactly within Babel, in fact it is almost likeable.

Once in 1973 Pierre came down to Wivenhoe from London with some good speed—we were young—on a Friday night. On Saturday morning I woke up and took some. I had been in a state of nerves for months and had a great tension and need. I suddenly saw a poem in my mind, that is I saw word for word the six-page, dense, long-lined or sentenced, complex poem that would be called "Your Dailiness" (see my selected poems, *Grave of Light*.) I saw every word of it more or less at once. I proceeded to write it down at various intervals during the day, I copied it from my mind, from its great slab in my mind. At the end of the day Ted, Pierre, and I met at the dining-room table to make a little tape-recorded reading of poems, and I didn't read it, I didn't even say, I have a new six-page poem that appeared to me in a vision this morning and that I have spent the day transcribing. I read some little dinky things, and I have very rarely told this story since. I now have the faintest of ideas that I might have, ever so slightly, "translated" it, for when I wrote it down in my notebook longhand, and especially when I typed it up on my typewriter, it looked a tiny bit different from the slab in my mind, the lines ever so much shorter. I translated it into two different kinds of writing, script and type, thus I changed it just, just a little. Or was the "original" "different"? However I didn't change any of the words (I don't think), and the writing down was effortless. Was the work dictated? Did it arrive via radio? No! *I* wrote it, and I have never questioned this fact. I know I wrote it.

But, Pierre's question might be, Was it already a translation when it appeared in your mind? (Pierre would certainly believe my telling of the experience, he has no problem with the existence of the inexplicable or magical.) And I say, I don't know exactly, but it was graven in stone already; it just *was*. At this moment we would need our friend (first encountered in that year, 1973), my later (second) husband, Doug Oliver, present to talk to us about the nature of an instant of time, and perhaps further question me as to whether the poem could by definition exist before it existed on paper, before I had taken the time to write it all down. Yes. In the sense that a poem, like a poetic stress, has a pre-existence and a just-post-existence (as well as an eternity ever after of existence), and you can never pin down where the stress is or when the poem exists. Do you dig? Whatever you might be translating *from* (in the mind) does continue well into the fact of the translation, and is there. But I, I didn't translate anything! Here is Pierre's lovely take on Doug's theories, a translation if you will:

a stress born in time
stands outside
a minor, eternal present, a
trembling instant
partly resisting the flow,
the line creates it
its very great fascination.

("A Calm Vademecum Dose" from
Five Elegies Preceded by a Meditation)

How about saying "it" like this? That the ur language is/isn't your language. It's self-translated—you are that self—or it, ur—translating it, unknowingly and decisively. You can also translate it into several languages at once, finding your true vehicle for it, say, in bilingual editions, with drawings and collages to punctuate the ur-slabs. For these books I refer to, *Aljibar* and *Aljibar II*, are incontrovertibly new, unique forms, with English (Pierre-English mixed with French and other) and a French translation, by Eric Sarner, running side by side as if the book were originally written that way. I mean the books look like they were first written in both languages.

Is it possible to uncover the primal language itself? But is there one? Yes. But *is* there one? Of course. It was spoken by all the animals, when animals and people weren't sure of their differences. All the indigenous peoples of America know this, as I do and am one, though I too am in exile. *Everyone* knows this, and one could go on and on in this way. But we've stumbled into the *time* place in this conversation. What time was before Babel, isn't it always now? The Zen Heads would say so . . . Ah, Franco Beltrametti! "j'emporte avec moi / a book to be called / Blows Against The Mother Tongue / a cura de (toi & moi) / (cosi cosi) / vos images / merci, mon ami . . ." ("telegrammatica per franco," again from *Five Elegies Preceded by a Meditation*). It's still, always, that time, but one doesn't remember it very well, except for where one wrote it, that page. But you wrote it before you wrote it, didn't you? You are before Babel, at the same time as you are in time: "time, time what we are / inside of, banging // our heads against yet / don't want to leave" ("Tuesday, May 23rd, 2000").

"Rafaél maì amècche zabi almi." "Rough hell may enmesh ease, a be-all me." is Pierre's homophonic translation of Dante's Nimrodian verse. Mine (not homophonic or anything) would be "The Angel, my friend, zaps our souls."

Pierre Joris—Cartographies of the In-Between,
edited by Peter Cockelbergh,
2011

Aljibar, Editions Phi, Esch-sur-Alzette, 2007.
Aljibar II, ibid, 2008.
Winnetou Old, Meow Press, 1994.

Alette Update 2013

I thought for this talk I would glance at some aspects of *The Descent of Alette* that I hadn't covered in the two previous essays I'd written on the subject, "Epic & Women Poets" (published in *Disembodied Poetics,* ed. Waldman and Schelling) and "The 'Feminine' Epic" (published in my book *Coming After: Essays on Poetry*.) I wrote those two essays around the time of the composition of the poem, in order to create an audience for it, it being different from anything I'd written before and also different from anything my contemporaries were working on, or that poets had written for quite awhile. The use of the quotation marks was irritating to a lot of people, but even more than that there was the very unnatural, unrealistic mien of the work. I often felt apologetic about it, but I couldn't stop myself writing it.

Now it is over 20 years later, and I see, rereading the previous essays, that certain aspects of the poem have still not been discussed or discussed adequately by me or others. So mainly before I read from it and we have discussion, I'm going to touch briefly on the following questions: 1. Who is Alette and what is 'the real' in relation to the work? 2. What is a measure? (I have talked about this before, but can never keep myself from going at it again.) 3. What was the immediate reception of the work like? 4. Besides the Inanna poem, what other materials did I read and research? What did I do as background for the poem?

One. Who is Alette? This question arises in relation to the fact that besides being an epic quote unquote, the poem is a dream vision quote unquote. In a dream vision—a form prevalent throughout medieval Europe—the narrator of the poem falls asleep, finds himself in a magical but rather natural landscape, meets up with a guide, and journeys through dreamlike or improbable events; then wakes up. In *The Divine Comedy*, the narrator doesn't fall asleep or wake up, nonetheless everyone agrees the poem is a dream vision. The first four words of my poem are "One day, I awoke", that is, the narrator/protagonist, who doesn't know her name until over three-quarters of the way through, *awakens* into the landscape of the subway—the subway and the other levels or landscapes presented are the whole "reality" of the poem. There is no reference to another reality.

A dream, it is important to note, is an *experience*. Dreams are part of one's life and continuity, and sometimes a dream is a very important occasion. In my real life I have had important real dreams that changed me. But it's a different kind of experience from events in waking life: you don't know "when" you enter the dream, and later you seem to "remember" it, but rather badly, usually: you were "asleep," whatever that may be. Dreaming is subject to different rules of time and space from waking life. Action may be telescoped and transitionless; landscapes may be composite; you are not you necessarily: you may be a person you have never been or will never be or who to your knowledge has never existed. Nonetheless a dream is a fact; and *you* experience it. But. You fall asleep, you cross a border and wake up in another reality. (The medievals loved these other realities that one seemed to have no control over the switch for, like dreaming and falling in love: you don't know you're going to fall in love, and then you do—you have become insane.)

Looking back, I can't remember why I wrote a dream vision, the way I do remember why I wrote an epic (again I'm saying the poem is both an epic and a vision). After my brother's tragic death, I began to ride the subways of New York as if looking for something, maybe a poem or maybe community with the other unfortunates. I began to see odd events in my imagination—that is the vision began to occur to me without my exactly asking for *it*—and I wrote the first few poems of the book: not the very first two though, I wrote those last of all, two years later. But subsequent ones, the ones involving animals, animal-humans, and metamorphosis. Then I realized each page or subpoem was a car, and I was proceeding from car to car, witnessing these strange scenes. This was the initial form of the poem, and the quest part of it, the search for the mother and father and the need to kill the tyrant, started to materialize from what was seen in the cars, and then subsequently in the caves.

Thence, the most essential rule of the poem, and the one that makes it most different from every other modern poem I know of: everything in the poem, though bizarre, is visualized and concrete. Nothing of it is created by language, in the sense that words produce more words out of their qualities *as* words. I repeat, Nothing of it is created by language, in the sense that words produce more words out of their qualities *as* words. Everything is seen and heard in immediacy. The words of the poem create a materially visualized, heard and spoken-in, participated-in landscape of people, animals, events. The reader isn't supposed to think about the writing, she or he is supposed to be right there in the vision. Despite the quotation marks, and most readers achieve this reading state.

But who is Alette? Is the narrator of a dream vision, which is always fictional and strange (to a greater or lesser extent), that is, unreal by definition—is that narrator the author? The narrator is always author-like; everyone knows that Dante is the protagonist of *The Divine Comedy*, though he is referred to in critical discussion by names such as "Dante's pilgrim." However, Dante did not descend into hell, and then ascend into purgatory and heaven. Or did he?

I assert that I am Alette—the name itself proclaims it; that I did descend into the world of the subway and the depths of heaven; that I did, at least that once, kill the tyrant. I lived the vision of the poem. (And I have also, in the past, asserted that I am not Alette; that she is a fictional character. Both are true.)

People talk as if a vision is, like, something you see, while you're standing there, staring off into space like a madwomen. Or in some cases it would seem to be a dream—certain native Americans might dream something while asleep and then say they *saw* it. I'm saying the poem *was* (and *is*) the vision and I lived in it for two years while I wrote it. I'm saying there's no difference between it and my quote unquote life; I'm saying that that is as much to be a visionary as to be Blake seeing angels in the trees while he's talking to one of his friends in quote unquote real life. I believe my poem; it's what I remember the most from those two years, it framed everything I did and was.

I developed certain techniques for writing it that stemmed from both dreams and visual processes. Sometimes there was a rule that I would close my eyes and whatever I saw first would be the first image of the next page or subpoem; I was then stuck with that image, however odd it was, and had to keep seeing and writing the subpoem from it: it initiated the action. I also kept track of my dreams, and sometimes the rule was that the first aspect of the previous night's dream that I remembered, sitting down to write, was what I wrote as the beginning of the new page (though I didn't recount the dream: I again used an initiating image.) This sort of rule I followed particularly in Books One and Two. In Books Three and Four, where the action is broader I allowed myself the indulgence of rational planning and tried to map out what would happen next. But I never knew very far in advance; I never had a detailed overall plan. Everything happened as I wrote the poem, as I, Alette and Alice, lived it. You may also have inferred that a basic rule was that I would allow myself to be very deeply embarrassed. The material was embarrassing, and the tone, and the measure.

So, Two. What is a measure? In the 20th-21st centuries the basic measure of the poem has emerged as the fact of the line itself, though there are exceptions—one thinks of the New Formalists and their exact use of old meters. And sometimes, as in prose poems, the line is the sentence. But the poetics that emerged with the Modernists proposed a line that *could* always be unique, that is, each line different from previous and subsequent ones in a given poem, in terms of number of feet, if one could even find them, or nature of metrical events: any line might sound different from any other one. The line break orders all the previous sounds in the line. Sometimes a poem appears to have lines of approximately the same length, sometimes the linear surface of a poem on the page is very broken, with lines of various lengths perhaps appearing all over the page; stanza breaks and/or white space give further clues as to how to read the work. The poet may be very sensitive to shapes on the page, to what the eye takes in as well as the ear. Or there may be a sequence of similar subpoems composing the poem, so that you carry from subpoem to subpoem a knowledge as to how the poem works. All of these qualities are part of measure, as is the replication of sound patterns—there are *always* repeated sound patterns in a poem, of one kind or another: repeated consonants and vowels, for example—letters, if you are more print-conscious; and repeated sound patterns that aren't feet, so-called intonation patterns, that are demonstrable with certain kinds of machines. If you record the raw sound—those graphlike machine scratchings—of people reading poems aloud, you will see similar clusters of rise and fall repeating and mirroring themselves in the poem, at wider intervals than the feet. A person with poetic talent internalizes all of these relations, as a person with musical talent internalizes relations between and among musical notes. A poet's talent is certainly as complex and mysterious and awesome as that of a composer of classical music.

I had ascertained from my ten, twenty previous years of reading long poems, epics, dream visions, that a consistent measure had been very helpful to all the authors of those works, up until the twentieth century, when measure changed—but that the authors of so-called twentieth-century epics weren't really putting the story in. They were doing a different thing, writing the modernist long poem for a supposed age of fragments, with what I considered to be a half-assed story thrown in; I felt totally uninterested in doing this. I wanted to do, as I have written in my essays, something closer to what Homer and then much later Dante did; and I wanted very much to write a public poem. My brother had died because of the Vietnam War—which had affected large numbers of people, whom I felt I was somehow writing *for*, even if they would never read the poem. I seem to believe that even though they don't read it, they do read it. But, though the poem has those pesky quotation marks, I was not writing for a coterie, or a poetry school, or in a more extended way, other poets. I was writing for the people on the subway, because I was one of them. I wasn't just writing for the half of them that were women, but I was determined that they would finally be included.

So. I had taught myself to scan the *Iliad* in Greek, though I couldn't and can't really read Greek. I had a sense of a long line divided into sound events that repeated themselves from line to line and that you could thus internalize. My own line came to include sound events that were similar, but also variable. I had, as I've written, previously used the form of phrases surrounded by quotation marks, but not precisely in the way of *The Descent of Alette*. The phrases became more pared down and orderly, there were three to four per line, and there came to be, in general, several four-line stanzas of those per page—I could work with that. I could tell a story with it. I probably needed the so-called feet laid out so transparently so that *I* could see them, as much as for any other reason I have described. I wasn't used to writing like this. When I wrote the individual poems in my notebook, by hand, I didn't put the quotation marks in, but

I did put the space around the phrases. I inserted the quotes when I typed the poems up. Without the quotes the phrases actually would have been read too fast; white space by itself just doesn't create enough space.

What happens is you start to think with the feet. I am normally very fast, I tend to talk fast and in general, though not always, I had previously written poetry in a very fast line containing a lot of linguistic events (which are different from sound events, though they merge with them.) I read my poems very very fast—Allen Ginsberg used to devote himself, each time he heard me read, to chiding me for this (the very last time he heard me read, from *Mysteries of Small Houses*, he said after complimenting me on the poems, "And you didn't read too fast.") I mention Allen because he was one of the group of men—they were all men, in fact—who seemed to get what I was doing with the measure, knew where it came from. After hearing me read from "White Phosphorus," a sort of precursor poem to *Alette*, he was heard to say, "Did I just hear dactylic hexameter?" In parts of that poem I used the Greek meter directly; I had not yet devised the simpler foot of *Alette* that I sometimes thought was too plain, not bombastic and sounding enough; though it was so good for telling *Alette*'s story.

The measure, and the quotation marks, slowed me down enough so that I could think out this poem in the way it needed it. The measure was a thinking tool, at the same time as it was a tool for keeping going, at length; it drove the poem and it drove my brain.

Question three. What was the immediate reception of the work? By this I mean, mostly, how it was received while I was in the process of writing it; for I unveiled sections of it as I wrote them, in a journal Doug Oliver and I published called *SCARLET*, and in readings given largely in bars and other small venues. This was probably part of my writing process. I had a group of fans who came to the readings, a rather small group admittedly, but nonetheless they existed and they were hooked—they had become involved in the story and wanted to know what would happen next. This group included the prose writer Johnny Stanton, the poets Jackson MacLow and Armand Schwerner, and the photographer/film-maker/painter Rudy Burckhardt. I think Rudy and Jackson showed up almost every single time. Armand once offered to explain the measure to me in case I needed it explained; I admitted that I didn't understand it analytically but told him I didn't want to yet. We never got to have the conversation about it; he, Jackson, and Rudy are all dead now. There was a sort of décollage for some people between hearing the poem and then seeing it on the page in *SCARLET*: certain ones really detested the quotation marks and told me so. We were still in the aftermath of the abstract-expressionist painters in New York, and everyone was passionate and forthright with their opinions. Johnny Stanton loved hearing it, but couldn't hear the quotation marks. Joe Brainard and Eileen Myles both told me they didn't like the quotation marks—and I think they just didn't like *it*. Leslie Scalapino, who was not in New York, quite simply hated the poem. The Language Poets, I felt, were quietly stunned: I had done something they couldn't have predicted, and it *looked* very radical. Barrett Watten claimed to be able to *hear* the quotation marks, and that was a rather good thing to say. It seems to me now that the first people actively to like it, besides my group of men, were people I didn't know—and whose names I can't recall this morning—who knew something about the tradition of the dream vision and/or ancient poetic practice. And high school students—boys who read comics and played video games—liked it. I also remember that certain gay men I didn't know—this was the era of many AIDS deaths—were deeply affected by it. I guess I was calling to them too; they were in the subway.

I did, as I've said, sometimes feel apologetic for changing my style so much, but I couldn't help it. I couldn't stop doing it the way I was doing it.

Four. Other books, materials, research, besides the Inanna material, which I have discussed in "The 'Feminine' Epic."

—Emergence myths. In the Southwestern United States (where I am from) there arose a fascinating group of Native American myths that deal with the emergence of the first people from successive underground layers. One might imagine them being influenced by living near the Grand Canyon, or on mesas, or in the amazing, layered geology of that area. I was particularly influenced by the Navajo material. There is a book called *Diné bahane'*, which is one particular gathering and translation of Navajo creation myths by Paul G. Zolbrod. There are successive underground worlds of different colors with different kinds of indigenous inhabitants—insects and birds for example—and the People themselves are being formed while ascending onto different levels of this world, often misbehaving, being disorderly, being kicked out or flooded out, going on up, until they hit the Fourth World, and finally the Fifth World, this world on the surface of the earth. They become the Earth Surface People. In ascending they gradually straighten out and come into contact with gods and holy figures that help them do right. First Man and First Woman come to be, and their children.This mythic material is incredibly beautiful, and I have taught it and forgotten it a couple of times. There is also the Hopi emergence myth, which only involves four worlds; a version of that material, *The Fourth World of the Hopis* has been assembled and translated by Harold Courlander.

—I read other books about Native American myths and customs, and also books about Australian Aborigines and their art, their modern paintings of the ancient songlines—the lines or maps that one traces with one's feet on long treks across that landscape, walking out the stories of the first events of the various tribes. In fact, my character the first mother, in my mind, originally looked like a photo that I kept seeing of a very young, naked Aboriginal woman holding a baby and balancing a wide basket on her head; but I later realized that the first mother had to be Lucy, the skeleton found by Louis and Mary Leakey in the Ulduvai gorge in Africa, which at that time was the oldest human skeleton known, a million or so years old. My first mother became a sixteen-year-old African woman. both younger and much much older than I.

—I read a lot of books about shamanism, but I conveniently forgot that. When people said that the tearing apart of Alette's body by the owl in Book Three was very shamanistic, I was astonished and denied it at first. Obviously it's true. And as I say that I lived the poem, I say now that my body *was* torn apart and reconstituted, though I'm not sure that I have demonstrable owl powers; however I do have a tattoo of an owl on my left shoulder, taken from an ancient Greek drachma, Athena's owl. I got it the year I turned sixty, with the help of Eileen Myles, who surely now approves of *The Descent of Alette* on some level at least.

—I read a lot of books about owls. I had never seen an owl in the wild, but I became extremely involved with the species in my mind and learned a great deal about their physiology and habits: I have since probably forgotten everything; forgetting seems to be important to the process of writing, at least for me.

—I read a lot of books about the Vietnam War. This was part of grieving for my brother, and it was also research for the poem, in which there has been much war and the protagonist is grieving.

—I rode the subway repeatedly, just riding it. I also visited repeatedly the Museum of Natural History in New York, with its lovely collection of Native American artifacts and its very many dioramas of different peoples in the world in naturalistic settings. At the beginning of writing the poem, I also happened to be in Paris for a week, and I spent some time in the Musée de l'Homme, which likewise inspired certain aspects of the poem, with its collection and its dioramas. The dioramas of both museums, in fact, were the inspiration for the tyrant's exhibits in Book

Four, the tyrant's house being largely modeled, physically, on the Museum of Natural History.

—For the landscape of Book Three, I used a couple of state parks in New York—one near Sebago Lake and one near Lake Mohonk, places I was somewhat familiar with. For the caves, I loosely used a site near my hometown of Needles, California—Mitchell's Caverns, a rather spectacular set of caves sacred to the Chemihuevi tribe.

—I did some research on masks and also made them. I would buy readymade masks and then paste things on them, collage them. For example, I found a mask of an owl and covered it with photos from National Geographic magazine of the opening ceremonies for the Vietnam War Memorial in Washington. These photos showed a lot of fireworks, and the owl visage of the mask appears to be on fire. (The mask is now in my archive at the University of California at La Jolla.)

—Finally I was living with a British poet, my late husband Douglas Oliver, who had written what he called a satire on Margaret Thatcher's England, a long poem called "The Infant and the Pearl." It is a *satiric* dream vision, based on the medieval poem "The Pearl," by Anonymous. That is, I was living with a poet previously involved in the same sort of project as I was—he subsequently wrote several other long poems. We showed each other our work and criticized and influenced each other in large ways that were never stated by either of us. He was the other part of my poetry movement at that time; no one has written about the connection, and I am hesitant to speak of it because it sometimes upsets me, since he is dead; but it was obviously an enormous *working* element in the actual writing of the poem.

I should perhaps add that I read no feminist writings that I recall, during this time. My feminism comes from my own experience and perception, and I don't feel a great need to read about the subject per se, though I do need to write about it. I would also like to say that I don't consider myself to be a great woman poet, I consider myself to be a great poet. That is an essential aspect of my feminism. In this statement I have placed myself in the grand tradition of poetry as we have received it for the past several thousand years. By including myself in the tradition, I have made it open to women. Perhaps it always wanted to be but didn't know how to find us—I have a certain trust in the great poets, though I don't always sound as if I do. Furthermore it does feel as if I have effected a change *backwards;* as if I could say that it is now a tradition that was always going to include me. I don't believe in time as a line. I believe in time as in the mind of god, though I don't believe in god, except to think that we are all godlike. I take this conception of time from my dreams, and from Boethius's *The Consolation of Philosophy*, Boethius being the originator of the dream vision.

2009,11,13 for talks given in Paris for
Double Change and at Naropa University

Dreams, Again

I've been using dream materials in my poems since I first began writing poetry in the late sixties. I've taken words, images, narratives, parts of narratives from my own dreams and repeated them, transformed them, commented on and sung them. I did this instinctively in the beginning, without a theory and not particularly out of literary precedent, though there is plenty of that. Partly it was clear to me that my dreaming self was better at some aspects of poetry writing than I awake was; my dreams would often surprise me when "I" couldn't.

In the early nineties, after having worked for a couple of years on the writing of *The Descent of Alette*, which draws to a large extent on dreams and on poetic techniques related to dreaming, I wrote an essay called "What Can Be Learned from Dreams," published in *SCARLET* in 1991. This essay posits "Dream" as a place or function in me I'm divided from, a place or function that knows things I don't know awake and is often the better, more imaginative maker. The essay discusses, briefly, the plasticity and the symbolic multiplicity of dreams, and the relationship between dream and myth; and it reflects on the part a sensitivity to one's dreams might play in making one's way through the egoism and manipulation of oneself and others abounding in daily life (after all you're *also* the pathetic creature you are in your dreams.) At this point, I began to write down my dreams every morning—I had done this once before for a couple of months, but my practice had generally been to write down only what was truly striking or mysterious. In the writing of *Alette*, I allowed myself to use anything I remembered from a dream no matter how humble or off-the-wall-seeming, but I wasn't recording my dreams on a daily basis, I was more remembering them each day.

Between sometime in the early nineties and now, 2008, I have written down all my dreams I can remember each morning. I haven't tried to write well, only to get down what I retain; and I have omitted a few dreams on the grounds that they're just too personal in a scatalogical or other way and I don't want them read—I don't know what's going to happen to my dream notebooks when I die: they aren't very interesting in themselves, but I might not get around to destroying them. I'm now rather fatigued with the recording of dreams and may give up the practice in this daily manner, though I doubt that I will ever stop using dreams as material. What I'd like to ascertain at this point is whether I've learned anything further from my dreams, whether I can articulate what I know beyond my previous essay.

First, I will state as a fact that dreams can be premonitory or telepathic: they *can* predict the future and receive information at a distance from the dreamer. They don't do these things in a way that can be easily evaluated, and they don't always do these things clearly, but they do do them. Many people recognize this truth but don't know what to do about it; I scarcely know what to do about it, I usually incorporate dreams into my poems rather than speculate on how dreaming works. If you're interested in a more scientifically explanatory tractate involving the curvature of time, a multi-dimensional universe, and other such comforting terminology (now dated, of course), along with a study of precognitive dreams, I suggest you consult *An Experiment With Time* by J.W. Dunne (Faber and Faber Limited, 1927). I'm not interested in proving something, I'm interested in meditating on what I know; and I now feel confident enough to say that dreams *are* predictive and mind-sharing.

Thus, in my dreams, I've been forewarned that people will die, told that I am seriously ill, or that a friend is having heart surgery thousands of miles away (about which I know nothing in my waking life). I've dreamed that someone is discussing her uncle, while she is in fact doing this, many rooms and one floor away in a thick-walled house; dreamed that my husband's letter of rejection for a Guggenheim is about to arrive in the mail (it did, the morning of the dream); dreamed that the antibiotics I'm taking aren't working and the symptoms only appear to be under control (that was true too). These are randomly recalled examples. And I have anecdotal evidence of the same sorts of dreams from other people. This is one part of what dreams do—communicate literal information of a more or quite less pressing nature.

But just as interestingly, dreams make you be somewhere where you apparently aren't, render you a character in a story that isn't yours and that you believe, in fact destroy your identity except for the most central core of the "I," since you are that self, the unnamed only I that remembers the dream. Daily detail melts, I remain. Dreams also meditate, they think while you're asleep, they ruminate in story and symbol form and go pretty deep doing that. They pun in the ways Freud said they do, and are parable-like in the way the Bible indicates: they can be "interpreted," but that's only one interpretation, isn't it? And some things that appear not to be sexual may be sexual, but on the other hand sex isn't always sex, it's rebirth for example (see the ending of Norman Mailer's *Ancient Evenings*—not a dream, but so dreamlike); and the dreams aren't always about you the dreamer, as the ancients knew but Freud didn't appear to. Sometimes one gets through a personal crisis by sleeping and dreaming a lot: dreams instruct and heal. I consciously use dreams that way. I also sometimes try to dream oracularly, asking myself, the dreamer, a question before I fall asleep, to see what answer I'll receive in a dream.

So, when I decided to write this essay and began taking notes, I thought to try to dream about what dreams are. I wrote down in my dream notebook (on January 3rd, 2008) TRY TO ASK DREAM ABOUT WHAT IT IS and then fell asleep and had a series of dreams. In the first dream I was walking in Place des Vosges, in Paris, with Karen Weiser, who said, "I don't have the cream." In the second dream, I heard the singing of the word "Deposuit," exactly as in a certain Bach choral piece—the Magnificat?, by a baritone voice, with much ornamentation. For the third dream I will quote from my notebook: "With an Asian tribe—the Guarami—in mts. They want me to show them which rocks (?) are weddıng rings; this one already is, I say. It's a large curved rock with a finger attached. The tribesman takes it eagerly." There was a subsequent dream that seems more personal and that I won't recount except to say it contained the name "Healey"—the name of a friend, whose appearance always signifies healing.

Some quick interpreting. Place des Vosges contains old arcaded buildings, I was walking in a secluded place with someone who was "wiser," probably stood for Dream and nonetheless didn't have the answer, but who managed to make a rhyme with the important, initiating word, "dream": dream/cream. "Deposuit"—in Latin—is from "deponere"—to lay down, to put down, to deposit. From those two dreams I get a sense that a word, or words, is, are, deposited and ornamented in a dream, as "deposuit" is so elaborated on in the singing of Bach's work. I woke up thinking that a dream is like an illuminated manuscript, in which words and letters are enlarged, made calligraphic, highlighted, painted, with stories and symbolic figures in the margins. I find the wedding ring dream harder to talk about. At some point we became wedded to waking consciousness, perhaps; and our choice is embedded (see how I've rhymed, unconsciously, "wedded" and "embedded") in rock and flesh, the whole finger. In waking consciousness we get a real, motile body, a stable one; in dreams we get a mind, though we also get an unstable, but often realistic, body. In the dream notebook, that morning, I also wrote: "Is dream an archaic way of thinking? Is it a memory of a way of being before time was sorted out? Do I have this memory?" I think the answer is, dream is an ongoing, major component of existence.

I grew up in the Mohave desert, in a town that overlaps with the Mohave Indian Reservation. The Mohaves, in a way that seems similar to the thinking of certain Australian Aborigines, believe that everything important was first dreamed in order to be. I am now going to quote from the preface and introduction to *Tales From the Mohaves* (University of Oklahoma Press, 1970), by Herman Grey, a Mohave from my native area:

> The Mohave clings to his belief in dreams as a basis for everyday life. Not only all shamanistic power, but all myths, songs, bravery, fortune in battle, and good fortune in gambling derive from dreams. Every special event is dreamed. Knowledge is not a thing to be learned, a Mohave will say, but something to be acquired by each person through his dreaming.
>
> All Shamans say that they received their power from Mastamho, when he was put here on this earth. So deep are these convictions that, when old age comes, a Mohave can seldom distinguish between the dreams he has been told by an uncle or brother and what he has

> himself experienced. The Mohave learns as much from other people as from his own experience. Conscious learning seems to him nearly impossible, and he is convinced he has dreamed for the first time, or has dreamed repetitiously, the things which all Mohaves know in common. . . .
>
> A man may give his song or story to his son or to some other close relative when he feels himself near to death or concludes that the person in question wishes to learn the story or song. Only one man may sing or tell a sequence of songs and stories, and thus the myths are inherited within the family and clan. A storyteller begins from a timeless source, with the statement that the story came to him from his uncle or brother and now belongs to him.
>
> Dreams, then, are the foundation of Mohave life. Dreams are always stated as if they had been cast in mythological molds. . . .
>
> A dream might be an actual nocturnal one, or it might be a continued thought or a flash of insight which gave a further comprehension and contemplation of the man's hopes and perceptions. Dreams might give foresight of some obstacle to the achievement of an end and might also reveal the means of overcoming the obstruction. Many times a dream foretold a coming event, such as the outcome of a raid or the fate of a warrior.

What strikes me here is first the intersection of all categories: shamanism, dream, myth, story, knowledge: these seem to coincide and then differentiate but never become totally distinct from each other. Dreaming and waking obviously aren't so different from each other either, in the Mohave world. One has a sense that time and consciousness are perceived as fluid, not compartmentalized into asleep/awake, past, present, and future. It's not that one is always in now—the Now that can be so fashionable, philosophically, to talk about—but the past is an important concept too, and the past goes on in an important way, and the future is accessible. Of course, I'm also interested in the sense that Dreams Know. I believe I've read elsewhere that when there's an important invention—or when there was: I don't know if Mohaves are as obsessed with dreams as they once were, as traditional—the invention must be incorporated into the tribe's dreams. It has to have been known about from the beginning, so it must have been dreamed about before. Somehow the innovation gets put into dream form and then one says, 'Yes I always knew about that, or we did.' Of course that's what it feels like anyway: who can imagine life before cars? Was there always going to be a car? (See the cars shown in the TV cartoon *The Flintstones.*—the previsionable automobile.)

I didn't know these facts about the Mohaves while I was growing up alongside them. I've found these things out later, as I've developed my own thought and discovered that it resembles theirs. Isn't that strange? The Mohave Desert is vast with space and one fills it with thoughts and dreams—or I did; I acquired certain habits of thought from growing up in this landscape. I came to wonder if so-called reality weren't malleable, creatable, long before I knew about the philosophy of the Mohaves or of the Australian Aborigines who also inhabit a desert.

It seems logical to me to quote a Mohave as an authority on dreams. Grey knows what it is to believe one's dreams, to use them, and to have dream-like flashes of inspiration (as a poet does.) And reality must have seemed flexible when you lived in a desert and didn't build things much: when you and those you were with were in a state of invention all the time. Imagine an early tribal existence in a desert. There's just the few of you, and you can say what is, what made it, and what it means. You're the poets of what you know. It's when people erect a lot of buildings and crowd together in large numbers that everyone has to agree on a version of reality that grounds the buildings drily and makes it possible for those from different backgrounds, or even cultures, to communicate blandly. However, if you take certain drugs, you will notice that the texture of wood and brick is in motion—though the buildings don't fall; that people's faces melt, and that nothing is as secure as you thought it was. As when you dream, things fall apart and the laws of science are violated. Occasionally, when you dream, an animal talks to you. Many Native American peoples posit an early time when humans and animals talked to each other and shared characteristics more blatantly, when time wasn't as fixed as now, and you could make things happen by "magic." (For a lovely, modern sci-fi take on this possibility, see Ursula LeGuin's book, *Buffalo Gals and Other Animal Presences.*)

Furthermore many people could tell you they have had dreams that have changed their lives. I have a long list of such dreams. They become mythic; they "happened" for real, to the extent that they have changed me. I count them as part of my knowledge and use them for guidance. Here is my retelling of an important dream, from the preface to my book, *Reason and Other Women* (Chax, 2010):

> In 1997, after I had been informed that Allen Ginsberg had died, I became afraid for him in death. I wanted—because he was my friend—to be sure that in death he was safe. I dreamed that night that my stepdaughter Kate, who is deceased and in dreams is often my messenger from the world of the dead, came for me, in a rich dark blue skirt and sweater, to take me to the 'second world.' I gathered that this second world was an afterlife with an active artistic com-

> ponent, for there was a professor there who was trying to achieve an intense enough red for the second world's mosaics. Then, my name became Ellen Goodman (yes like the columnist), so I knew that I was Allen, the good man, and I waited in a small apartment to die. To die being to lose the power of one's vocal chords, no longer to speak . . . A knock at the door as 'they' came for me, I approached the door knowing I had used my vocal apparatus for the last time and would now learn to communicate telepathically; then I woke up. Allen was safe; for I understood there was an expansiveness beyond that of the voice. And I could now write with authority, of the first and second worlds, and the colors blue and red. The soul must be red. And Kate, the messenger was dressed in blue, for reason: as reason is the working through of 'messages,' or is perhaps the voyage of the messenger.

This dream enabled me to write my book, providing a sense of a double world, and also a color symbolism, plus a notion of telepathy: in *Reason and Other Women* I overtly expect the reader to get what I'm saying via a sort of telepathy—the reader must go with the rhythms and odd usages of my mind as I present it, in order to know further things, attain a new state of consciousness with its own materials and details, coaxed from dreams and words. You might well say that that is what poetry is—an art form based on telepathy, a sending of complex messages through an almost immaterial presentation—a few words on a page?; or you might say, that all communication is like that. And isn't it? Aren't we always communicating telepathically? So much of what we tell each other is told via air: to talk about "cues" and "body language" is to be perfectly limited: it's in the very air between us, everything we know and try to say to each other. We read each other's minds all the time.

Anyway, the dream presented these ideas to me, as well as the knowledge that Allen was whole and well, and that it would be good, probably, not to have to use one's vocal cords any more: there was a bigger better language, if you want to call it that. The dream remains important to me: it's part of who I am and what I know; it's part of my relationship with Allen and with everyone else. For me it is a work of great beauty in itself, though it terrifies me as well. The opening of the door at the end was a vast moment, to step into infinity without being able to speak, never again to write poetry.

If dreams are telepathic or precognitive or knowledge-imparting or otherwise "extraordinary," then do they exist to fill those functions, or are those functions a by-product of dreams? Or, more likely, are dreams and those functions part of a similar flexible fabric we keep trying to push away from our world of clearcut surfaces? Dreams are certainly a part of our condition of being alive. But how do they work? Why do we accept the fact of dreaming, as we accept walking and talking, without ever asking ourselves how, physically, we can be in another place, identity, and story while we lie in bed sleeping? We accept dreams but do not accept premonition. Do we have to accept dreams? Or did we? For sometimes it seems as if we are always creating who we are, selecting which of our abilities we want and pretending not to have others. We opt for dreaming—some scientists would say "select for it"—but do we have to dream? We're always dreaming, perhaps. Some people think an unconscious part of us dreams while we're awake—and I have personal experience of this. There is a wall in ourselves between sleeping and waking that dissolves at night, but we're always dreaming; and a part of one is always awake. The dreamer is awake in the dream.

How *are* we able to experience dreams at night as a physical reality as we do? This seems to me to be a much stickier problem than the fact of premonition and telepathy in dreams. I mean if you accept dreams in all their impossibility, you might as well accept something like premonition. Why does it seem acceptable to you that you can dream you're married to someone you've never seen in waking life (you realize when you wake up)—in fact a mean drunk—in an apartment you've never been in? Oh yes, that's normal for dreams, you say. How is that normal? Somehow our senses are working, but what are they stimulated by? Where did this guy come from? He and the apartment were rock solid and he was, absolutely, my husband. The dream was scary and intense. I incorporated it into a poem (that I've never published) twenty-seven years ago. It still upsets me to think about the dream. I can interpret it, if I want to, but I can't explain the physical reality of the tall thin man with slick almost pompadourish red hair and the apartment with its twilit psychic emptiness, and I can't explain the fact that I *was* that story. I wasn't myself, but I was.

As no science explains adequately how dreams work, no one can explain how a poem works. Where is a dream, sure, but where is a poem? I believe somewhat in Williams's formulation that a poem is a machine made out of words, but, finally, the poem isn't where the words are. The poem is somewhere between the words and the reader, or it is the words taken into the reader, who exists within the general society and its history. You enter the poem when you open to its page or remember it, having memorized it, but it is a much larger world than the page. It is transformed when you say it out loud; and it changes from reading to reading—you the reader change it, for one thing, as you change, or is it that it changes for you? If you are reading a poem by Catullus, you are in no way the same as an ancient Roman reading it: you are not that person—that kind of person, though it is that poem, as those words. But even if you know Latin, you don't "speak Latin," and you haven't much feeling for what it was like to be a Roman. A poem, like a dream, has an odd relation to time: it is in time, like a poem by Catullus, but it is timeless, as an object made out of words. A dream lasts a moment but endures as a memory might: but it didn't *really* happen. A memory can be backed up but no outside observer can find the particulars of a dream in time and space (evidence of REM or whatever isn't evidence of what happened in your dream). A poem didn't or doesn't happen, it's a still group of words on a page; and a story doesn't really happen either. We say that dreams, poems, and stories occur in the imagination, or the psyche, or whatever word we're using right now, to invent another entity that doesn't concretely exist to put them in. But doesn't the "real world" exist in some collective category like that? All we do is dream; we live in poems and stories we invent.

I'm interested in how caught up I can be in a daily comic strip in the newspaper, given four meager frames a day, of "unreal" actions perpetrated by line drawings who speak in balloons. For the last couple of years, reading *Doonesbury* on a daily basis in the *International Herald Tribune*, I have felt completely involved in the strip whenever the character B.D., whose leg was shot off in Iraq, enters this amazingly sketchy, involving world. Recently another character, Toggle, has been shot up—shot in the head—has aphasia and has been transferred from Iraq to Walter Reed Hospital in Washington, where B.D. is visiting him. I was recently in New York, and reading the comics one morning I said to Jess Fiorini, "It looks like Toggle is finally about to make it to Walter Reed." "Oh, yes," she replied seriously, "I saw that." Toggle is probably more real to me than Barack Obama or John McCain are; I am commenting on my imagination, not on them. I read, on a daily basis, *Doonesbury*, reruns of *Peanuts* and *Calvin and Hobbes*, and sometimes *Dilbert*. The world of *Peanuts* is worth reentering many times—it grows more beautiful as time passes, the drawing always seems more interesting and the situations more poetic: it has become literary and artistic, in time, though I suppose it always was; but these qualities are becoming more evident. I miss the comic strips of my earliest childhood though; I remember being entirely caught up in *Dick Tracy* during the saga of the angel girl whose name I can no longer remember; I can still see her radioactive angel-winged hair. None of this ever happened.

Suppose you admit that the world, physical reality, going on from day to day, is, in some long-term way, plastic, malleable. You can conceive of existence as a field you are involved in shaping. You can think of yourself as almost totally shaping it on your own, or reshaping it; refusing to accept the names people give to its shape automatically transforms it straight off. We are dreaming together, but we are dreaming separately too. Some of us are writing poems, and sometimes the poems are dreamlike. For example, there has been a school of poetry, Surrealism, inspired by the apparent mechanics of dreams, that contributed single words to the culture—"surreal," "surrealistic," and also furnished a way of viewing the overall story we may be in: "This war is surreal." For a very long time in Western civilization, there existed a literary form, sometimes called a dream vision, sometimes called an apocalypse, in which a lady appeared to a protagonist in dire circumstance and urged him or her not to give in to despair, instead to grow strong and conquer fear and doubt. The vision of the lady, from Boethius, through Dante, Christine de Pizan, and Chaucer, and more recently in poets like D.G. Rossetti and T.S. Eliot—that's almost two thousand years of these visions—is a powerful poetic event, still. The dream is as real as the words that describe it, as when the three ladies appear to Christine, in *La Cité des Dames*, who is despairing at the misogyny of the world and wondering if the female sex is indeed the inferior one:

> Lost in these painful thoughts, my head bowed in shame, my eyes full of tears, my hand supporting my cheek and my elbow on the pommel of my chair's armrest, I suddenly saw a ray of light descending onto my lap as if it were the sun. And as I was sitting in a dark place where the sun could not shine at this hour, I was startled as if awakened from sleep. And as I lifted my head to see where this light was coming from, I saw standing before me three crowned ladies of great nobility. The light coming from their bright faces illuminated me and the whole room. Now, no one would ask whether I was surprised, given that my doors were closed, and nevertheless they had come here. Wondering whether some phantom had come to tempt me, in my fright I made the sign of the cross on my forehead.
>
> Then the first of the three began to address me as follows: "Dear daughter, do not be afraid, for we have not come to bother or to trouble you but rather to comfort you, having taken pity on your distress, and to move you out of the ignorance that blinds your own intelligence so that you reject what you know for certain and believe what you do not know, see, and recognize except through a variety of strange opinions.
>
> (As translated by Blumenfeld-Kosinski and Brownlee, in *The Selected Writings of Christine de Pizan*, W.W. Norton & Company, Inc., 1997.)

In a typical dream vision the lady or ladies tell the seer or dreamer that she or he must not believe the world, or give in, mentally, to its brute force by acceding to abjection; that there is an evident truth that she knows for herself and that will now be proven to her, by Lady Reason, or Dame Philosophy, or whoever. The dream is right, you see, and the world is wrong; the poem knows, and the lady will now impart its highest knowledge. When I read this kind of work, I am always startled when the lady appears, I find her as beautiful as the writer does, and I believe in her reality absolutely, though she is most often "an allegorical figure." That's what we call her: Reason is not real, it's an "abstraction." In fact, Reason is as real as Lady Reason is, as real as the vision of her arising from the words on the page; she is real at that moment, the writer is real, and I am not there, the only one present who is real, the one who will remember that last moment when she appeared to me, when I identified with the protagonist. In fact there seems to me to be nothing truer in *this* world and *these* times than Christine's despair at the world's misogyny 600 or so years ago; nor anything as true as Lady Reason's defense of women.

We are constantly remaking the world from the inside out. As I say at the end of *The Descent of Alette*: ""I will change the" "forms in dreams"" . . . / ""Starting" / "from dreams," "from dreams we" "can change," "will change" . . . If we can be clear that reality is changeable, we can change it; and we can understand better both what our dreams are and what poetry can do for us. Dreams remind us that we can shape the world, that it doesn't fit into the categories we tend to make for it: we think and observe with our dreams and communicate with unconscious others, moving about in a time and space whose walls are down. Poetry is our conscious attempt to reshape the world, which is, as Philip Whalen says, "by nature wicked." We make it and remake it over and over. It's practically all we're doing; I mean, poetry is practically all that we're doing.

(2008, revised in 2013)

Published online in *Talisman*. Given as a talk at Naropa University, and also the Vermont Studio Center.

On the Poetry Talent

Poetry is an art form requiring tremendous skill, though it can also be practiced by someone who simply wants to write a poem (it will not be a very good poem, but maybe that doesn't always matter.) The talent for poetry is as particular as that for composing classical music . . . You can't - just - do it! And as peculiar to define. To get to a discussion of the talent, one might try to define the art, though it shifts and confuses, because it resembles speech.

Poetry is measured and compressed language, but so are certain kinds of charts and documents. Poetry is beautiful—oh what is that? Poetry is based on the fact of the rise and fall of the voice—repeated intonation patterns. It isn't always measured according to stress: in a language like French stress is variable and weird. Poetry is a bunch of sounds and meanings meant to be alive and give pleasure (sometimes a hurtful pleasure: it depends on what it says) and to offer a form or shape that someone might like to receive. Sometimes no one wants to even when it is very good. Who judges whether it's good? I might, I often do

A poem might do any of the things it's always done, or, more likely, a combination: tell a story, express feelings, make a picture, titillate the ear and mind, amuse, present a philosophical point, an aesthetic point, a conceptual point, etc etc. It will not do this in the language of the novel or philosophy or essay, it will do this in poetry. It will be compressed even when it looks garrulous—a lot is *supposedly* being left out. It will effect its hits all over itself, between two words or within words or grabbing an almost forgotten word and joining it with one much further down (as in rhyme). There are minutiae of experience in saying a poem if it is any good. Each syllable, each letter counts. It just does.

Poetry's about vibrations—of the voice, and doesn't everything in the material universe vibrate? It isn't like music, you have to think harder. Music tends to make you mushy. But poetry isn't like philosophy because its traditions seem to be up for grabs at any instant (philosophy is of the academy and thus conservative), and it's more about the act of thinking than of concluding. It selects sounds, words as it's thinking and you're inside thinking with it, as if thinking were what we are always in. When it tells a story it truly doesn't have to put everything in. And generally you don't need all that crap though some people, novel-reading people, like it. I detest it unless it's Chaucer.

How do you have a talent for poetry? It starts when you're about four years old though you don't usually know it. You "get things"—you're always getting things and then you say it. You try to think of the best way to say it, but maybe as you're saying it you go to another place where the words take on their own force. They present themselves as you say them. You still aren't measuring. Or maybe you are. You haven't thought about the line though it's been there in front of you on pages or in the voice of a reader if you can't read yet. You never ever question the fact of the line when you see it on the page. It is primordially logical. It is a shape that makes as much sense as your body does.

One of my first favorite poems is a nursery rhyme called "Little Jenny Wren." Robin Redbreast takes in the sick Jenny Wren, feeds her and cares for her, and then she gets well, tells him she doesn't love him, and leaves him. "Robin being angry, / Hopped upon a twig / Saying out upon you, fie upon you, / Bold faced jig." I didn't know what a jig was (I still don't really, it's an obsolete usage), and I couldn't make that last word last long enough. I would always say Out upon you fie upon you bold faced Ji-ig! I had to draw the last word, whatever it meant, out. Also I was never quite clear how to group the words of that line and would say Out upon / you fie upon / you bold faced ji-ig! My mother said I would say you bold, faced, jiyug! There's a u mixed in. I understood the story itself clearly, at four, five years old. There was a picture in the Mother Goose book as well with Robin bringing food to Jenny sick in bed. Two birds in 18th-century clothes.

I had a late development as a poet, I couldn't make a connection between the fact of a poem and writing one. I thought you were supposed to write stories, though I wasn't sure how one might do that. However in high school lit class I automatically memorized all the poems. Listen my children your father is dead, from his eyes we will make buttons? No it's listen, children your father is dead, from his coat we will make jackets . . . That became the story of my life as everyone died. Life must go on, I forget just why. Christ! What are patterns for? And God stepped out into space and said I'll make me a world.

The first work I remember writing was a collaborative play when I was eleven. The sixth-grade teacher got sick of teaching one day and made everyone do projects in groups. She sent me and some other girls, Freddie, Kathy, and Barbara Madison, outside to write a play. We decided it would be about the Salem Witch Trials—this in Needles, California in the Mojave, and everyone started saying what should be in the play but they couldn't write it down. I knew I could write it down and I seized the piece of paper and pencil and began to write down all the dialogue as they had ideas (different people speaking, different voices, has since been a strength of mine). Then the teacher said we should put it on, and I played the witch and they played the bewitched girls; they mostly rolled around on the floor, they had wanted to do that all along! I made myself up to be as old as I am now and recited lines protesting my innocence. There were small parts for boys, but a couple of boys made a few changes to the production (nobody changed *my* lines.) The most striking change being the creation of a character, a drunken bum who wandered into the New England courtroom disrupting the proceedings. The drunk was played brilliantly by Zeke Mesa, a Hualapai boy with spiky black hair and a constant sense of humor. I loved it. I had been inside of and witnessed Creation. I still haven't told you much about the poetry talent, but during the making of this play it became evident that I had the writing talent. I saw it and took it, though I subsequently kept forgetting about it.

One day in high school this girl was reading Amy Lowell's "Patterns" aloud—Christ! What are patterns for?—and she slipped up somehow and made it sound like "the Lady" in the poem, in a brocade gown, peed on her brocade gown. Everyone started laughing, because . . . everyone was paying attention. Why?

It's a pretty good poem as I remember it. It tells a story, it messes with tense and time, and it makes you remember the lines. It's not precisely as if you need it, but you like it. It occupies your mind. (I have had the theme from *Gilligan's Island* playing through my mind for the last few weeks, so it's possible I don't have good taste. The millionaire and his wife, the movie star, the professor and Mary Ann, here on Gilligan's Island.)

I got interested in William Blake in high school, just a poem or two. I've always liked "The Sick Rose." This is just to show you I have taste, before I go off on some tangent about farout vibrations. "The Sick Rose" can be read really really fast, aloud, and then be over with. In college I wrote an "Auguries of Experience," countering Blake's "Auguries of Innocence," for a literature class—I got an A minus because I introduced Yeats into the work, and it was supposed to be an imitation not a satire, so I couldn't have the A. I still didn't know I was a poet. And no one in my hearing had ever tried to explain what poetry was. We took it for granted; we should have. But then it becomes hard to change poetry when it needs it.

Once when I was a little girl I told my mother I had an "excruciating headache." I was four or five years old. I had no headache but I wanted to say "excruciating." She burst out laughing and said No you don't. It was embarrassing, but I got to say the word. There are always words in my head waiting to be said like that if I can relax enough and not think about what I'm *supposed* to say in a poem.

It's all made out of words: sometimes I believe that and sometimes I don't. A poem is made out of words—is it? Words are made out of me and you. Nothing is made out of anything, nothing is made out of. Words are electric and change shape as you say them, and the world changes shape as you speak. That's more like it. I am changing you, I am causing you or me. I am changing us. I am making us transform, come to new life, forget the old stuff so hurtful. If this poem hurts you, you will still have some distance from it, even I will, even if it appears to shatter me. Because it's more material than my feelings are that can be nightmarish, that is, unreal. This poem is more real. Do I believe that? Yes, that's why I'm a poet.

There are certain things I should never have to go through again. Some aspects of experience are unbearable. Poetry can change them. The novel can't, it's too sentimental, music can't it's too sentimental, what about painting? I find it of use because it's so hard. Poetry can be hard because the words of it are hard. They stay there though you're always almost distorting them with your voice.

I still haven't explained it, though whenever I say a line of poetry it gets explained. Her love is only itself. Each poet is only a human girl who must die. When a snake was our mother, when a snake was the train. Hang me up by the old corral / hang me up by the old church wall / and I'll never go home again / and I'll never go home again. That's a song I dreamed and it came with a tune. [sing] As did the following lines I dreamed come with a tune: new bluebonnets in the underworld / new bluebonnets in the overworld / new bluebonnets / new bluebonnets / new bluebonnets in the underworld. Also: do I rise / baby just as long as I rise // do I sing / baby just as long as I sing // do I write // baby, just as long as I write.

That is, those are three little songs I dreamed whole with their tunes. The first two, particularly the first, work without their tunes, the third doesn't seem to exist apart from it and I can't say it without singing it. But I DREAMED them, I wrote them in my sleep ten or twelve years ago. I am incapable of forgetting their tunes. I have never written a musical tune awake.

I wrote the following poem when I was thirty-one:

WHEN I WAS ALIVE

When I was alive
            I wore a thin dress bare
shoulders the heat
            of the white sun

and my black thin
            dress did envelop me
till I was a shell
            gladly and breeze

ruffled and filled
            against good legs
the translucent fabric and my
            heart transparent

as I walk towards Marion's
          and Helena's as my
skirt fills empties and fills with
          cooling air

This poem has a poetry tune, it has a stanza shape a traditional one which is a superficial part of the tune, but the real tune just rises up from the words as I read it. I think it was an imitation of a poem by William Carlos Williams. But it is so much itself now that I can't remember anything about how I wrote it. No one else but me could have written it. Repeat that. No one else but me could have written it. It is sentimental because I wanted it to be, but it is more than that, it is a unique life form. It is also true. It is about being on the way, not being there, and that's why it's more than sentimental; but it's more than sentimental because it's its words. Completely. It refers to no other form even though it's an imitation. If you talk about consonants and vowels, or intonation patterns, or even word choices, you won't get at why it works.

I can remember walking to Marion's and Helena's on that day in 1977. Did I make the world over in some way by writing this poem?

Probably a form of telepathy is involved in poetry. I write the poem and the reader is then inside me. Or I am inside the reader, and I have "told" something but it is continuously transformed as it is told or read each time, particularly as it is read aloud since it always comes out slightly different. It is possible that the essential process of the world or universe is telepathic, mind within mind, interpreting what is being experienced, seen or felt; it is possible that poetry is the essential expression of this process. It is possible that the universe is nothing but interconnected poems, vibrating, and that the poet's talent is for locating these poems. But the poet is also creating the poems, or world or universe, as she or he writes them, in conjunction with the minds of everyone and everything else.

When I wrote my epic poem *The Descent of Alette* in the late '80s of the last century, I created a measure for it though it was not a particularly consistent measure. It is musical but different from music because it would never sound better sung.

> "One day I awoke" "and found myself on" "a subway, endlessly"
> "I didn't know" "how I'd arrived there or" "who I was" "exactly"
> "But I knew the train" "knew riding it" "knew the look of"
> "those about me"

It's very liquid when I say it but that isn't it. It's extremely compressed and that's more of it, but finally it takes over your mind and you think it. One day I awoke and found myself on a subway endlessly . . .

> "As the old man lies dying" "in his bishop's robe and gown" . . .
> . . ."We will be dead" "With emerald rings"
> "Green stones upon our" "fingerbones" "That is our love"
> "Must be our love" "that we will be dead &" "he"
>
> "will live forever" "on exhibit, in his museum"

And god stepped out in space and said I will make me a world.

> "The roses" "were sumptuous," "soft, & yet," "slightly waxen"
> "as if red paraffin" "had been lightly—" "almost" "imperceptibly—"
> "brushed over them" "The darkness behind the mask" "was an emptiness"
> "I could see nothing in" "Yet all of this—" "mask & voice behind—"

> "seemed alive," "electric," "the mask a" "sort of deity—" "some divine" "neuter principle" "I felt love &" "awe for it"
> "Or rather" "its lush roses" "seemed to" "become" "my feelings of love & awe"

Because where words and the mind start or stop and the so-called outer world starts or stops is not clear. This is one of the things poetry continuously makes clear.

One time my mother was sorting and dusting all the records—78s—and my younger sister kept getting into them, and so my mother swatted her across her diaper with a 78 record and broke it. My sister didn't even notice. It was my father's favorite song "The Ballad of Rodger Young." There is no point in my telling this story, except that I wanted to change the world again and bring the tone down. Also I want to recall things about my mother, who died recently. "Rodger Young" was the special song of the army infantry, which my father wound up in twice trying to get to World War II, both times finally being rejected because of flat feet. I can remember a little of the song, And to the everlasting glory of the infantry, stands a man stands a man named Rodger Young. And is there a reference to the Battle of Verdun, which was in World War I? My nearest métro stop in Paris, Gare de l'est is also named Verdun. But I haven't heard the song "Rodger Young" since my mother broke the record over my sister's butt when I was four, how can I remember this swatch of it? It fills the mind, and that is what the mind seems to be for. I think it is poetry and not prose that allows you all of these associations, as if in trying to remember everything you are both recreating and creating these new sound structures that may be a paragraph, a conversation, a poem finally: *is* everything a poem finally?

The talent is for gathering all these things together, but all these things are everything, including the trembling of the smallest so-called molecules or particles of sound or light heard or seen now being created or remembered. It was he who drew the fire of the enemy . . . I have just googled the song and discovered that there is no reference to Verdun in the song, I made that up, because Verdun almost rhymes with Rodger Young. I also misremembered the last two lines. I re-created it.

In my book *Culture of One*, which I call a novel in poems, I say, sort of, that each person's brain isn't a brain but a codex, a manuscript of all the things that that one knows and thinks, a sort of illuminated manuscript beautiful (though not always) but composed of all the garbage from the dump of cultures. Each one is her or his own culture. But the dump is everyone's. The the.

The poet is responsible to every bit of thought and matter to the extent that that is possible. The universe moves and makes tiny noises all the time, or if you can't hear, it does something else. I once met a blind painter who saw colors. The senses are not finitely distributed and there are more of them than have been defined. The poet's job is to be attuned to as many as one can be; the fact of the line is an organizational pitch that by limitation makes it possible to gather more material. I believe this woman, the blind painter—I think she was blind from birth, was a cognitive psychologist as well, or that had been her first profession. I went to a show of hers in a coffee shop on the Lower East Side in New York. She was an older woman by then. I can't remember her name. The paintings were abstract and full of brilliant orange-reds. She told me that she always knew what color clothes she was wearing. Henry Schuman, the oboist, introduced us. He helped promote and perform the music of Moondog—do you remember—the composer of strict canons, who used to stand on 48th Street selling his scores wearing a Viking helmet and lederhosen? But finally he became an accepted composer and his work was performed at the Brooklyn Academy of Music.

What *about* the fact that I can dream a song, tune and lyrics, a small but complex art work coming whole to me while I'm asleep and without my asking? Incontrovertible. Where did they come from? Did I receive their gift from the poetry talent, from the musical talent as if it floats about looking for a receptacle? Is it perhaps the case that the human talent has not been in the least adequately defined? Who knows what a dream is anyway, a detailed and lived-at-the-time (somewhere in sleep) experience of what one would lamely call another reality? The fact must be that I as a poet am in touch with aspects of life that most people refuse to face and reflect on. If one is talented enough and (in my opinion) has suffered enough (at the time of the dreamed songs I had recently been widowed for a second time), one may be granted unexpected gifts. But suffering isn't enough to make you a poet. And do you, as I am describing it, really want to be one ?

I am sure my mother never wanted me to suffer, as I have never wanted my sons to. Or wanted her to. I don't think she quite understood who or what I was when she was raising me, though she also knew me very well. She herself went fairly far into the poet's experience sometimes. On her deathbed she saw words everywhere and she shouted to them as if she knew them, though she was also identifying them. One of the last things she said was, Peter said everyone heard in their own language. That is, on the Day of Pentecost (my mother was a fundamentalist Protestant) the apostles spoke in tongues, but everyone present—people who spoke a lot of different languages—heard them, the apostles, each in his, the listener's, own tongue. This may be what the poet is always doing, working in a fundamental language, speaking in tongues, that each reader has the capacity to understand as her or his own person.

The gift of the poem comes from everyone and everything. It comes whole and in its own form because oneself comes whole and in one's own form. When you're totally battered and too tired to think the poem through you may just "dream it," get it whole. After all you yourself are not linear, why should it be? And why can't you just know the future—

the poem as it exists in the future—sometimes? It's *there* somewhere. One morning in 1973 I saw a five-page, long-lined, dense poem as a whole entity, word for word, in my mind and spent the rest of the day writing it down, in between periods of taking care of my baby son. It is called "Your Dailiness," and I consider it to be one of my best poems.

When I was four I followed my dad around the house as he memorized a Masonic rite. I memorized it with him, until my mother said it was supposed to be a secret and I shouldn't say it to anyone. I now can't remember a word of it. However my mother taught me the Hopi corn maidens chant and my father taught me the Apache dog dance chant—they had previously belonged to an organization of white people committed to helping Native Americans preserve their rites—and I can still sing the chants though very badly. Versions of them are whole in me, in languages I don't know, which I must butcher terribly when I sing the songs. I was *supposed* to remember them.

I am not being mystical, I am being matter-of-fact.

Momma used to get me to memorize parts of the Bible, though I don't remember these passages in their entirety now. But at one time I was able to recite the Beatitudes, various of the Psalms, first Corinthians thirteen, and the temptation of Christ (which I found baffling. I didn't understand why anyone would want what Satan was offering, essentially the world. I guess I thought that was just a word.) If you know a lot of things by heart you can participate very well in literature; you might be a rememberer, rather than an overt maker—why not? Or you might be both. Memorizing scripture of one kind or another is a traditional and efficient preparation for being a poet.

I believe Whitehead said the world is the organ of novelty, though he might have said that the mind is. You keep remaking each moment so it will be different enough from the previous one that you can go on. When you're dead you do something different. I'm picturing a poem right now as being like when you dig a hole in the earth and tunnel through out onto the other side of it in China—remember that image?

One year Daddy and I used to go out in the backyard every morning to see how high the morning glories had grown on the trellis. We only did it the one year. One time when we were out there I told him I'd just seen a giant moth, and he said it was actually a hummingbird. I realized I'd been Seeing Hummingbirds for a long time without knowing it, and I wanted the other times back, to experience again but with my knowing it. Once, when I was in my 50s, visiting my mother in Needles I told my youngest sister who was also there that the birds at dusk she'd always thought were birds were bats. She was disgusted.

In the poetry talent you connect with as many minds and voices as you can though you aren't thinking that you are while you're doing it. You are Hearing Everything in your mind. Everything might unify into one thing, a talking about one thing. But the whole thing's there at the time, because of what you're like. You are, oneself is, the unity everyone is always seeking, as you go about whatever, but you can't stop acting as if you're constantly in the process of finding out what it is. Or at least that's what I'm like. In the meantime I am, say, brushing up on classical meters or reading Racine or rereading a bunch of detective novels and trying to convince myself that I'm working at being a poet by doing so.

Towards the end of my mother's life, she and my aunt would sit around talking about what their parents had been like. It was their favorite thing to do except for gambling up the river at Laughlin. Momma would tell the story of when Grandma said, You know, when I'm sick a little girl comes and stands beside me; and Momma said to her, Do you think it's your little sister who died when you were young? And Grandma said, I don't know. Well I jus' don't know.

This is from a poem of mine called "Sandpaper" (*Culture of One*, Penguin Group, New York, 2011):

> He was in a hospital one of whose names is La Pitié, to have spinal
> surgery. The other bed in the room occupied by a young
> man injured in a car crash: a French kid whose ambition
> had been, truly, to become a kickboxer: he'd walk now but couldn't ever
> be an athlete. Full of self-pity and despair. His mother came to
> sit with him, calm him, as I was showing a poem to my husband, who said
> that he found it difficult. You have to hear it I said and read a passage—
> in English of course. And then the other guy's mother said, Mais
> ça, c'est très beau! She got it from its sound. Poetry is la pitié. Everyone
> was quiet.

There is an aspect of the poetry talent no one ever *ever* talks about, the poet's ability to be vividly present on the page. Critics either talk about "style" or deny the fact of "presence" (probably because they don't know how to do it.) I've recently engaged in a correspondence with someone (David Need) about where the voices in my poetry come from. Here is something I wrote to him:

> When you start to write a poem you empty yourself out mentally of everything but the potential poem, and words are then produced on the page; you are somehow transferring yourself, as a live being, to the page. It is at this point that other voices—besides the one you associate with yourself and that you usually hear in your head—seem to find it possible to enter the act of writing. Because "you" aren't there.

If you can't let go of yourself and transfer yourself to a page you can't be a poet. Not that you are talking about yourself, rather, as you write, you are now being the poem. It is a total experience. Sometimes you become someone else, maybe more than one.

No I don't believe the lies of the live. I am a spot of light in
order to find out, hanging on because it wasn't revealed in
death. I know what happened to me, she said; bleeding I
lay there unblessed. Do I want a blessing now, or a god to
rebuild me? We have gone beyond god or new lives, or death, or
tribes. I am working on this lace light at present; I accept the
drop of blood to propitiate me. One piece of you at a time
is all I need. I am letting you feed, I say, because I know this has
always been. You've been telling me for years
We needed you, if no one else did. We have this project to
change our silence into the beautiful city of a voice.

That is from a poem about genocide called "Millions of Us." (From *Songs and Stories of the Ghouls.*) The idea is that I can help the genocided dead find their voices or voice, their new city. I offer them each a drop of my blood (an oblique reference to the new sacrifice required by Artemis, a drop of blood rather than a life, in Euripides' *Iphigenia at Tauris*) but really I offer them my voice and my poem.

The poetry of one person can be a large endeavor, bigger than a government. Maybe I am your leader, whatever "your" and "leader" mean.

I used to stare at my brother's head from the back as he sat on the floor with his legs splayed out from the knees. I was fascinated by its roundness and by the indentation at its nape. He would be drawing two fighter planes attacking each other and would make shooting and explosion noises that were quite variable and shapely. Somewhere between electronic music and farts.

When I took a course in contemporary poetry in college, the teacher, well-known outside the institution, was a pompous narcissist. He made all the poets – their bodies of work—harder than they were because he didn't approach the poems through their form and as poems, he talked about them as if they were each an esoteric body of theory, derived. Luckily I had already read *The Waste Land*, liked it and knew it was dead easy. It was voices. He made a mess out of Pound and Stevens, and I couldn't read them for several more years. I was sure I wouldn't be able to understand them. When I became a poet, I just read them.

Once my mother was in a casino in Laughlin, playing computer poker, and she did something, made some movement that caused her to declaim to the equally aged man next to her, whom she didn't know, Tennyson's line "My strength is as the strength of ten." I picture her lifting a tub of quarters and saying it: "My strength is as the strength of ten." To which the man replied with the subsequent line, "Because my heart is pure." She was thrilled that he knew it, and this became one of her late anecdotes.

Once my father took me up in his little Tri Pacer airplane, a two-seater with a steering wheel in front of each seat. After we had been in the air for awhile, he removed his hands from his wheel, forcing me to try to fly the plane with the wheel in front of me. You have to do it, he said, and he would tell me how to turn it, this way that way. But the wheel would never do what my hands tried to make it do. Finally he said, "It's on automatic pilot." I took my hands off, and he and I sat watching both wheels turn by themselves.

Talk given at Poets House circa 2013

The poem "When I Was Alive" may be found in *Grave of Light: New and Selected Poems, 1970 - 2005* Wesleyan University Press, 2008.

The No Poetics, or The Woman Who Counted Crossties

The important thing about poetry and poetics is never to confuse the two. Poetry is ruthless, amoral, self-sufficient and potentially destructive—"revolutionary." Poetics isn't. It's moral, and often self-serving—it justifies, it creates value. I am amorally and ruthlessly a poet. I serve my talent. I have suffered and been chastised. So?

Diogenes – anyone writing must mention Diogenes—was told by the oracle at Delphi to devalue the currency. I have done that all my life, hardly having any currency, and that is certainly to devalue it. My poetics, if I have one, is to live without a job besides my poetry. Nonetheless, it's possible that I'm a world leader. I will tell you more of this later. Diogenes was a bag lady. The character Marie in my novelistic book of poems *Culture of One* is a fictional rendering of a bag lady, named Marie also, who lived in my home town, Needles, California, at the municipal dump, when I was growing up. Needles, in the Mojave Desert, is slightly less hot than Death Valley; Marie's shack that she built of palm fronds was not air-conditioned, and she would eventually die of exposure. She supplied herself with items from the dump and walked about with her several dogs. The phrase "bag lady" was not in our vocabulary then, and according to my mother's friend Bernice who would sometimes give Marie a lift into town, she was lucid and happy with the way she lived. She wasn't an artist, as I make her in my book. She didn't make collages from garbage as I myself do.

I've always been fascinated by Marie since she so created the details of her own existence, and I first wrote about her in my early twenties, when I was a student in fiction transitioning to poetry, in Iowa at The Writers' Workshop. I had just taken a break in my studies and gone to Morocco. In my story about Marie—Old Marie I called her—she sets out from her shack at the dump to walk to Africa. She walks on the train tracks counting the crossties and inserting the word "Africa" in each number she says, one-thousand-and-Africa-one, one-thousand-and-Africa-two . . . The story was quite short and had no particular resolution that I can recall: she thought and walked and counted the crossties. There is a similar woman in a long poem I'm writing right now who is dead and counts crossties in the afterlife. What is a crosstie? In the poem, written in long lines, it is something like a poetic line. In the story I wrote before I called myself a poet it is perhaps an intersection to each point in a nauseating linearity, at cross-purposes to it: a preview of the poetic lines I would write. One counts off time, moments, endlessly and counts off certain other items, as in the folksong "On Top of Old Smoky": "They'll hug you and kiss you and tell you more lies / Than crossties on the railroad or stars in the skies." That is what false-hearted lovers do.

I've lived in three places that have deeply affected me and my poetry: Needles, New York City, and Paris, France. I've lived in them both chronologically and simultaneously (mentally), traveling back and forth between the first two after I grew up and then among all three after I moved to Paris. I and my poems represent an experience of all of them compressed into myself the body or symbol you see and the ones made by my poems. I am a primal and universal consciousness (like anyone) flowing forever in one place, representative of myself and absolutely existent as myself. I used to think my poems could not contain three such divergent places or sources of poetry and that as a person I probably made no sense. I don't feel that way anymore. The world is, rather unfortunately, not local now except as a planet. But also I have accepted myself and the fact that a person makes no sense.

I haven't quoted from a poem yet. Here is a poem from *Culture of One*:

The Decline of Memory in Our Time

I can't remember why I wanted to make a codex.
Marie doesn't know the word "codex." But she tries not
to remember, by making what she makes containing
all her memories and yours, o garbagers: your

product is my medium, have I a choice? I have no
values. But I can't help doing this: it keeps me from
the bug-jawed memories that eat one, dead already
since adolescence. I make my mementos mori. Because
I have no values. And block memory when I can—

what could anyone remember? The relation of this
skull to the tissue adhering that's supposedly me?
I don't value brains, poem of the master of taxonomy:
His Same Old Glow. But it's in the Trash. I don't
value the trash. I use it, I value myself, keeping on.
            I want to get even. With the

men in yesterday's, today's, and tomorrow's editions. I judge
them guilty, to elect themselves again.

The woman is gluing the senescent oppressor's creepy love—
his past jewel—to a tin-can pull ring. I pledge my troth, because
            I was born.

Poetry isn't anything like what you think it is. It is more than a human invention and has little to do with a learnable thought process; it has a lot to do with mind and form; it hates your ideas about it; it hates your ideas. It is the primal formal mind insuring the coherence of the universe (which we all are, so-called animate and inanimate); it is our formality, our just one remove from chaos—as we make sure our universe goes on via the communication that holds it together, all us thinking and talking in strange and resonant forms. Any idiot knows this. Matter manages to stick together because its constituents communicate while moving.

Where I grew up, in the Mojave, there are glyphs everywhere incised into rocks and into the earth, in shapes you can make out as animals and people, but also abstract shapes, the familiar emergence spiral, phosphenes (the geometrical shapes you see under your eyelids when you're high), and so on. At the end of our street, where my mother lived until her death last year, there were glyphs on boulders, with shapes more writing-like than pictorial. My brother "discovered" them and told a local lady about them, who arranged that they be named for her not him—we are all still miffed. Fifteen miles outside of town is an enormous spiraling intaglio maze with hedgerows engraved into the ground, called the Topock Maze or the Mystic Maze by the whites. The Mojave Indians, whose reservation overlaps with my home town and whose ancestors made the Mystic Maze, probably call it something else. Just across the river in Arizona and also further south close to Blythe, California are more intaglios, enormous drawings that can only be seen from the air: they were "discovered" by an aviator in 1932. My brother took Ted (Berrigan) up in an airplane once in the '70s to see what he called the Giant Man and the Giant Woman. Ted came back from the outing looking very bemused. What did they look like? I asked. A giant man and a giant woman, he said, they can only be seen from the air.

They are messages, drawings, forms, addressed to whom? Who are your poems addressed to? I don't always know. These figures are in the middle of nowhere, a stark hot-as-hell nowhere. They are peculiarly modest, looking like everything else; despite their size they blend in. They weren't exactly an idea; they are not Spiral Jetty. They are messages to the sky. There's you, and the sky. Period. I don't believe in god, but I believe the dead are still alive; they could be up there or somewhere down here, somewhere; it's all kind of the same thing, you can see that. Life, death, sky, ground, same. Make a little art, or make a big artwork—what's scale in the desert? Is there really such a thing as size?

There's no obvious money in the desert, hardly any currency, nothing you'd want to buy unless you were a billionaire already. So the railroad came through in the 19th century and started to mess up the Mystic Maze. They were going to lay their tracks down right through the maze. The railroad said there was obviously no maze, it was nothing but dirt and rocks. The people of the area—they are white, Mojave, Latino—rose up against the Santa Fe Railroad and made them change the course of the tracks. The maze was obviously sacred, any fool could see that, and is since a protected site; if you live around there for any length of time you know what and where the sacred is. The natural landmarks called sacred by the Indians are sacred to everyone, the strangely shaped mountains, the special washes, the springs with the wild grapevines where the rattlesnakes live. It's obvious.

When I would return to Needles to visit, especially when my mother was ill last year, I would often stay in a room that was a sort of store room. My mother, a hoarder, stuck a lot of stuff in there. On one shelf was my late Aunt Edna's collection of insulators, those ceramic or glass items a couple inches high, domelike, placed on top of poles for electrical power lines. In the middle of the night, every night, the freight train would go through town. The tracks were down the hill about a mile away, but the train could still be heard. I would wake up and the glass insulators would be vibrating and gently knocking against each other like sounds inside words inside poems. Freight trains are long. I would lie there and wonder things such as why words sound the way they do in a poem, as opposed to the way they sound when you're just talking. The letters and syllables set each other off, and that makes it be a poem; if that doesn't happen it isn't a poem. Your voice changes when you read a poem aloud, if that doesn't happen it isn't a poem. Neither subject nor concept nor a poetic form make it be poem, *that* does. It isn't music, you don't have to play it or sing it. As hardly any songs are poetry. The whole art is in the ability to make this vibratory setting-off occur; it can't be taught and can barely be discussed. It has nothing to do with dramatizing or chanting the poem when you read it. It has a little to do with measure and line, but that's certainly not all of it. I know I know how to do it—having this ability must be why I changed from being a fiction writer to being a poet. It's maybe like, instead of describing an object, making you hear its atoms spin. So far there's no good way to talk about it. Poem excerpt:

> believe in tunnel except as piece of poem itself except as poem when everything to me
> manifestly overlaps a machine made of tubes sending messages all night all night but
> thats i think we're erasing poetry with a movie or video camera which shows nothing
> shadows it seems i have a lot c a lot of cash in my pocket but we will buy bees instead.
> in exchange for chips of coral and jade which i have earned along my lifeline and all
> night i the two bodies i lie in bed and create the real body which is

light its where i life
exactly its i and next to its the other body this white body is the real body and is really
there this is a body and that i participate in its construction lying there in the dark, all
night i lie in bed and create the real body which i see as light layer on me its exactly i
body its where i lie and next to its the other the other body aside there this they are
bodies and i participate exactly in the construction of this the real body me where i am
lying in bed in the dark. am i always hes holding up the building which is the library

(from Growth of the Light Flat upon Her, *Reason and Other Women*)

When I moved to New York, first to go to college and then back again in the mid-70s to be part of the Lower East Side poetry community, I was confronted by masses of voices, in a way I hadn't been before, a vast number of people who talked to each other all the time, who were often out on the street, delighting to be in each other's faces. Or at parties. Or at readings, before and after—or at concerts, dance performances. Everyone in groups, everyone talking, or couples fighting in the street at 2 AM; or the crazy person shouting nonsensical speech; or the kids shouting playing football right in the street between the departure and arrival of the crosstown bus. And everyone, anyone and everyone, in my apartment. I became attuned to more and more vocal qualities and adept at remembering conversations. And I began to think that voices were everything and everything had a voice, all objects secretly vibrating since everything is in motion, as you find out from taking LSD.

New Yorkers get faster and faster and louder and louder—all ethnic groups; as if about to spin in place and then levitate. You can barely understand anyone when this happens unless you're inside the conversation—also a possible occurence in Paris. I recently had a rendez vous with my Parisian GP in which she finally talked to me as if I weren't a foreigner, so fast I could hardly believe I was keeping up. It's of course like plays, like opera, and like flying. In New York I wanted my poems to be like plays, like opera and like flying. I wanted to extract poetry from all the voices around me. People talked slowly at home in Needles; everyone who met my mother said she drawled. You don't talk so fast when it's 115 degrees out—you talk to each other more telepathically. One word suggests a whole anecdote you both already know and you laugh.

Here is one of my New York stories. Around 1977 I used to go to an Italian butcher shop on First Avenue run by two fairly young guys, near a lot of other Italian-American owned shops. One of the two butchers was quite handsome and smooth-faced with black hair. So we go to Needles—Ted and the boys and I—for a couple of weeks in summer to visit my mother, and one night I dream about him, the good-looking one, I simply *see* him in a black suit standing in a closetlike space. So we return to New York, I go out to buy some meat a few days later and they aren't there, the two guys, the butcher shop's closed for good. I ask the guy in the Italian grocery next door what happened to the butcher shop. Those two guys are dead, he says, they were gunned down by the Mafia: shot on their lawns in their houses out in the suburbs. Couldn't repay their loans.

I will always *see* him in his black suit. It was around this time I began really to understand I wasn't a poet of the so-called quotidian; that I was going to receive disruptive communications from the non-quotidian; that the quotidian in any case didn't match what I'd been led to believe. My ear is not normal, my dreams are not normal. You are a visual amalgam of choices made by everyone as to how to see you, you are a symbol of your reality. One choice is to see you as completely still and stable in one place in linear time. A handsome man with a smooth forehead under dark hair standing in a black suit in a closetlike space, an upright coffin? I didn't even know his name. You are standing in. You are standing in for yourself, when you seem to live an everyday life. Better to be Marie; but I am on track, five billion and the future thirteen. A poem is in the simultaneous time we are really in. And I know the dead have something like voices, because they talk to me.

POEM

Is he here? yes he's here the
dead butcher whom I
didn't know even his
name. I didn't think I'd be
shot for chrissakes offstage
three bottles of whisky and a fascist
hangover. Bruno's finally gonna
repaint our apartment not
the living room 'too much crap in
here' he says works by Guston
Burckhardt Schneeman Brain-
ard and Warhol. People have no space
inside them, they only have talk
but sometimes when the one uni-
versal vocal cord we are vibrates I
remember the dream of disap-
pearing through a black quarter-
tone to death whatever that is.

Later Doug says 'It's alright, it
always is, isn't it?' Yes, I know it is.
But you have to tremble to hear yourself properly.

(I just wrote that New York School poem trying to remember how to do it, Aug. 4, 2013)

Perhaps Marie is really walking towards the beginning of the universe. At the beginning there's movement—explosion, moltenness—which would be intensely painful to the human-like element in the pre-universe, that is surely present. There are all the reverberations . . . vibrations, overtones—my ears and voice and mind hear them now. I myself was walking to Paris.

When I got to Paris I didn't know the lingo; since arriving here twenty years ago I've been increasingly more unsure of who I am except this voice, that indeed hardly ever gets translated: I have never fit in anywhere I've lived. It's possible I don't fit in in the entire universe, like Marie. She could have arrived anywhere in it, and never been of it; and being entirely alone, still love. I have to change it, the whole goddamned universe. I can't change Paris, or French, but I can fucking well change the universe. That is my poetics for today. The beginning of the universe was a painful wounding explosion creating vibrations still felt, and heard in our voices and shaped into poetry. Everyone has been trying to communicate with the beginning since we were cut off from it, scattered into pieces. Poetry is the best language for this since it employs the very sound of the primal separation. We are still hearing what happened . . . I will glue everything back together . . . I will lead all us pieces to a new universe.

There's a man here in my quartier who is a bit like Marie. He has an old, portable newspaper kiosk which he keeps filled with used books that, as far as I know, aren't for sale. He lives somewhere near the kiosk, I don't know where; has only one name, like a French pop star but I've forgotten it; and once wrote a book that I neglected to buy the one time I saw a copy. For years he kept his kiosk near the bouche de métro of métro Poissonnières just around the corner, but then he moved it up to a space in front of l'Eglise St. Vincent de Paul, across from Place Liszt. So I hardly ever see him now. He would generally stand near his kiosk; you could ask him for directions, I have; and I once saw him in conversation with André Glucksmann, a philosophe who lives around here. They are both soixantehuitards. But really he's a bag lady. He has his books, a kiosk full instead of a bag. He hangs near his books. He, Glucksmann, and I have been subliminally aware of each other at times, though I don't think they know I'm a poet but you can never tell. The man who runs the librairie where Glucksmann and I buy *Le Monde* (for which Glucksmann writes occasional gloomy political pieces about Eastern Europe) knows that I am a poet. He is originally from Madagascar, and it is a quartier of immigrants, the 10th on the border of the 9th. Anyway M. Abdoulaly might have told M. Glucksmann that I am a poet. Everyone keeps an eye on everyone though being Parisian one doesn't necessarily say hello. In a certain way everyone knows who I am. I have very slowly become of the neighborhood, that is my habit.

Once a few years back I was walking on the rue de Chabrol, which is two blocks long and on which I habitually do things. I was there near bd Magenta—I can't believe this, I've lived around here for 17, 18 years—I saw a street behind rue de Chabrol that I'd never seen before, as if inside the walls. You know how this is possible in Europe, a hidden street, passage de la Ferme St. Lazare. An entire other world, at one end of it an abandoned electricity building—electricity plant?—with the words "Electricité de France" painted thereon. I'd only ever seen the outer wall, hadn't known what it was. In the middle of the street was the entrance to what turned out to be a hospital, Hôpital St. Lazare, closed. I subsequently determined that the whole area, my whole area of which this street was a tiny part, had been called l'Enclos de St. Lazare, dated back to around 1100, and had been a refuge for lepers. The hospital that still stood—it was about to be converted into a maternelle— possessed a much shorter history associated with prostitutes and their diseases. And there had been a prison close by or connected. And, in the 1600s St. Vincent de Paul too had been active with lepers *right here,* right around here. I of course began to write a narrative poem that took place on a sort of ghost street, involving a group of dead people and a soi-disant savior, myself, who met there to compose a bible. The characters are a leper, a whore, a pickpocket, a gangster, a fortune-teller, a raped and murdered teenage girl, an immigrant, and the savior —they are from various centuries. The book is called *A Voice: Our Bible.* The characters are somewhat empowered by the empty electricity building; they speak via the savior figure, who transcribes their stories into Elizabethan English. Their voices—her voice—has a tendency to break up into overtones and crackle. No part of this book has been published yet.

How speaketh we in the new? saith the savior *into* the tangible electricity.

That we heareth *all* the tones, saith the pickpocket, in our *mental* speaking pronounced by thee, and written.

Tell me of thyselves in the new, saith the savior.

I speak/think it as it seizes/seizeth me/one/her, saith the whore;

and there are glisssaaandi of sig ni fi ca tion in the orchards/orchids/ orchestras straw/strobe of sooundz. Butitneedstobequickersometimes;

I must CONTROL IT.

What dost thou think it is *for*? saith the savior.

I oh I   am less *local*   BUT I must be local enow to   talk   as   my   self.

Art thou endddlesss in each WORD   rising and fallling?

Yea. I wishest that thou *hear* what I *hear*   butImustsaymorequickly or thou willst *forget* what I wast *meaning.*

In this hooolinessss.

I was *in* it,   saith she,   but I return.

Poetry is about there being one time. Prose is about there being a particular time with socialized details—that make me so impatient. What then is there to express, if not those? What is "express"? It's possible that I'm simply filling up time, living, counting crossties, except for the poems. Poets have a rare, exact talent. My vocal cords connected to my brain are in the possession of a lot of voices, people, who are somewhere between dead and electric. This is not a poetics popular with literature departments at the moment. My paragraph becomes slightly dislocated at this point, so I may be getting somewhere. Poetry requires no help as an art, it is innate to the practitioner, who doesn't even have to write the poem down—is it the most organic, indigenous, of all the arts? Is it an expression then of what everything is? Expression for chrissakes. I don't accept a lot of words—I like there to be a hard thing in the middle of it, the word. A tangible, if vibrating, seed thing. I have this book about the decipherment of languages that I seem to read whenever I write a long poem: I'm interested in decipherment. The rock art symbols. The hard place in the word. It's less that you know what something means though than that you know what you do when you say it. You make noises out of your mouth and maybe move your body. When I dream I speak I don't know what I said, later; I just know I spoke. But poetry comes out of an empty electricity building. Or you are thinking to me and I'm writing it down. Allen Ginsberg told me that when he wrote poetry he felt his vocal cords vibrate. Each of the crossties is a line and you can feel the train coming before it gets there. I am an enormous room full of people and other beings and formations speaking constantly and overlappingly; their words hold us together. We are each exact individuals or realities. Poetry makes us unchaotic, just about. So you, one says, as the coordinator of vibrant words are overtly holding everything together. Just about. That is, I am a world leader.

It is important not to want what you are told you want. The only possible revolution is to cease to want what they say to. If "they" includes "you." I mean it does. So they will cease to want it too. What do you want? To continue counting crossties without a poetics. To listen to and transcribe the electric words of all you.

When my mother was diagnosed with terminal cancer and returned to her home after surgery, she was supposed to receive hospice care there, but Governor Jerry Brown cut off all hospice care in Needles as part of his end-of-the-year budget cuts (people in the desert don't exist), and she was left on her own. She had no doctor, in fact. At some point I dreamed that her doctor was the voodoo god Baron Samedi. I looked him up and discovered that besides being (as I knew) the loa of cemeteries and, like Legba, a loa of crossroads, he was also a very particular kind of healer, a god of healing before death. I.e., I thought, you need to be healed in order to die. I flew back and forth several times in the months of my mother's illness, watching her heal. Sometimes she was very sick; sometimes she was well enough to go gambling at the casinos in Laughlin. As she neared her death, she began to have what they call hallucinations: as all dying people do she saw things no one else could see. However unlike any other dying person I've been near, my mother saw words. She would call them out, or call to them: "iris" was one. She shouted "Iris!" She called out "Scrub!" and "Curb!"—near anagrams, she had done a lot of word puzzles. She called out a lot of words I can't recall. I wasn't present when she finally passed, but among her last utterances was the sentence: "Peter said everyone heard in their own language." This is a reference to the Day of Pentecost, Acts 2, 2:

> And they were all filled with the Holy Ghost and began to speak with other tongues, as the Spirit gave them utterance.
>
> And there were dwelling at Jerusalem Jews, devout men, out of every nation under heaven.
>
> Now when this was noised abroad, the multitude came together, and were confounded, because that every man heard them speak in his own language.

That is, the miracle of Pentecost is that nothing said in tongues needed to be translated. I think this means that when my mother died she was heard and understood, she went home.

This is the heart of poetry for me, but I can't explain it—as with the insides of words setting each other off. I can only tell you the story, for I have become full of stories as well as poems. Sometimes I call them songs. When? Sometimes when they look the most like prose. Who cares? Who cares about life? Fuck it and heal.

> This song lifts you. Way above the black coat. Way above your self-identification of the night high golden moon, an image.
>
> I am flying, for you're sick.
>
> After my injection, like any folk shaman of the path.
>
> In the beginning when young I tried and failed; and as I suffered more and more, improved. Now in my defect I'm best of all. In my earlier injections, I was the twin of this now. I took on the stories I am casting away like old medicines.
>
> The songs are inside within small red cells. The stories, once coiled into snakes, I cut to pieces. They're trembling words which connect vibrationally.
>
> His tears are old. And now that they're flames I can use them. In the dissolution, of my wrong location.

From the dark blue dock of the spine. Cast off. Shook it broke it.
Tears are old spine.
It's good that you're trapped in your illness.

I'm going to find your soul
I'm going to find your soul

This is the oldest song.

(From "In the Pines"—13)

If I find your soul who will be it? There are a lot of poetry gangs. It's like a medieval structuring of a small portion of this medievalistic world of corporations and political groupings. But we all know this. The poetry gangs promise belonging, the truth or something, transitory recognition, the possibility of a job. These are territorial incentives; you might build up a small online empire or fit, with your friends, into a supposedly important anthology. Internet is a sack of shit: scads of material that people read every fifth word of and then make pronouncements about. People have been allowed to not read my books and then make lying pronouncements about them, rather often lately. Nothing is at stake online. Anything you say drifts and disappears, remaining forever somewhere but unnoticed; it isn't attached to anything concrete, why not lie all the time? But in fact all of this is nothing, the most nothing of nothings. The web is neither a desert nor a mind, it is transparent like nonexistence but without force. I've lost track here. I'm counting tracks, just counting crossties. I don't know what anyone should be doing. There are no shoulds. But I do want to lead everyone invisibly on these tracks somewhere that is fabulous, not just adequate (like graduate school poetry or art school art) but a place where we can transform the universe by rearranging the smallest constituents of sound and trembling, so that we and they are no longer in the position of flinch and trauma assumed after the first explosion. You perhaps wouldn't do very much to do this. You would mostly listen and hum. I think I'm serious, I'm pretty serious. Though I'm not totally sure what I'm saying. Maybe it's a poem and I don't fucking well have to be sure. But it's possible there could be a new kind of leading and following, with just a very few indications. With nobody much saying they're leading and following. The reason it should be me leading is that personally broken I have trembled more than anyone I know, and I have definitely devalued the currency. I have these skills. And I am older and haplessly not exactly anyone, but I'm not a jerk. As you walk along the tracks counting it becomes impossible to be a jerk. When I occasionally stand still, I realize I'm probably already home. My talent isn't teachable or transferable, but what I know may be. Use me.

Talk first given at Moving Back and Forth Between Poetry and/as *Trans*lation, Nomadic Travels and Travails with Alice Notley & Pierre Joris—an international poetry seminar held at Université libre de Bruxelles, November 7-8, 2013

Culture of One, Penguin Group: New York, 2011.
In the Pines, Penguin Group: New York, 2007.
Reason and Other Women, Chax: Tucson, 2010.

Published in *Among the Margins,* ed. Fox Frazier-Foley & Diana Arterian, Ricochet Editions, Los Angeles, 2016.

Allen Ginsberg: An International Poetry, Its Genius and Its Particles

(To Bobbie Louise Hawkins, tonight in the air above us)

That Allen Ginsberg is thus far the one truly international poet that has ever lived, I mean making of his person or speaker or point-dot of location in the poem a verticality or stack of conditions across the globe, as one knowing about any number of places and kinds of consciousness at once. That his doing this foreshadows our great need for such a way of being now in what almost everyone knows to be global crisis; that a poet might aspire to know all in the sense that each individual probably does, even if it's nothing, even if everything is nothing. That the local certainly is part of the international, that the singular self is larger than the planet, that righteousness is disgusting, that the human animal bound to the globe in its suffering—which would seem to be its knowledge, but why?—must face its suffering as an entity self-invented eons ago and not caused by others for it (one) is the other. Please listen.

I dreamed I asked Allen what he wanted me to say in this keynote, and he said "I want you to tell them how hard I worked at the poetry." That part is easy to do, for I always saw Allen working hard at the poetry and so can tell you—the multiple versions (finalized with the date of first draft), the concentration on each word (as brushstroke c.f. Cézanne, his master for detail and plastic space), the research into vocabulary (looking for exact Miltonic usages for "Plutonian Ode," with Miltonic dictionary nearby, for example), the research into traditional metric (his giving

me a manuscript once of poems in sapphics throughout western literary history), the obsession with how music and words go together (Allen as singer/songwriter), breath—the breath, the obsessive journal-keeping, note-taking not about self-celebration but about research: research into life's minutiae being research into the particles of poetry, everything you do or see or say or think, intermixed, forming the particles. But I keep going back to this sense I have of Allen as international, as global, that he is the one poet people in many different countries have heard of, know, want to read . . . Or this was the case, when I was informed in 1997 that he was dying. I was in Paris, as was Kenneth Koch and we met for coffee and to talk, and I said something like "Allen is the one international poet." And Kenneth himself was an internationalist, a traveler, an appreciator of other cultures; but he agreed. He told me I should write about it! write a whole book about Allen's poetry, but then I didn't; and we were sad, Kenneth and I, where was that cafe? near métro Iéna, a bouche de métro named after one of Napoleon's battles in Germany . . . I had left New York in 1992, but had seen Allen two or three times since in Paris. Also the States, but he came to Paris to visit, to read, to manifest himself, once receiving an honor from the French government; once reading in a large hall at Trocadéro, he still filled it up! I went with him and others (Doug, Peter Hale) to the l'Orangérie to look at paintings, among them the Cézannes, the last time he was here. He gave me his name-tag for le Salon des Livres, and I have pasted it into one of my collage-fans recently, my own collages reminding me now of Allen's works where you build and pile on detail after detail, keeping the energy consistent across it (most important that), until you have completed the entity, which in its consistency of energy of details is like the world. Or a person, vivid.
I decided, two weeks ago, to select ten poems at random in Allen's *Collected Poems*, to see how "international" they were. They weren't all were, but the very first one certainly is, I see—I am going to proceed by

listing these poems and saying whatever about them, but may I say, what a pleasure! Please please listen—poetry is a pleasure! (c.f. Kenneth "The Pleasures of Peace").

The first poem I selected by chance was "Vulture Peak: Gridhakuta Hill" . . . written in Benares, April 18, 1963, so we are already making my point—have made it, but who wants to make points? The first line is a natural opener "I've got to get out of the sun"—he's walking uphill and it's hot, but the third line is "walking up crying singing *ah sunflower*," Blake going through Allen's head because the traveller's journey will soon be done, at least the one in the heat to the top of the hill! towards the sun. Humor, but something contrapuntal has been set up and Blake phrases occur later, holding the experience together, English poetry in the head of the New Jersey Jew in India. The poem whirls in its layout with staggered indentations, and when Allen gets to the top of the hill he turns round and round in circles:

> Till when I stopped the earth
>   moved in my eyeballs
> green bulge slowly
>   and stopped

You see, because what you see is in yourself, until you see—pure Blake and Cézanne's *petite sensation*—with references to Indian history, American place names, Peter du Peru (who I think is Orlovsky in South America). To be anywhere and be there, is the point, be sensitive to place and self but also this one moment of being there, alive,

> All the noise I made with my mouth
> singing on the path up, Gary

Thinking all the *pale youths* and
virgins shrouded with snow . . .

What poetry does, that prose cannot, is make the one thing, the one time that lasts, composed of its details. A poem is a stacked entity, a poem, as Ted used to say, is a list of lines—it is also a list of words and of details, and it whirls in place. Allen traveled a lot, with long stays in India and Mexico (you have to risk missing out on being here! in New York or Frisco), and he wrecked himself and his health doing so, in order to know what the world was like and to say it. The poem ends

My thirst in my cheeks and tongue
back throat drives me home.

"Back throat drives me home," that's pretty good.

The second poem selected by chance (I am opening the book randomly, plonk, trying to be vaguely chronological) is "Going to Chicago"—dated August 24, 1968, so this is on the way to the famous Democratic convention in Chicago nominating Nixon and characterized by violence on all sides, street demonstrations, mean cops and a later court trial of demonstrators, at which Allen sweetly testified and honestly (as honest as you can be and be funny) answered all questions, remember? Going to Chicago: "22,000 feet over Hazed square Vegetable planet Floor" so immediately this is not just an American situation, this is the planet of hazed air. Allen continues:

Approaching Chicago to Die or flying over Earth another 40 years
to die—Indifferent, and Afraid, that the bone-shattering bullet
be the same as the vast evaporation-of-phenomena Cancer

Come true in an old man's bed. Or Historic
Fire-Heaven Descending 22,000 years End th' Atomic Aeon

Chicago, a dangerous place to approach this day in 1968, is a point on the globe, and the near future a point in vast-void time, and maybe he'll be shot or maybe die of cancer forty years later—it was more like thirty, wasn't it?—or maybe there will be an atomic is it? holocaust . . . There are two more six-line stanzas, braiding together the strands of the Convention (pun) as politics and "Conventional police"; the color blue that's the sky, "Our Father," and Lake Michigan; and the poet's self identification as the "Angel King." I think. This poem is not as immediately clear as the later Allen might have wished, but it is masterfully compressed, beautiful and pertinent:

Democratic Anger is an Illusion, Democratic Joy is God
Our Father is baby blue, the original face you see Sees You—

This is an airplane poem, a genre that has not been remarked upon or anthologized yet, to my knowledge, but there exist a number of examples among my friends' poems, a poem in which the speaker is temporarily above the country and globe, often recording details within the plane (Allen briefly alludes to "papers & Noses"), but being above it all, and in a spiritual expanse. Remember Georgia O'Keefe's 1965 paintings from above the flat clouds!—this was a new kind of thing to experience. When you are above the globe, you can think about it too, and remember Allen has said "flying over Earth" the planetary, this is planetary even cosmic consciousness not the American poetty-boo keeps discovering America, joys and problems. Phil Whalen has a version of this where he simply leaves his body: "I soar / Face down high above the shore & sea" ("Self Portrait Sad 22:ix:58"). There is another one I can't find where

Phil says "face-down over America." It's a position I took permission for implicitly, from Allen, in my own poem "At Night The States."

For poem number three I got landed with (in emotional storm of) "Hymmnn," the poem after "Kaddish" (1959) that is in fact part of it, the "caw caw" one. "Kaddish" being Allen's saying of the ritual in his words, for his mother so far un-kaddished, though she had died a few years previously, mentally-ill, lobotomized Naomi, for whom there had been no real memorial, now one of the most famous mothers in poetry. Born in Russia she was, so the internationalism starts here and oneself is always part of a diaspora somewhere along the line, as we represent each of us global criss-crossings from over a million years and if time is one time, a compressed every time and all the time, these criss-crossings are happening now, oh they are:

> O mother
> farewell
> with a long black shoe
> farewell
> with Communist Party and a broken stocking
> farewell
> with six dark hairs on the wen of your breast
> farewell
> with your old dress and a long black beard around the vagina
> farewell
> with your sagging belly
> with your fear of Hitler
> with your mouth of bad short stories
> with your fingers of rotten mandolins
> with your arms of fat Paterson porches

with your belly of strikes and smokestacks
with your chin of Trotsky and the Spanish War
with your voice singing for the decaying overbroken workers
with your nose of bad lay with your nose of the smell of the pickles
  of Newark
with your eyes
with your eyes of Russia
with your eyes of no money
with your eyes of false China
with your eyes of Aunt Elanor
with your eyes of starving India
with your eyes pissing in the park
with your eyes of America taking a fall

I don't have to make my point. Except I'm saying Allen often wrote out of deep trauma . . . But who is saying Kaddish right now for the dead of Ghouta? (March, 2018) in Syria, abandoned by America and all the world. Allen would. Naomi says "the key is in the sunlight" . . . the mote in the sunlight, Allen says, of which a word would be one. One mote. Oh Allen, "we are led to believe a lie / when we see with not through the eye . . ." (Blake) And he would say maybe, you can't see through it without seeing where you are exactly physically—though the word order is optional, as long as each word is equal to the other. Poetry is democratic on its tiniest levels, as matter is, and the spiritual or limitless holds all. Each word equal in energy, applied to the page or voice. Allen's practical poetics, the words are equal. In his lifetime his word order becomes increasingly, *whichever order best energizes each word.*

I will now totally speed up with list. But first I will go to sleep and dream I lose my purse (I learned to record my dreams from Allen and

Jack Kerouac) but then I realize I am dreaming so I haven't really lost it with all my bank cards and such—do I still have my identity, and my *credit*? (I in fact don't have a credit rating.) Thus having awakened, in the dream, I am now sitting talking to a woman whose vocation is to teach Old English. And Allen is there. I then *really* wake up remembering that Allen once told my mother I was a genius, when I introduced her to him in 1977, at the Basil Bunting (British poet!) reading at New York's 92nd Street Y—a statement that was helpful to her to remember while I was poor (am poor) and unstatused. I say New York's 92nd Street Y though I am giving this talk in New York, because I'm writing it for everyone, and Allen would never assume his reader knew where the 92nd Street Y was which city, having a readership among Bangladeshi poets in long white robes, French German Swiss Spanish Korean Peruvian Italian Chinese Belgian Russian Dutch Japanese poets and scholars for example, whom I have met, as well as among my Mojave Desert mother, a fundamentalist Protestant Christian of Northern European descent with some Cherokee. We, Ted and I, gave her Rafael Soyer's etching of Allen, kept on her wall until her death six years ago, because she also admired Soyer's work, another Russian Jew transplanted to New York, with whom I once discussed the poetry of Marina Tsvetaeva, the great Russian poet, modeling for him in his studio in 1970 . . . there is only one interconnected, possibly damaged world.

So the next poem up is "Northwest Passage," from 1969, with its history-book title. This poem I hadn't attended to before is a gem, written in Boise, Idaho on a supposedly specific day April 24, 1969, describing local pollution, beauty, companies and industrial reach—money and industry creating a financial, materialistic Northwest Passage across the continent, though by now, 2018, a veritable true Passage has been created by the pollution Allen describes, since the polar cap is melting. "*We just invented throwaway Planets!*" Allen's poem screams prophetically. Boise data is dovetailed with the ongoing saga of Sirhan Sirhan (whom I once passed in a high-school corridor)—the assassin of Bobby Kennedy, and news from Europe "May Day parade canceled for Prague / says Police Radio to / the old King of May faraway —" that being Allen: "And I am the King of May," Kraj Majales,1965. And the Vietnam war goes on. Allen is able to handle all of this information from so many lands and places and crisis centers through his metrics, that he worked on so hard throughout his youth, keep everything in air floating musically, that's how you do it:

> Green salt waves washing Wall Street
> Rain on gray sage near Standard
>   Oil junction Eltopia,
> Static at Mesa! Yodeling ancient
>   Prajnaparamita
> Gaté Gaté Paragaté Parasamgaté
>   Bodhi Svaha!
> Way Down Yonder in the Bayoux
>   Country in Dear Old Lousian,
> Hank Williams chanting to country
>   Nature, electric
> wires run up rolling brownplowed wheatfields—
> Wallula polluted! Wallula polluted! Wallula polluted!

I'm moving on, I'm a travellin' on (wrong Hank—mine's Snow) through my ten poems fast now, I'm running out of pages. Next poem, "Reflections at Lake Louise," 1980, the Naropa Poetry Wars, hey I was there! I understand these lines:

Scandal in the Buddhafields
The lake's covered with soft ice inches thick.
Naked, he insulted me under the glacier!
He raped my mind on the wet granite cliffs!
He misquoted me in the white mists all over the *Nation*.

Nation in italics, the political rag. Allen has officially become a Buddhist by now, with a Tibetan guru, Trungpa enscandaled, whom he co-exists with in Boulder, Colorado, at Naropa University, with Anne Waldman, of course: "She coordinates the J.K. School / of Disembodied Poetics with / the left pinkie and a / nervous breakdown full of personal / per-fumo". Who is not an internationalist? except all of America right now, I'm trying to remind you that the World exists. Or does it? Those lines turn it all to geologic eras older than people and their tiresomeness of being shocked—human disgrace, what a funny invention!

Poem 6 is a song, "Industrial Waves," that is to be sung (and I don't know the tune)—"And I know Allen will follow me round the world with his terrible singing voice" Ted wrote, but it wasn't that terrible at all.

Freedom for Indonesia to murder half million
Freedom for South Africa to stabilize the Bullion
Freedom for South Africa to slave her Blacks
Freedom for Korea's corrupt party hacks
Freedom for America to kick plenty Ass
Allende Lumumba yass yass yass!
Freedom for Martin Luther King it's a gas
Freedom to forget our bloody Indochinese past!

This is 1981. God, it was so much fun when Allen sang and chanted! Even I, who refuse all group activity whenever I can, chanted and sang in the audience when Allen bade me. There is that continuum in which speech becomes chant becomes song, and Allen explored it and played with it along its length, becoming a consummate performer—performance being the currency of international communication. But he exploited his line variously, in skill and pleasure, exacting the secret underlying melody against the metrical foot, using capital letters for vocal emphasis, eliminating punctuation, and finally riding that line. "Freedom for South Africa to slave her Blacks" but also "Freedom to forget our bloody Indochinese past"—which is elegant and undulant despite what it says. Allen could do a lot with his voice, from demotic New York-y wit intonation to baritone solemnity to shouting . . . Your own voice from your own throat is your most basic material.

Poem 7 is "Cosmopolitan Greetings," which is dated 1986, but I seem to remember Allen working endlessly on this list of injunctions and axioms. "Catch yourself thinking." . . ."Subject is known by what she sees." . . . are two that strike my eye, though there is a lot of poetry advice in this rather short poem. "Mind is shapely, Art is shapely." Then there is "Remember the future." . . . which as I have already demonstrated, Allen did. Internationally speaking, the poem is dedicated to *Struga Festival Golden Wreath Laureates & International Bards, 1986*—I believe that is Macedonia. These are "Cosmopolitan Greetings," and anyone in any city would want to know these things: "Consonants around vowels make sense." "Candor ends paranoia." Repeat, "Candor ends Paranoia." Candor isn't screaming at others, you know. It's Candor, purity of openness.

Poem 8—I have somehow selected backwards in time to 1966—turns out to be Allen's remarkable elegy on the death of Frank O'Hara, "City Midnight Junk Strains." This poem is completely local, in the big way O'Hara was local, it takes place in Allen's mind in his room, with Peter Orlovsky there, figured twice—"Delicate Peter loved his praise"—

> Peter stares out the window   at robbers
> the Lower East Side   distracted in Amphetamine

I mean that Peter is used almost as a poetic device to make a picture for Allen's being distraught; I always remember this poem with Peter's image there at the window, Peter haunted and a ghost. The poem ends with a signature line, at least for me, "a common ear /for our deep gossip." I would quote it often. Do you know any gossip, any deep gossip today? I'd ask. (Allen knew plenty.)

> I see New York thru your eyes
> and hear of one funeral a year nowadays—
> from Billy Holiday's time
> appreciated more and more
> a common ear
> for our deep gossip.

New York is a geographical point, you see, and not the mainstay of Allen's consciousness, though one's consciousness might be of it and immense in it. But kind of, a city is a thing, among things. Oh and this, the one poem randomly selected with sexual frankness in it . . . but that is, too, the gossip.

Poem 9, likewise backwards (my hands are awkward trying to operate by chance) and likewise an elegy, "Death News," on hearing of William Carlos Williams' death, in Benares 1963:

> Quietly unknown for three weeks; now I saw Passaic
> and Ganges one, consenting his devotion,
> because he walked on the steely bank & prayed
> to a Goddess in the river; that he only invented
> another Ganga-Ma. Riding on the old
> rusty Holland submarine on the ground floor
> Paterson Museum instead of a celestial crocodile.

All my points are made. India and New Jersey are one.

Poem 10, "Porch Scribbles," totally Boulder, 1980. Three- and four-line takes connected by sets of three-asterisks, as

> I want that brick house on Mapleton,
> it's for sale "Moore Real Estate"—
>   But price too high,
> I'm too drowsy to go to the telephone.

I go around all week with the line "But price too high" in my head, it really spreads though it's so simple. Which price is too high for you? price of what? Allen, by the way, was totally generous with his money.

> "Everyone loves the rain, except those caught in their business suits . . ."

Not really a put-down that line. Allen taught everyone how to be open, I have forgotten to say. Anyone might drop their guard.

The vocation is to destroy yourself for it
The vocation is to destroy your health in every country
Because health is an illusion like satisfaction
The vocation is to become more and more specific as your body lets
you down
The vocation is to record farts shits piss throughout the Milky Way
The vocation is to destroy yourself opening all the gates, you thing
All the gates doors windows closed in you Open
The globe that speck in nothing to become an utter transparency
Or uttered   The vocation is not to win dominate or boss
The vocation is not to cheat by not destroying yourself
The vocation is not to cheat by not erasing your cultural identity
On a globe of fools pretending they aren't the same animal
Pretending they are dignified screw dignity   The vocation is
To ignore everyone's sensitivities which are mere transparencies
The vocation is to ignore how bad or sad you make everyone pretend
to feel
The vocation is to destroy yourself for it over time
The vocation is to destroy time, exactly
The vocation is not to go through time, it is not to be
In a local place   It is not to be anything a teacher can pin down
The vocation is to avoid the Teachings
The vocation is to be faithful to your mother and your old lovers
The vocation is never to be asleep when you sleep
The vocation is to not know who you are, while naming yourself in
Every country of the world   The vocation is matter, the globe to pass
Through as you pass through your form towards your reader in your poem
The vocation is to leave, not say goodbye, and come back
The vocation is to be embarrassing

The vocation is to follow your own embarrassment to beauteous hell
The vocation is to preach to and convert the damned
(poem by myself)

"I write poetry because it's the best way to say everything in mind within 6 minutes or a lifetime."
("Improvisation in Beijing," 1984.)

I was at a conference in Madrid a few years ago, La Memoire de la Memoire—The Memory of Memory, talks in English, French, Spanish and Portuguese; and there was the guy who gave the impenetrable (to me) talk in Portuguese, on Portuguese Renaissance metrics was it, looking very very severe . . . Then later, at lunch, I was trying to explain to him—we spoke in English—the what I was as poet in the world, and said I'd known Allen Ginsberg, and this guy suddenly cracked. He grinned and grabbed my hand and said he wanted to touch me, someone who had known Allen, and told me how important Allen had been for him and everyone. No more defenses? Learn yr metrics, and drop your defenses, and then, again, go with the metrics (broad use of term: rap, jazz, or Oulipian, self-made, improvisatory, even traditional, whatever.) Don't be afraid. Don't you never be afraid, as Woody Guthrie's sister said to Woody Guthrie.

The weather in Paris this winter so strange, two months solid rain, flooding of the Seine, an historic snowfall followed by record cold, then a record April heat wave. The world worse than it was when Allen was alive, that is the human-mind world, for the planet in depth as a giant rock-soul keeps its own agenda, the universe supposedly has a life-span, within what Anaximander calls the Unlimited. One tries to touch the Unlimited with mind connected to the meat-body we somehow contracted for millions of years ago. There are rules in Religions for correct procedures for contacting the Unlimited, with smug footnotes deeming correctness incorrect and so on, all in the mind. Allen's poetry knows all this, and free to move about wherever, on the earth-map, the sky-map and the unmapped map, frees the reader from constrictions as well. People like to feel free, and Allen's poetry is beloved among people I meet everywhere, because he gives them this release, this deep relaxation . . . He performs, page or stage, and then you are freed from your own performance; you don't have to be the one everyone said you had to be—because he was once crazy—after all, his mother was—and traumatized by signing her lobotomy papers, traumatized! worked hard at his poetry, became enlightened, lost track of having to conform in any way, and having learned the form of his own poetry thoroughly, gave it to you in joy and glee. I mean it's less that everything in mind got said than that . . . And what is that that? Poetry itself makes you feel good, maybe. Because it's poetry—imagine that! It's its own inspiration, and if you work as hard at it breaking self and body, as Allen did, you might . . . even if you're worried that the planet is collapsing . . . write one; as there's nothing for us except here, where we all are on it. Or are we? Where are we? "Vat's the qvestion?" he asked a few weeks before he died. When he knew he was going to die and was excited about that (as Bob Rosenthal told me) . . .

KEROUAC

I can't answer;
reason I can't answer
I haven't been dead yet
Don't remember dead
I'm on 14th St & 1st Avenue

Vat's the qvestion?

Talk for The Allen Ginsberg Symposium,
May 3-5 2018, held at The Poetry Project

All quotations from Allen Ginsberg are from *Collected Poems 1947-1997*, Harper Perennial, 2007, except for "Kerouac," which is from *Wait Till I'm Dead, Poems Uncollected,* Penguin Random House, New York, 2018.

OTHER TITLES FROM THE SONG CAVE:

1. *A Dark Dreambox of Another Kind* by **Alfred Starr Hamilton**
2. *My Enemies* by **Jane Gregory**
3. *Rude Woods* by **Nate Klug**
4. *Georges Braque and Others* by **Trevor Winkfield**
5. *The Living Method* by **Sara Nicholson**
6. *Splash State* by **Todd Colby**
7. *Essay Stanzas* by **Thomas Meyer**
8. *Illustrated Games of Patience* by **Ben Estes**
9. *Dark Green* by **Emily Hunt**
10. *Honest James* by **Christian Schlegel**
11. *M* by **Hannah Brooks-Motl**
12. *What the Lyric Is* by **Sara Nicholson**
13. *The Hermit* by **Lucy Ives**
14. *The Orchid Stories* by **Kenward Elmslie**
15. *Do Not Be a Gentleman When You Say Goodnight* by **Mitch Sisskind**
16. *HAIRDO* by **Rachel B. Glaser**
17. *Motor Maids across the Continent* by **Ron Padgett**
18. *Songs for Schizoid Siblings* by **Lionel Ziprin**
19. *Professionals of Hope: The Selected Writings of* **Subcomandante Marcos**
20. *Fort Not* by **Emily Skillings**
21. *Riddles, Etc.* by **Geoffrey Hilsabeck**
22. *CHARAS: The Improbable Dome Builders* by **Syeus Mottel** (Co-published with Pioneer Works)
23. *YEAH NO* by **Jane Gregory**
24. *Nioque of the Early-Spring* by **Francis Ponge**
25. *Smudgy and Lossy* by **John Myers**
26. *The Desert* by **Brandon Shimoda**

27. *Scardanelli* by **Friederike Mayröcker**
28. *The Alley of Fireflies and Other Stories* by **Raymond Roussel**
29. *CHANGES: Notes on Choreography* by **Merce Cunningham** (Co-published with the Merce Cunningham Trust)
30. *My Mother Laughs* by **Chantal Akerman**
31. *Earth* by **Hannah Brooks-Motl**
32. *Everything and Other Poems* by **Charles North**
33. *Paper Bells* by **Phan Nhiên Hạo**
34. *Photographs: Together & Alone* by **Karlheinz Weinberger**
35. *A Better Place Is Hard to Find* by **Aaron Fagan**
36. *Rough Song* by **Blanca Varela**
37. *In the Same Light: 200 Poems for Our Century From the Migrants & Exiles of the Tang Dynasty,* translated by **Wong May**
38. *On the Mesa: An Anthology of Bolinas Writing (50th Anniversary Edition),* edited by **Ben Estes and Joel Weishaus**
39. *Listen My Friend, This Is the Dream I Dreamed Last Night* by **Cody-Rose Clevidence**
40. *Poetries* by **Georges Schehadé**
41. *Wings in Time* by **Callie Garnett**
42. *Two Murals* by **Jesús Castillo**
43. *Punks: New & Selected Poems* by **John Keene**
44. *ABC Moonlight* by **Ben Estes**
45. *Star Lake* by **Arda Collins**
46. *The Maybe-Bird* by **Jennifer Elise Foerster**
47. *Seriously Well* by **Helge Torvund**
48. *Dereliction* by **Gabrielle Octavia Rucker**
49. *Bookworm: Conversations with* **Michael Silverblatt**
50. *April* by **Sara Nicholson**
51. *Valley of the Many-Colored Grasses* by **Ronald Johnson**
52. *The Sphinx and the Milky Way: Selections from the Notebooks of* **Charles Burchfield**